Intellectual Property Law

BUTTERWORTHS CORE TEXT SERIES

Intellectual Property Law

Jennifer Davis MSc, PhD
Fellow in Law, Wolfson College, Cambridge

Series Editor

Nicola Padfield
Fitzwilliam College, Cambridge

Butterworths
London, Edinburgh, Dublin
2001

United Kingdom	Butterworths, a Division of Reed Elsevier (UK) Ltd, Halsbury House, 35 Chancery Lane, LONDON WC2A 1EL and 4 Hill Street, EDINBURGH EH2 3JZ
Australia	Butterworths, a Division of Reed International Books Australia Pty Ltd, CHATSWOOD, New South Wales
Canada	Butterworths Canada Ltd, MARKHAM, Ontario
Hong Kong	Butterworths Hong Kong, a division of Reed Elsevier (Greater China) Ltd, HONG KONG
India	Butterworths India, NEW DELHI
Ireland	Butterworth (Ireland) Ltd, DUBLIN
Malaysia	Malayan Law Journal Sdn Bhd, KUALA LUMPUR
New Zealand	Butterworths of New Zealand Ltd, WELLINGTON
Singapore	Butterworths Asia, SINGAPORE
South Africa	Butterworths Publishers (Pty) Ltd, DURBAN
USA	Lexis Law Publishing, CHARLOTTESVILLE, Virginia

© Reed Elsevier (UK) Ltd 2001

A CIP Catalogue record for this book is available from the British Library.

ISBN 0 406 89591 0

Printed in Great Britain by Cromwell Press, Trowbridge, Wiltshire

Visit Butterworths LEXIS *direct* at: **www.butterworths.com**

Preface

Once a subject encountered only occasionally by students, the law of intellectual property is now widely taught. Debates surrounding intellectual property—for example, about gene patenting or copyright on the internet—have found their way into the popular press. A generation raised on the computer and the logo will appreciate the growing significance of intellectual property and the law which relates to it in modern society. The law of intellectual property has changed as rapidly as the character of the global economy. Information and its surrounding technologies, biotechnology and branding have all become increasingly important in international trade. Intellectual property has come to acquire a central position in the global economy.

The purpose of this book is first to provide a basic understanding of the law of intellectual property. It deals with the six areas of law conventionally understood as falling under its rubric: patents, copyright, industrial designs, unregistered and registered trade marks and confidential information. To fully understand the nature of the law of intellectual property, it is important to be aware of the wider context in which intellectual property is produced and the law applied. Throughout this book, I shall be attentive to this wider context. The chapters which follow will recognise the economic and social influences on the development of the law of intellectual property. They will also examine some of the ethical questions which are raised when the law is used to protect intellectual capital. The author hopes that the reader will come away with a better understanding of the legal protection afforded to intellectual property rights. The book also aims to convey to the reader some of the excitement which naturally arises as the law of intellectual property advances into what are often uncharted territories, whether it be of human creative endeavour or international commerce.

A number of people have contributed to the completion of this book. Nicky Padfield was patient and supportive throughout. I would like to thank Yvonne Cripps, David Freedman and Catherine Seville for reading parts of the manuscript. I would also like to thank Paul Taylor, who was so generous with his own considerable knowledge of the field, and Bill Cornish for his support and encouragement. My thanks also go to Neeta Thakur and Kiaron Whitehead. Finally, I owe a debt of gratitude to Raj Chandavarkar.

Jennifer Davis
January 2001

Contents

Table of statutes

List of cases

xvi

PARA

F

G

PARA

Decisions of the European Court of Justice are listed below numerically.
These decisions are also included in the preceding alphabetical list.

CHAPTER ONE

An introduction to intellectual property

SUMMARY

The definition of intellectual property

The development of intellectual property law

The justification for intellectual property rights: the 'Law and Economics' and 'labour' justifications and their critics

The international dimension to intellectual property rights: WIPO and TRIPS

Remedies for infringement of intellectual property rights: damages, an account of profits, delivery up and injunctions

Pre-trial relief: interim injunctions and search orders

Defining intellectual property

1.1 The subject of this book is intellectual property. The following six chapters each examine a separate area of intellectual property: patents, copyright, industrial design rights, unregistered trade marks (passing off), registered trade marks and confidential information. The first question to ask is what brings these very diverse areas of the law together under the rubric, 'intellectual property'? The World Intellectual Property Organisation (WIPO) has offered one suggestion. According to WIPO, intellectual property refers to the 'products of the mind: inventions, literary and artistic works, any symbols, names, images, and designs used in commerce.' In a similar vein, the World Trade Organisation (WTO) has offered its own definition: 'Intellectual property rights are rights given to people over the creation of their minds.' It goes on, 'Creators can be given the right to prevent others from using their inventions, designs or others creations. These rights are known as "intellectual property rights" '. But even these very general definitions of intellectual property and its associated rights are problematic. They exclude, for instance, the most basic product of the mind, ideas, which are not generally protected as intellectual property. At the other extreme, confidential information is conventionally viewed as a type of intellectual property, even though it is difficult to see how a secret, for instance a marital secret such as a lesbian affair (*Stephens v Avery* (1988)), constitutes a 'product of the mind', although it may certainly have commercial value.

The abstract nature of intellectual property

1.2 Another way to think about intellectual property is to ask not what it is, but rather what the various kinds of intellectual property, patents, copyright, industrial designs, trade marks and confidential information, have in common. One answer has been to point to the abstract or intangible nature of intellectual property. Unlike a piece of land or a car, for example, intellectual property has no material existence. As a consequence, while it would be possible to write a book about a body of land which describes its picturesque and plant-yielding qualities but entirely ignores how it is owned and who has the right to use it, a book on intellectual property law could not take the same approach. Patents and trade marks, for example, cannot be discussed except as a form of property, for they come into being precisely at the point that they are legally recognised (for a discussion, see Drahos *A Philosophy of Intellectual Property* (1996) ch 2).

1.3 Although intellectual property may be intangible or abstract, once in existence intellectual property rights bear much in common with the rights associated with real property. For the most part, intellectual property rights can be assigned or bequeathed. Those who 'trespass' on another's intellectual property can be held to account. Ownership generally gives an exclusive right to exploit the property or to give others a licence to do so in a variety of ways (Litman 'The Public Domain' [1990] Emory LJ 971). It is also the case that while intellectual property is itself intangible, it will be embodied in real objects. A Coca Cola sign, a best-selling novel, a new wonder drug may each constitute the physical embodiment of an intellectual property right: a registered trade mark, a copyright and a patent respectively.

2

The boundaries of intellectual property

1.4   The analogy with real property breaks down again however when the question is raised of how to mark off the boundaries of intellectual property. The area of a piece of land may be measured in metres. But given its intangible nature, how is one to demarcate the area of protection conferred by an intellectual property right? Can one determine, for instance, the size of the monopoly offered by a patent or the extent of a trade secret? This is a question which will be raised throughout this book in relation to each of the rights discussed. However, a general point may be made at once. Such boundaries may not be identified unless and until they are legally challenged. It useful to offer an initial example. X manufactures and sells crisps under the registered mark 'McTatties'. Y starts to sell crisps under the mark 'McTatties'. By selling crisps marked 'McTatties', Y will clearly have trespassed upon X's registration and X will have the right to stop him. Having learned his lesson, Y instead sells crackers under the mark 'McTaggies'. X brings infringement proceedings against Y. It will now be up to the court to decide whether the rights in the mark 'McTatties' accorded to X by registration extend to his preventing Y from using a different mark on different goods. In making its decision, the court will take into account a range of factors such as the distinctiveness of X's mark, its reputation or how both goods are sold (all of which may, themselves, change over time). In the end, the court must make a judgment. It is the result of this judgment which will mark out the boundaries of X's rights in the mark 'McTatties', rather than the mere fact of its presence on the Trade Mark Register (see below, Chapter 6 on Trade Marks).

The development of intellectual property law

1.5   Each of the diverse intellectual property rights covered by this book has, of course, its own separate history. The first patent for an invention was granted as early 1565. Registered trade marks were only brought into existence by the Trade Marks Act 1875. The design right was introduced as late as 1988. In the last three years, the UK has acquired a database right, which although examined here in the chapter on copyright is actually governed, in part, by quite different legal rules and procedures. Obviously, each of these areas of intellectual property law has been shaped in response to changing economic and social conditions, and these changes will be mapped in some detail in the relevant chapters. More generally, it has been suggested that the idea that there is a discrete body of law which can be placed under the rubric of 'intellectual property law' and which can encompass such diverse legal areas as patents and copyright, trade marks and industrial design rights emerged in the UK only in the second half of the nineteenth century. Its emergence has been attributed to a shift way from seeing intellectual property rights primarily as rewards for mental labour to instead viewing them as important economic assets. Under the latter view, it is, of course, possible to place copyright, traditionally understood as a reward for individual creativity, side by side with trade marks which might be viewed rather as products of the market than of the mind. Once this view of intellectual property had taken hold, its remit could easily be stretched over time to include, for example, sound recordings, cable programmes or, most recently, electronic databases, whose production may involve no intellectual creativity at all (Sherman & Bentley *The Making of Modern Intellectual Property Law* (1999) Part 4).

The justification for intellectual property rights

1.6 Undoubtedly, most 'new' intellectual production draws from a common stock of knowledge, language and ideas. If intellectual property rights are too widely drawn then this common stock will be depleted, impoverishing intellectual life and inhibiting intellectual production, whether it be of useful inventions, new cultural works, books, music, films, or trade symbols. To protect this common stock, limits have been placed on the protection afforded by intellectual property rights. In principle, for example, it is not possible to own a copyright in an idea, nor to patent a discovery. The law defines a number of circumstances in which it is possible to make use of another's intellectual property, without infringing his rights, such as the fair dealing provisions in copyright (see **3.66**). Furthermore, in contrast to most other property rights, ownership in intellectual property is time limited. At the end of the period of protection, the intellectual creations, protected by these rights, will return to the common stock, or public domain, as it is often termed. Once in the public domain, it may be used by others to produce new intellectual capital. Nonetheless, despite these limitations, there continues to be intense debate as to what belongs in the public domain and, by contrast, what should be available to private ownership. These debates, as they relate to individual intellectual property rights, will be examined in the course of this book. There are, however, two general arguments which are commonly advanced to justify the private ownership of intellectual capital, which are worth an initial examination.

The 'Law and Economics' justification

1.7   The 'Law and Economics' approach to legal studies is generally concerned with the role of the law in the efficient allocation of economic resources. Those who favour this approach, have noted a particular problem in relation to the creation of intellectual property. Because of its intangible nature, intellectual property poses what economists refer to as a 'public goods' problem. Intellectual property can be costly and time consuming to produce and may require a considerable degree of inventiveness or originality. Yet once this 'mental' investment has been embodied in a material form, it may be relatively cheap and easy to reproduce. Furthermore, there may be no limit to the extent to which it can be copied without depleting the value of the original. Without intellectual property rights, it is argued, what is to prevent others from taking advantage of (or 'free riding') on this intellectual capital, without incurring its original costs. As a result, according to this argument, intellectual property rights offer an important incentive for the creation of new intellectual capital. Without them, individuals and companies would be deterred from making the necessary initial investment to produce intellectual capital and hence the market would be impoverished. Furthermore, in the long term, without the incentive to produce offered by intellectual property rights, there would be other social costs. The public domain would inevitably be depleted, since eventually this intellectual property would be expected to become part of the public domain and to form the basis for future intellectual production (van den Bergh 'The Role and Social Justification of Copyright: A "Law and Economics" Approach' [1996] IPQ 17).

1.8   To take an example, a pharmaceutical company, Thermo Ltd, invests several years and many millions of pounds in developing a chemical compound which can cure the common cold. It sells the compound in tablet form, the physical ingredients of which are inexpensive and easily acquired. To recoup its investment and to turn a profit Thermo Ltd will want the price of the tablet to reflect not simply the cost of manufacture but also the price of development. A rival pharmaceutical company analyses the tablet. It can manufacture and sell the tablets far more cheaply than Thermo Ltd but nonetheless at a huge profit, because it has no need to recoup the costs of the initial investment in the development process. It can, in effect, 'free ride' on Thermo Ltd's creative effort. If, however, Thermo Ltd had patented the invention, it would have been able to prevent its embodiment in any tablets except those manufactured or licensed by itself. The cost of the licence would in effect be a charge for the use of the patent over and above the cost of producing the tablets, which may in itself be negligible. The same point can be made about best selling novels, CDs, videos or trade marked sports shoes, where, in all cases, the cost of the materials may be far outweighed by the value of the intellectual property which they embody.

Intellectual property and competition

1.9   The application of intellectual property rights may be seen to offer a solution to the public goods problem. Nonetheless, it may also have social and economic costs. The enforcement of intellectual property rights may be viewed as anti-competitive. For instance, in the example cited above, Thermo's patent will of course raise the cost of the drug to consumers by preventing cheaper competitive products going on the market. If Thermo has a monopoly on the drug, it may, if it chooses, raise its price beyond one which the majority of the public is able to pay. Others may be deterred from exploiting similar inventions to the general benefit of the consuming public because of fear of possible legal action by Thermo, whether or not it would be successful. Indeed, it is fair to say that there is an inherent tension between intellectual property rights and free competition, which has been widely recognised in the prevailing law, and which will be considered in the course of this book.

The 'labour' justification for intellectual property

1.10   Despite this tension, the 'Law and Economics' approach to intellectual property rights has generally been favoured by advocates of free-market economics. It rests on an underlying assumption that rational individuals will seek to maximise their economic gains and will be disinclined to act if they expect to receive only a marginal economic benefit. Hence, there is the need for intellectual property rights to solve the public goods problem. An alternative and highly influential justification

6

for intellectual property which embodies a more rights-based approach, rests on the ideas of the eighteenth century philosopher John Locke. The Lockean approach, derived from his *Second Treatise of Government*, begins from a different premise: that individuals have a right to the fruits of their labour. Put briefly, this approach assumes the existence of an uncultivated common which is characterised by an abundance of goods. Property rights are granted to those whose labour adds value to the goods they take from the commons, provided that as a result of their labour the common stock is also increased, or as Locke put it, provided 'enough and as good' is left in the commons for others to enjoy.

1.11 It is easy to see how the Lockean approach might be applied to intellectual property. In the case of intellectual property, the commons would be represented by the public domain. The public domain retains those intellectual goods which either nobody may own or exploit (such as ideas or discoveries, which if they were extracted would not leave 'enough and as good') or conversely those intellectual goods which are free to be expropriated as intellectual property, provided the necessary labour is expended upon them. In essence, this would mean that the finished 'intellectual product' would leave the public domain once it meets the relevant legal criteria for protection, for instance as a copyright work or a registered trade mark. Advocates of the Lockean view usually maintain that such expropriation from the public domain will not breach the 'enough and as good' imperative. Instead, over time, intellectual property rights will actually serve to enrich the public domain. Intellectual property rights encourage individuals to place their creations before the public. Once these creations become public, they will themselves engender new ideas and encourage further creativity. Eventually, given the time limited nature of intellectual property rights, these intellectual goods will return to the public domain (for an account of the Lockean and the alternative Hegelian approach, see Hughes 'The Philosophy of Intellectual Property' [1988] Georgetown LJ 287).

1.12 The rights-based approach to intellectual property has long been favoured by continental countries and the US. By contrast, as was suggested above (see **1.5**), the development of intellectual property rights in the UK has largely reflected more pragmatic considerations, particularly the protection of economic investment. The Law and Economics and the labour justifications for intellectual property rights are, of course, neither mutually exclusive nor contradictory. Indeed, all three approaches have been vulnerable to the same general criticism which centres on the extent and treatment of the public domain. In particular, it is argued that the present international intellectual property regime fails to recognise that some intellectual capital may be produced and exploited co-operatively, and, as a result, social justice demands that it should be protected against private ownership. For instance, it happens that the chemical compound that constitutes Thermo's cold cure actually occurs naturally in the leaf of a tree which is indigenous to India. The leaf has been used in India for many centuries as a cold cure. Aware of this fact, Thermo has analysed the chemical make up of the leaf and reconstituted it in its laboratories. Susan visits Chile and overhears a 'folk song' which is widely sung in the villages, although no one is sure of its origins. Susan returns to England, translates and arranges the song which becomes a best seller. The argument goes that an intellectual property regime which rewards Thermo and Susan, with a patent or copyright respectively, but provides no mechanism for rewarding the farmers of India or the villagers of Chile is unjust. Indeed, for a current controversy in just this area, the reader is referred to the debate surrounding attempts by a multinational chemical company to patent products derived from the Indian neem tree, long known by local farmers to increase soil fertility.

1.13 While much of this criticism emanates from developing countries, which may be seeking to protect what is often characterised as 'traditional forms' of knowledge, this is not exclusively the case. For example, similar controversy has been provoked in both in the UK and the US over the possibility of conferring a private monopoly over words and symbols which also have a wide popular meaning. A prominent example was the successful attempt by the US Olympic Committee to prevent a San Francisco gay rights group from using the word 'Olympic' in promoting the 'Gay Olympic Games' (*San Francisco Arts & Athletics v US Olympic Comm* (1987)). Critics of the decision argued that given its long history and the positive associations which have, over time, been embodied in the word by the public at large, 'Olympic' should be freely available. More recently, in the UK, the CA denied the estate of Elvis Presley a registered trade mark for the singer's name in relation to memorabilia. The decision relied in large part on the CA's recognition that given the singer's enormous popularity, the public had now attributed its own meaning to the name Elvis which it should be free to use (*Elvis Presley Trade Marks* (1999); see also **6.97**).

1.14 Both in terms of domestic law and at the international level, there has been growing pressure to frame intellectual property protection in ways which recognise the co-operative production of knowledge or the common ownership of its raw material. An example is the UN Biodiversity Convention, a product of the 1992 Earth Summit in Rio de Janeiro. Following pressure from developing nations, the Rio Convention sets out as one of its aims to preserve and protect the knowledge, resources and practices of indigenous communities. At Art 15(9), it recognises the sovereign rights of states over their natural resources, so that the authority to determine access to genetic resources should rest with national governments and be subject to national legislation. The Rio Convention has not found universal favour, not least because of its potential challenge to patent rights. However, in a parallel development, a number of governments have come to separate agreements with companies seeking to exploit their natural resources for the purposes of research. In perhaps the most publicised example, Iceland, through a company, DeCode Genetics, negotiated a $200m payment from a major biotechnology company for access to that country's gene pool. The company plans to use the Icelanders' highly uniform DNA to develop new drugs and diagnostic tests.

The international dimension to intellectual property rights

1.15 Although many intellectual property rights are territorially based, so that a UK trade mark registration protects that trade mark only in the UK, intellectual property has always had a strong international dimension. As will be seen in the course of this book, European Community law has had a transformative impact on intellectual property rights in the UK. International agreements and the resulting organisations which are concerned with individual intellectual property rights, such as the European Patent and the Community Trade Mark, will be discussed where appropriate. However, two international organisations WIPO and the WTO have been concerned with intellectual property more generally and their role is considered below.

The World Intellectual Property Organisation

1.16 The beginnings of WIPO are to be found in two nineteenth century international treaties relating to intellectual property. The Paris

Convention for the Protection of Intellectual Property (1883) covered inventions, trade marks and industrial designs. The Berne Convention for the Protection of Literary and Artistic Works (1886) dealt with copyright in a range of works, literary, artistic and musical. The effect of these conventions was to confer reciprocal protection on signatory countries, so that their nationals were accorded the same intellectual property rights in other member states as were accorded in their own. Initially, the Paris and Berne conventions were administered by separate offices and then together in Berne. In 1974 WIPO was established as a specialised agency of the UN charged with the promoting and administering intellectual property matters on behalf of its members. Today, WIPO administers a range of treaties apart from Paris and Berne. Among the most notable are the Patent Convention Treaty and the Madrid Agreement relating to trade marks, both of which offer signatories a simplified route to obtaining protection in other countries (see **2.1** and **6.13** below). WIPO also administers a number of classification systems for international property rights, such as the Nice Agreement which classifies goods and services for the purpose of trade mark registration.

1.17 Since its inception, WIPO has provided a forum for its members to discuss issues relating to intellectual property, and a base from which to launch international agreements. As the value of intellectual property grows in relation to world trade, it is inevitable the WIPO will see its importance enhanced. For example, since 1994, WIPO has provided an Arbitration and Mediation Centre for the settlement of disputes relating to intellectual property. The Centre is well placed to deal with the increased opportunities for conflict inherent in the spread of global information systems and e-commerce, such as the rising number of disputes over internet domain names, now a key area of the Centre's work.

The WTO and TRIPS

1.18 In 1996 an Agreement between the WIPO and the WTO came into force. The purpose of the agreement was to provide for co-operation between the two bodies in the implementation of the TRIPS agreement. TRIPS (Trade-related aspects of International Property Rights) was the product of the WTO's 1988-94 Uruguay Round of trade negotiations. It came into effect in 1995. Its broad purpose is to harmonise the manner in which intellectual property is protected world-wide and to provide a mechanism for settling disputes between WTO members.

1.19 The effect of the TRIPS agreement is to set out the minimum standards to which member states must adhere in relation to intellectual property rights of all kinds, including copyright, patents, trade marks, industrial designs and trade secrets. It also seeks to ensure that member states have adequate mechanisms in place to enforce these rights. While in a number of areas the standards of protection specified by TRIPS reflect those contained in earlier intellectual property treaties, such as the Paris and Berne conventions, in others the standard of protection required by TRIPS is more rigorous, while it also covers intellectual property rights such as databases which may not be covered by earlier treaties.

1.20 For its supporters, TRIPS is viewed as a crucial tool in protecting what has come to be one of the most significant areas of world trade and therefore a potential source of damaging disputes between nations. A product of free market ideology, TRIPS ensures that owners of intellectual property rights will have a level playing field not just at home but overseas. It aims to minimise the barriers to free trade which might be thrown up when different countries offer different levels of protection to intellectual property. Inevitably, TRIPS has also attracted criticism. In particular, while countries such as the UK and the US will in most respects find little conflict between their own intellectual property regimes and the TRIPS requirements, for many developing countries implementing TRIPS will involve major transformations of their domestic law. At one level, the provisions of TRIPS has taken account of this anomaly. While developed countries were given a year after TRIPS took effect to ensure compliance, the agreement allowed transitional periods of from five to ten years for 'developing' and 'least developed countries' to do the same. Nonetheless, it has been argued on behalf of these latter countries that a level playing field in relation to intellectual property rights may not be universally beneficial. For example, many developing countries, as has already been suggested, offer a wealth of resources which might be exploited by pharmaceutical companies in search of new products. These same countries may not however have the technical expertise or financial resources to develop these products domestically to the point that they would receive the extensive patent protection which ensures compliance with TRIPS. Instead, such protection may find its way to foreign-based multinationals. TRIPS has also been criticised for failing to recognise that traditional forms of knowledge may need a different type of protection than that offered in prevailing intellectual property regimes. To a considerable extent the debates surrounding TRIPS encapsulate the wider issues concerning the measurement of the public domain. As intellectual property becomes ever more valuable and hence the drive for stronger rights to protect it more intense, it is inevitable that the debate will remain central to how the law of intellectual property develops in the future.

Remedies for the infringement of intellectual property rights

1.21 In succeeding chapters, this book will examine those issues relating to remedies, which are raised by particular intellectual property rights. However, it is possible to make some general points at the outset. The first concerns jurisdiction. Most intellectual property cases are brought in Chancery Division of the HC (High Court). Patents and registered design cases are heard in the Patents Court. In addition, the CDPA 1988 established the Patents County Court, which offers a cheaper and more speedy forum for patent disputes (see **2.91**). Copyright cases may also be brought in the County Court. The 'Woolf Reforms' introduced by the 1999 Civil Procedure Rules are generally applicable to intellectual property cases. Following the incorporation of the European Human Rights Convention into domestic law by the Human Rights Act 1998, there seems little doubt that it too will play an increasingly important role in intellectual property actions. In particular, Art 1, Protocol 1 (the right to property), Art 8 (the right to private and family life, home and correspondence) and Art 10 (the right to freedom of expression), all have obvious relevance to a number of intellectual property rights.

1.22 In certain cases, copyright and trade mark actions may also be brought in criminal courts. The use of the criminal law has been largely aimed at activities such as the pirating of copyright materials, for example videos or CDs, or the use of trade marks on counterfeit goods, which may be extremely lucrative and carried out on a considerable commercial scale. Criminal actions can have a deterrent effect. They give the rights holder the assistance, where necessary, of state agencies such as the Trading Standards Office to ensure enforcement. They may not be as costly as civil actions. However, criminal actions also carry disadvantages. They can take time to initiate and they will not carry the range of remedies both pre- and post-trial which are available in civil actions (see for

12

example, the recent case of *Unic Centre SARL v London Borough of Brent and Harrow Trading Standards Office* (2000) concerning forfeiture).

Civil actions

1.23 A common feature of many intellectual property actions is that speed is of the essence. The claimant's aim is generally to stop a threatened or an on-going infringement of his rights by obtaining an injunction against the alleged infringer's future activities. Furthermore, once a claimant obtains an interim (or pre-trial) injunction, the defendant may have little incentive to contest the action further. If, for example, he is using a trade mark on a new product which the claimant alleges is infringing, he is unlikely to suspend the marketing of the product pending the outcome of a trial. Instead, he will almost certainly seek to cut his losses, chose a new trade mark and reach a settlement. As a result, most intellectual property actions are settled at the pre-trial stage and the usual remedy, where the claimant is successful, is a permanent injunction together with costs. Injunctions are looked at below (see **1.29** et seq).

1.24 Apart from injunctions, the main remedies in intellectual property cases are: delivery up, damages and an account of profits. For the reasons suggested above, the latter two remedies are comparatively underused in intellectual property actions (see **1.23**). In most intellectual property actions, liability is determined first. Where the claimant chooses to continue, damages are usually determined or an account made at a separate hearing. The third remedy, delivery up of infringing articles, is particularly appropriate where the intellectual property is embodied in a material form, and may accompany the other two.

An account of profits

1.25 A claimant must chose between damages or an account of profits. In order to assist in making the election, a claimant is entitled to the disclosure of relevant information by the defendants, such as financial records (*Island Records v Tring* (1995)). It is relatively unusual for a claimant to opt for an account of profits, not least because the process of reckoning may be complex and the outcome uncertain. Furthermore, in copyright cases, where a claimant opts for an account of profits, he cannot then seek exemplary damages under s 97(2) of the CDPA 1988 (*Redrow Homes v Betts* (1998) HL).

1.26   An account of profits considers the profit made by the infringer rather than the harm suffered by the plaintiff (*Celanese v BP* (1999) per Laddie J). According to Laddie J in *Celanese*, the purpose of an account of profits is not to 'punish' the defendant but to ensure the he does not unjustly enrich himself at the plaintiff's expense. The defendant is treated as if he has 'conducted his business and made profits on behalf of the plaintiff'. An account of profits raises the same issue of causation as is raised in assessing damages (see **1.27** below). The question to be asked is were the infringer's profits a result of his infringement of the claimant's rights (*Imperial Oil v Lubrizol* (1997)). There is strong authority that a defendant cannot lessen his liability by arguing that he might have made the same profit by following a non-infringing course. Nor can a claimant argue that the defendant should have made higher profits than he did (*Celanese*). There has been debate as to whether profits should be assessed incrementally (by looking at the difference between actual profits and those which would have been made without infringement) or alternatively whether they should be apportioned, that is paid only from that part of the defendant's business which is infringing. In the most recent case, *Celanese*, which concerned patent infringement, Laddie J preferred apportionment. In *Celanese*, the invention at issue although useful was 'small' and contributed less than 20% of the profits of the plants in which it was used. The result was that the defendant was ordered to pay a sum less than it had already admitted as being appropriate based on an incremental approach. It remains to be seen whether the *Celanese* approach will be endorsed by a higher court.

Damages

1.27   Damages in intellectual property actions are assessed following the same principles as other torts (*General Tyre v Firestone* (1975) HL; also *Gerber v Lectra Systems* (1997) CA). The victim should be restored to the same position he would have been in if no wrong had been done. Furthermore, the victim should only recover loss which is caused by the defendant's wrongful act and is a reasonably foreseeable result of it. In the case of damages then, the court will look to see how the claimant would have profited without the defendant's infringing acts, rather than, as with an account of profits, looking to the infringer's profit. While the imposition of damages is not intended to punish the defendant, nonetheless 'the defendants being wrongdoers', damages should be liberally assessed (*General Tyre* per Lord Wilberforce). The onus is on the claimant to prove the extent of his loss.

Assessing damages

1.28   The two most obvious ways a claimant may profit from his intellectual property are that he may exploit it himself or he may license it to others. In the first case, the plaintiff will seek to recover damages based on his loss of profit. Quantum can be difficult to assess. For example, in circumstances where the plaintiff and the defendant are not alone in the market and there are others competing with them, the extent of the claimant's loss attributable to the defendant's activities in particular may not be immediately apparent (Moss and Rogers 'Damages for Loss of Profits in Intellectual Property Litigation' [1997] EIPR 425). The question as to what damages should be attributed to the infringement also arises. In *Gerber*, a patents case, the CA held that the plaintiff's loss need not necessarily be restricted to those activities which constituted infringement of the patent. It could extend to loss of sales on articles which were commonly sold together with the patented goods. By contrast, in the copyright case, *Work Model Enterprises v Ecosystem* (1996), the HC found that the defendant's infringement of the plaintiff's brochure did not effect the plaintiff's sales of its products, which were advertised in the brochure. Despite its infringement of the brochure, the defendant competed perfectly lawfully with the plaintiff when selling its own goods. The situation is rather more straightforward where the damage is for loss of a licensing opportunity. Damages will follow the cost of the license. In the third case, where the claimant neither profits from manufacture nor licences his product, the court will assess damages based on a reasonable royalty. This too can be difficult. In one copyright case, it was described as 'a judgment call' (*AEI Rediffusion Music v Photographic Performance Ltd* (1998); see also *General Tyre*). In cases before the Copyright Tribunal, the Tribunal will look at comparable licences.

Injunctions

1.29   Damages and an account of profits are awarded for past misconduct. By contrast, injunctions look to the future. They are designed to restrain threatened breaches of the defendant's rights (*Coflexip v Stolt* (1999) per Laddie J). In general, once liability has been established in an intellectual property action, the claimant may expect to be awarded a final injunction. Exceptions may arise where there has been a long delay in bringing the action or the court has taken the view that there is no likelihood of a repetition of the infringing act, but examples are few. There are also particular problems raised in relation to confidential information (see **7.59** below). In an interesting recent decision, *Coflexip*, Laddie J questioned the appropriateness of final injunctions in intellectual property actions which are characteristically broadly drawn to restrain all future infringements of the claimant's rights by the defendant. He suggested instead that in certain cases a 'narrow form' injunction which restrains the repetition only of the infringing act for which the defendant has been found liable, might be more appropriate. The latter approach has the advantage of certainty for the defendant, particularly in patent actions, such as *Coflexip*, where the scope of the protected invention may not always be entirely clear. A broad approach was taken by the HC in *Microsoft v Electro-Wide* (1997). In that case, the HC granted an injunction to restrain the defendants from reproducing a substantial part of *any* operating system software in which the plaintiff had copyright (not just the software they had already infringed), because the HC took the view that the defendants were interested in copying whatever operating systems software was currently saleable.

Interim injunctions

1.30   An interim injunction prohibits the defendant from carrying out the allegedly infringing act until trial. Although an interim injunction precedes a finding of liability, its effect is frequently to bring the matter to a close. The guidelines for granting an interim injunction were set out by the HL in *American Cyanamid v Ethicon* (1975). Before *American Cyanamid*, the courts had habitually looked to the relative strength of the plaintiff's case as the main factor in deciding whether to grant an interlocutory (now an interim) injunction. The plaintiff had to show a (serious) prima facie case before the court would go on to examine the balance of convenience in favour or against granting an injunction. In *American Cyanamid*, a patents case, Lord Diplock held that there was no such rule. Instead, the court need only be sure that there was a serious question to be tried. Once that had been established, the court should go on to look at whether the balance of convenience lay in 'granting or refusing the relief which was sought'. In particular, according to Lord Diplock, the court should look to see whether the plaintiff would be adequately compensated by damages if he were to succeed at trial and in the meantime the defendant continued its alleged infringement or, conversely, whether, the defendant would be adequately compensated at trial by damages if prevented from doing the allegedly infringing acts until trial. The ability of either party to pay such damages was another important factor. Where these questions were evenly balanced, the court should look at the comparative strength of each case.

1.31 Following *American Cyanamid*, there was some debate as to whether and to what extent courts should continue to assess the strength of the parties' cases in determining whether or not to grant an interim injunction. In *Series 5 Software v Philip Clarke* (1996), Laddie J said that it should continue to be one of the four 'major' factors which the court should bear in mind. The others are the extent to which damages are likely to be an adequate remedy and the ability of the other party to pay, the balance of convenience and the maintenance of the status quo.

1.32 An example of an action where the plaintiff failed to obtain an interim injunction was the passing-off case, *Dalgety Spillers v Food Brokers* (1994). The plaintiff sold 'Golden Wonder Pot Noodles'. It accused the defendants of passing off their product 'Nissin Cup Noodles' as its own, because of similarities in the packaging. The plaintiff sought an interim injunction, which was refused on the balance of convenience. In particular, the HC was impressed by the defendants argument that if an interim injunction was granted preventing them from selling their 'Nissin Pot Noodles' in the UK, the commercial uncertainty of waiting for a trial would force them to change their packaging not just in the UK (as a result of the injunction), but in Europe where their product was also sold. Having done so, they would be unable to change the packaging back and as a result an interim injunction would effectively determine the action.

Other pre-trial relief: Mareva injunctions and Anton Piller Orders

1.33 The Mareva injunction (now called a freezing injunction) prevents a defendant from disposing of assets on which a claimant may have a claim, both before and after judgment. It is often combined with an Anton Piller order. Like the Mareva injunction, the Anton Piller order (now called a search order) is a powerful weapon in the armoury of any claimant, and has been particularly widely used in intellectual property actions. The Anton Piller order requires the defendant to allow the claimant (or his representatives) to enter his premises to search for, seize or take copies of, as the case may be, relevant goods and/or documentation. The defendant may also be ordered to provide information about allegedly infringing acts. The order is granted at an *ex parte* (without notice) hearing, and is intended to be used where there is a genuine risk that the defendant, if he had notice of the search, might destroy the relevant materials. The claimant cannot enter the defendant's premises without his permission, but the defendant may be in contempt of court if that permission is refused (see, for example, *Taylor Made Golf v Rata & Rata* (1996)). The Anton Piller order thus entails potentially serious inroads into the defendant's rights and since its introduction in the 1970s has been hedged with an increasing number of safeguards for the defendant.

1.34 The Anton Piller order was first developed by the CA in *Anton Piller v Manufacturing Processes* (1976), which concerned, inter alia, passing off and confidential information. In his judgment, Ormrod LJ set out the three criteria for granting the order, which still pertain today. The claimant must have a strong prima facie case. There must be clear evidence that the defendants have in their possession, incriminating goods or documents, and if put on notice, there is a genuine risk that they might destroy them. Third, the potential damage to the claimant must be very serious. Following the *Anton Piller* case, the order was adopted enthusiastically by claimants seeking to preserve incriminating evidence in intellectual property actions, which they believed might otherwise be lost, but it also came in for a strong measure of judicial criticism (*Columbia Picture Industries v Robinson* (1986)). A key area of concern was the difficulty faced by many defendants of obtaining expert and urgent legal advice upon the service of an order, particularly if it occurred outside of business hours. This was a point taken up by the Vice Chancellor in *Universal Thermosensors v Hibben* (1992) which concerned confidential information. In *Universal Thermosensors*, the order was served in the early hours of the morning at the defendants' homes and their business addresses. At one house, a women was alone with her children when the order was served. Following a claim by the defendants for damages relating to the effects of an interim injunction granted with the order, the Vice Chancellor set down a number of guidelines which must be followed in executing an Anton Piller order. These have now been incorporated into a standard form of the order set out in a 1996 Practice Direction. Perhaps the most important is that the order must be served and its execution overseen by an independent Supervising Solicitor. In addition, the order should be executed in business hours and on a weekday to ensure that the defendant is able to obtain legal advice.

1.35 Anton Piller orders frequently require defendants to provide self-incriminating information. For instance, the defendant may be ordered to disclose the whereabouts of allegedly infringing material or to provide other information about alleged infringements. Following a number of successful legal challenges, including one which went to the HL (*Rank Film v Video Information Centre* (1982)), the privilege against self-incrimination in civil proceedings was set aside by s 72 of the Supreme Court Act 1991. It however continues to apply in criminal proceedings which might be brought as a result of complying with the order.

1.36 In the period since its introduction the courts have become far more sparing in their willingness to grant Anton Piller orders. Indeed, compared to its earliest incarnations, the Anton Piller order can no longer be seen as overwhelmingly favouring the claimant. A challenge to the Anton Piller order was mounted in the European Court of Human Rights (*Chappell v UK* (1989)). It was based on the right to privacy guaranteed to by Art 8. The Court rejected the challenge, holding that the order, as it had been developed by the UK courts, did not violate the plaintiff's rights. Nonetheless it is submitted that it may still be open to criticism. For example, a defendant served with an Anton Piller order, especially a private individual living outside a metropolitan area, may find himself unable to obtain the level of expert legal advice which would place him on a level footing with the claimant during the execution of the order.

1.37 The Anton Piller order is, of course, of purely domestic origin and application. The role of the UK and, indeed, of foreign courts in enforcing intellectual property rights infringed overseas and granting 'cross border injunctions' or 'extra-territorial injunctions', is a complex one and beyond the remit of this book. Suffice to say, given the enormously important international aspect of so much intellectual property, it will be an area of increasing importance. It has already been noted that the WTO and WIPO are taking a key role in settling international intellectual property disputes. It may well be that the international enforcement of intellectual property rights will be a key area both for political initiative and judicial intervention in the future.

Further reading

J Boyle *Shamans, Software & Spleens* (1996)

W R Cornish *Intellectual Property* (3rd edn, 1999)

W Landes & R Posner 'Trade Mark Law: An Economic Perspective' [1987] Journal of Law and Economics 265

Self-test questions

1. Is the optimum level of legal protection for intellectual property compatible with the existence of a healthy public domain?

2. To what extent can intellectual property rights be treated as a largely domestic concern?

3. 'The courts have finally found the correct balance between the interests of the claimant and the defendant in granting Anton Piller (search) orders and interim injunctions'. Do you agree?

CHAPTER TWO

Patents

SUMMARY

The Patents Act 1977 and patent law: its development and justification

Routes to international protection

Obtaining a patent

A patentable invention: excluded inventions, novelty, the inventive step, and industrial applicability

The need for sufficiency

Infringement and defences

Losing the patent and enforcement

Patents in the international context

Introduction

2.1 The patents system in the UK is governed by the Patents Act 1977 (PA 1977). There are also a number of relevant provisions in the Copyright, Designs and Patents Act 1988 (CDPA 1988). The PA 1977, which succeeded the Patents Act 1949 (PA 1949), was intended to harmonise UK law with that of the European Patent Convention (EPC), the Community Patent Convention (CPC) and the Patent Co-operation Treaty (PCT). The PA 1977 is organised into three parts. Part I sets out the domestic law relating to substantive matters such as patentability, infringement and registration of patents. Part II covers international matters, principally the EPC and the CPC. Part III contains a number of general provisions relating to the working of the PA 1977 and like matters.

Development and justification

2.2 At its simplest, a patent may be thought of as a monopoly right to the use of an invention. The first patent for a new invention is thought to be Aconicio's Patent, for a grinding machine, granted by the Crown in 1565. From being within the power of the Crown to grant at its discretion, the patent was declared a creature of the common law by the Statute of Monopolies 1628. However, as an increasing number of Acts dealing with patents were passed in the 19th and 20th century, it effectively became a creature of statute. The longevity of the patent suggests its critical importance to the economic concerns of governments. It also means that the justifications for and the relative utility of the patent regime have varied depending upon the political and economic climate in which it has operated.

2.3 There are three broad justifications which are today most often canvassed for the existence of a patents system. The first is based on justice for the inventor, since it rewards him for the labour which has gone into his invention by preventing others, who have made no similar investment, from 'free riding' on it. Some have questioned the cogency of this justification since justice would presumably require any number of inventors of the same invention to be granted equal patent protection as long as their inventions were independent of each other (as is the case with copyright protection). In fact, patent protection is granted only to the first to file a patent application (Cornish *Intellectual Property* (4th edn, 1999) p 129). It is worth noting that in the US, by contrast, patent protection goes to the first to invent. Furthermore, if patent protection was designed largely to ensure the inventor received his just reward, then the relatively short period of protection which patents provide would be difficult to justify when compared to that granted by copyright or trade mark registration. The second and third justifications may be said to have more to do with the broader economic aims of the patent system: to encourage (investment in) innovation and, through the publication of patent applications, to disseminate information on the basis of which others may further innovate or compete. In the latter case, the patent system is said to gain its justification through an exchange by which the inventor is given a limited monopoly to exploit his invention in return for making its workings public, information which, without patent protection, he might be tempted to conceal. The fundamental importance of the patent as a disseminator of information may be seen in the courts' insistence that a valid patent application must contain an 'enabling

22

disclosure', which enables the reader to reproduce the invention which is its subject (see *Asahi Kasei Kogyo Application* (1991) per Lord Oliver).

2.4   The question of whether patents are also necessary to encourage investment in innovation has been hotly debated and the evidence is unclear. Over the 20th century, companies have dedicated increasing resources to research and development by specialists. Today, this policy is most visible in the biotechnology industry, but it has also characterised the development of other 'cutting edge' technologies in the past. Patents may be justified as encouraging expensive and speculative research by companies, in the knowledge they alone will reap the initial rewards, and hence recoup their investment, if it is successful. However, it is the exceptional invention, such as the recent anti-impotence drug Viagra, which brings exceptional rewards. It is possible that these rewards would in any event have been earned by the invention's being first on the market, even without the benefit of patent protection. It has been suggested that there may be a fourth justification for the patent system. It can be an important instrument of competition policy. It is probably true that most technological advances occur incrementally, and few such advances involve a real 'inventive step' (a necessary criterion for patenting) which carries it beyond the existing know-how. Nonetheless, the EPO has chosen to grant broad protection for patents which have been characterised less by a clear inventive step than by the fact that their development involved major financial investment and resulted in a breakthrough in a highly competitive international field, biotechnology. An example is the EPO's decision in *GENENTECH I/Polypeptide Expression* (1989), which presents an interesting contrast with the more cautious and narrow approach taken by the HL in *Biogen v Medeva* (1997))(see **2.47** below). By giving broad patent protection to technological advances in Europe, the EPO can be seen to be promoting the competitiveness of European industries against their international rivals, most notably in the US, where similarly broad patent protection is available (McInerney 'Biotechnology: Biogen v Medeva in the House of Lords' [1998] EIPR 14).

Routes to international protection

2.5   The protection given by a patent is generally territorial. It is limited to the country in which it was granted. However, it is possible to obtain patent protection in more than one country through a single application.

The Patent Co-operation Treaty (PCT), under the aegis of WIPO, provides a route by which an application can be made through a 'receiving office' (the UK Patent Office (PO (UK)) is one, as is the European Patent Office (EPO)) for patent protection in any of the contracting states. The appropriate bodies of each of the states named by the applicant decides, on the basis of their national patent law, whether to grant the patent (which is a national patent). A second route is through an application for a European Patent to the Munich-based EPO, which was established by the EPC. In contrast to the procedure under the PCT, the EPO makes its own decisions, on the basis of substantive law set out in the EPC, as to whether to grant a patent application. If approved by the EPO, a European Patent (EP) will be granted for each of the contracting states designated by the applicant. An EP has the same status as a national patent. Thus, an EP (UK) is treated as if it has been granted under the PA 1977, and questions of infringement and invalidity are decided by the domestic courts. The Community Patent (CP), which has yet to be introduced, is intended to be a single unitary patent for the EC (much like the Community Trade Mark). The Paris Convention (to which the UK adheres) ensures that nationals of one member state will have the same level of patent protection in any other member state which the latter grants to its own nationals. In addition, as a signatory to TRIPS, the UK has made some alterations to its national patent law to meet the minimum requirements laid down in the Agreement (the Patents and Trade Marks (World Trade Organisation) Regulations 1999, SI 1999 No 1899). The changes relate primarily to the granting of compulsory licences (see **2.88** below).

UK patent law and the EPC

2.6 Specific sections of the PA 1977, primarily those dealing with patentability, infringement and validity, 'are so framed as to have, as nearly as practicable, the same effects in the UK as the corresponding provisions of the EPC, the CPC and the PCT….' (s 130(7)). The UK courts have frequently followed EPC decisions or have sought to interpret the PA 1977 so that the same meanings are given as to equivalent provisions in other EPO countries or by the EPO. For example, in *Gale's Application* (1991) in relation to computer programs, Nicholls LJ said: 'in all respects material to the current case, the test for patentability under the Convention is the same as the test for patentability under the 1977 Act.' Nonetheless, there remain important areas where UK and EPO interpretations of the relevant law are at odds (for example, see **2.73** on construction). In part, this is because the EPO is not concerned with questions of infringement or invalidity, although, unlike in the UK, it is possible to oppose the grant of a patent by the EPO. Nor is it possible to appeal from the PO (UK) or courts to the Board of Appeal of the EPO, just as the latter's decisions are not open to appeal in the national courts. It is arguable that full harmonisation between domestic patent regimes and the EPC has been delayed by this absence of any final court of appeal concerning the interpretation of the relevant law in all jurisdictions.

Obtaining a patent

2.7   Any person may apply for a patent, but the broad principle is that a grant will be made only to the inventor (or joint inventors). There are exceptions. The inventor may transfer his rights to an invention by specific agreement, such as by assignment. The right to the grant of a patent may also pass to others through the operation of the law, most notably in the case of employee inventions.

Employee inventions

2.8   An employer may be entitled to ownership of an invention in two circumstances. First, if it was made by the employee in the course of his normal duties or in the course of other duties specifically assigned to him *and* the circumstances were such that an invention 'might reasonably be expected to result' from carrying out those duties (for example the employee has been hired specifically to undertake research and development) (s 39(1)). Secondly, he may be entitled to the invention if the employee had a special obligation to further his employer's interests and the invention was made in the course of his duties (s 39(2)). An invention not made in any of the above circumstances belongs to the inventor, as in *Harris' Patent* (1985), where the employee's invention could not reasonably have been expected to result from his duties in sales and service, and his status in the company was not sufficiently responsible to place him under any special obligation to his employer. There are however provisions for the employee-inventor to be compensated if the employee can show that the patent (not the invention per se) has been of 'outstanding benefit' to his employer (s 40) (*Memco-Med's Patent* (1992)).

25

The application

2.9 Patent applications are filed at the PO. A complete application includes an application form, the fee, the specification, which is made up of a description of the invention and the claim(s), plus any drawings, and an abstract (s 14). The specification must disclose the invention clearly and completely enough to be performed by a person skilled in the art (s 14(3)). The description tells a person skilled in the art how to work the invention. The claim(s), which delimit the extent of the monopoly being claimed through the application, must be clear and concise, be supported by the description and relate to one invention or a group of inventions which are so linked as to form a single inventive concept (s 14(5)). Generally, the patent will have a first broad claim, Claim 1, and then a number of subsidiary claims. It is possible to amend the claims in certain limited circumstances, once the application has been filed. An application must cover only one invention but it is possible to 'divide' the application if it covers more than one (s 14(6)). If the specification and/or the claims fails to fulfil the standards set down by the PA 1977, the application may be rejected for insufficiency. Whether or not an application will fail for insufficiency depends upon the application of the relevant legal rules and case law. The substantive conditions necessary for a finding of insufficiency will be considered below when the validity of patents is examined (see **2.62**).

The priority date (s 5)

2.10 The date at which an application is filed is its priority date. The priority date provides the cut-off point for determining what is included in the 'state of the art' (see **2.27** below), against which the novelty of the claimed patent is measured (s 2(2)). If an application is filed after the priority date of an earlier application for the same invention, the later application will fail. The priority date of an earlier application filed in countries covered by the EPC, PCT and the Paris Convention will be the priority date for a UK application, provided the latter is made within certain specified time limits. An early priority date may also be obtained by filing a skeleton application at the PO, which need meet only minimum conditions, most notably by including a description, but not the claim(s) or the abstract (s 15). The earlier priority date, obtained by a skeleton application, will hold good only for material in the later full application which was also disclosed in the earlier description (*Asahi*). Furthermore, the skeleton application, like all patent applications, must contain an 'enabling disclosure', that is sufficient information to enable a skilled person to work the invention (*Asahi* ; see **2.61** on what constitutes an enabling disclosure). If the full application is then filed inside a specified time period its priority date will be that of the first informal filing. Because it takes time to prepare a successful patent application, the earliest inventor may want to ensure that his patent claim is not defeated simply because a later inventor submits an application more quickly. The skeleton application allows him to secure an early priority date although he may still be unsure about the full implications of his invention.

Preliminary examination and publication

2.11   Within a specified period (now 12 months) following the filing of either the full application or the earlier application establishing priority, the applicant must request a preliminary examination and a limited search by the PO. The preliminary examination determines whether the application complies with the formal requirements of the PA 1977 and that it covers only a single invention. Within a specified period (18 months) from either the filing of the application or an earlier priority date, the application is published. Once the application has been made available to the public, it becomes part of the prior art. This means, for instance, that if this application is subsequently withdrawn and the *same* applicant re-submits it or a closely related one, the later application will fail because it has been anticipated by (its own) prior art.

Substantive examination and acceptance

2.12   The applicant must request the substantive examination within a specified period (now six months) from publication. It is during the second examination that the examiner will decide whether the invention meets the substantive requirements for patentability (see **2.17** et seq). A patent may then be granted or the examiner may raise objections. If the latter, the applicant has an opportunity to put his case to the examiner, either through correspondence or at a hearing, and also to make some limited amendments, for instance by limiting his claims so they avoid overlapping with prior art. If the applicant is finally unable to meet the objections within a specified period (now four and a half years from the priority date or date of filing) or 12 months from the first substantive examination report, the application will fail.

Length of grant

2.13 Patents are granted for four years in the first instance and are renewable for up to 20 years. Certain patents for pharmaceutical products or processes may gain up to five years' additional protection through the EU's supplementary protection certificate procedure (SPC). These SPC's (granted by national patent offices) recognise that many pharmaceuticals must undergo a prolonged period of government testing after the patent grant and before being placed on the market, cutting into the full 20 years of patent protection. According to ECJ, the SPC's object is to encourage research in the pharmaceutical field by offering this additional protection (*Farmitalia Carlo Erba SRL's SPC Application* (2000)).

Patentability

2.14 Patent protection is given not to all inventions but only to patentable inventions. As Lord Hoffman noted in *Biogen*, the PA 1977 does not define an 'invention', supposedly because the parties to the EPC could not agree on one. Instead, it sets outs the necessary characteristics of a 'patentable' invention (s 1(1)), and identifies excluded categories for which a patent will not be granted either because they are not considered to be 'inventions' for the purpose of s 1(2) or because, despite being 'inventions', a patent should not be granted on public interest grounds (s 1(3)). A patentable invention may be either a product or a process.

A patentable invention

2.15 The act identifies four attributes of a patentable invention. They are:

* it must be new (it must not have been anticipated)

* it must involve an inventive step (it must not be obvious)

* it must be capable of industrial application

* it must not fall within any of the categories excluded by s 1(2) and (3).

However, it is important to remember that even if an inventor believes his invention is a patentable invention, because it has all the positive characteristics listed above and does not fall into any of the excluded categories, he may still fail to obtain a patent because of some insufficiency in the application itself. The four attributes of patentability are looked at below, beginning with the excluded categories.

Patentable inventions I: The excluded categories

2.16 The PA 1977 sets out four broad categories which 'among other things' are not considered inventions to the extent that the patent relates to that thing 'as such' (s 1(2)(a)-(d)). Each of these will be considered in turn.

Discoveries, scientific theories or mathematical methods (s 1(2)(a))

2.17 Discoveries and ideas are not patentable, but discoveries or ideas which have a technical aspect or make a technical contribution are (*Fujitsu's Application* (1997)). It is the practical application of a discovery which leads to patentability, even if that practical application is inherent in the discovery or is obvious once the discovery has been made (*Genentech's Patent* (1989)). In *Genentech*, the discovery was the gene sequence of t-PA, a protein which might be used as an anti-coagulant. The patent failed, inter alia, because it did not set out, sufficiently, claims for the practical application of the discovery or was too speculative as to what those applications might be. Natural laws, for instance Einstein's theory of relativity, are not patentable. Or, as was put in one famous judicial example, by Lindley LJ: 'An invention is not the same as a discovery. When Volta discovered the effect of electric current from the battery on a frog's leg he made a great discovery, but no patentable invention' (*Lane-Fox v Kensington and Knightsbridge Electric Lighting* (1892)). However, if an inventor employs a natural effect, such as an electric current, as part of a new method to produce a new product, he could patent the method.

2.18 The dividing line between a discovery and a patentable invention is highly contentious, no more so than in the field of biogenetics, as the recent debate over the EC Directive on the Legal Protection of Biological Inventions (98/44/EC; incorporated into UK law by the Patents Regulations 2000, SI 2000 No 2037 in July 2000) illustrates. Much of the debate has focused on the question of whether a gene sequence is a discovery or an invention. The Directive states that genes and gene sequences, as they exist in nature, are not patentable because they are discoveries, but goes on, in Art 22: 'biological material [such as genes] which is isolated from its natural environment or processed by means of a technical process may be the subject of an invention even if it already occurred in nature', provided a use can be ascribed to it. Processes used to isolate genes and gene sequences and therapies involving, for example, delivery of these genes to the body were already patentable inventions before the Directive. The PO (UK) has stated that the Directive does not change UK patent law nor lead to anything being patentable in the UK which was not already patentable (see for example, *Biogen*; *Chiron Corpn v Murex Diagnostics Ltd.* (1996)). For those who argued against the patenting of genes, a major concern was that academic and non-profit organisations, which cannot muster the resources of private companies, will be deprived of the opportunity freely to undertake genetic research and to employ its results, for instance in the area of diagnostic tests for genetic diseases. Others have answered that because genetic research is so expensive, those who invest in such research must be able to count on some monetary return from their investment through at least a limited monopoly, otherwise such research would not be undertaken and the public would not benefit from its results. Another telling argument in favour of the Directive was that the US already granted patents in this area and the failure of the EC to follow suit would damage the competitiveness of its biotechnology industry. The implications of the Directive's approach to the patenting of gene sequences has been particularly intense because of output of the Human Genome Project, which recently achieved its object of identifying the DNA sequences of the entire human genome. Interestingly, the UK Prime Minister and the US President, responding to these concerns, issued a joint statement on 14 March 2000 endorsing the idea that raw fundamental data on the human genome, including the human DNA sequence and its variations, 'should be made freely available to scientists everywhere.' Cynics might note that beyond this statement of best practice, the law of patents as it now stands both in the UK and the US was left unaltered.

Literary, dramatic, musical or artistic works or any other aesthetic creations (s 1(2)(b))

2.19   These are, of course, protected by other means, most notably through the provisions of the CDPA 1988. Original computer programs which are excluded from patent protection will be protected by copyright.

Schemes, rules or methods for performing mental acts, playing a game or doing business, or a program for a computer (s 1(2)(c)) and the presentation of information (s 1(2)(d))

2.20   These are not patentable. The issue of computer programs is looked at separately below (see **2.21**). Generally, a 'mere idea' is not patentable, but a method of putting a principle or an idea into effect might be. An example of a rejected application was for a method of lessening the noise on a jet engine, which the court viewed merely as a flight plan and 'as much outside the operation of any of the useful arts as would be a trainer's direction to a jockey in his control of a racehorse' (*Rolls-Royce Application* (1963)). Whereas, a method of presenting information in shorthand by means of notations on a printed sheet was held to be patentable as possessing a definite mechanical purpose (*Pitman's Application* (1969)). It has been suggested that a computer program might, itself, qualify as a method of performing a mental act (even if the human mind could not do the act on its own (*Fujitsu*)).

Computer programs

2.21   It is in the area of computer programs that the problem of what constitutes a 'technical contribution', which separates a patentable invention from the excluded categories, such as a discovery or an idea, has been most acute (*VICOM/Computer-related inventions* (1987)). The boundary has not been easy to locate. In *Fujitsu*, the claim was for a method and an apparatus for modelling a synthetic crystal structure through the manipulation of a computer program, where previously this had been done by hand modelling. The technical contribution claimed by the patentee was either the processing of images of real objects or, alternatively, the provision of a labour-saving tool. It was held that a method for the production of images of real objects did not on its own provide a technical contribution. It was also held that, although the program did indeed avoid the labour and error which came from hand modelling, this was not a technical contribution since avoidance of labour and error was precisely the sort of advantage expected from a computer program. *Fujitsu* can be contrasted with *VICOM* (decided by the EPO), where the claimed invention also involved the processing of real images by a computer program, but the technical contribution was held to be the generation of an enhanced picture. In the latter case, the application was approved. Courts will not refuse to patent an invention merely because it is implemented in the form of a computer program, if the 'novel effect' goes beyond the computing process or the operation of the computer itself (*Gale's Application* (1991)). In *VICOM*, the means for implementing the invention had been through a computer program, but the invention was held not to be a computer program 'as such'. Instead, it was a technical process, with the computer set up to operate in accordance with a specified program for controlling or carrying out a technical process. Conversely, the courts had in the past rejected applications where the invention claimed was for computer hardware, but the essential novelty lay in the software it embodied (*Merrill Lynch's Application* (1989)). The recording of a series of instructions for calculating square roots on a ROM was held not to be a patentable invention since it did not contain a technical contribution; the ROM was merely the vehicle for carrying the instruction (*Gale's Application*).

'The thing as such' and computer programs

2.22 In *VICOM*, a technical process which was implemented by a computer program was not held to be a computer program 'as such'. However, following *VICOM*, EPO practice (and that of the PO (UK)) was based on the understanding that claims that specifically recited a computer program, even if it was the program which delivered the patentable technical effect, were not to be granted patents. In effect, the EPO and the PO (UK) were admitting claims for methods which were implemented by computer programs but disallowing claims for the computer programs themselves or for other 'carriers' of such methods (Davies 'Computer Program Claims: The Final Frontier for Software Claims' [1998] EIPR 429). This apparent anomaly was deplored by producers of computer software, not least because two of their major competitors, the US and Japan, offered patent protection to software. In *IBM's Application* (1999), the Technical Board of Appeal (TBA) at the EPO held that this practice could not be sustained. It was not logical to refuse claims to a program or carrier, if the running of the program involved a technical contribution, provided the claims were properly defined and delimited the program in question. As was put by the TBA, the exclusion of a computer program should only mean the exclusion of a program as such, meaning exclusion of a program which lacked a 'technical character'. A technical character was the effect of the execution of the program where the software solved a technical problem.

IBM's Application and the international dimension

2.23   Following *IBM*, both the EPO and the PO (UK) have altered their practice in relation to claims which are framed in terms of a computer program (Patent Office Practice Notice (1999)). These will no longer be rejected provided that the program is capable of bringing about a technical effect, which goes beyond the 'normal' physical interaction between the program and the computer. Although the change in practice undoubtedly broadens the patent protection offered to computer programs, the PO (UK) has pointed out that its effect has certainly not been to rescue 'inherently unpatentable subject matter from its fate merely by changing the semantic form of its claims.' In other words, the claim must still fulfil all the other criteria necessary for patentability. The decision in *IBM* undoubtedly brings patent protection for computer programs in the UK (and Europe) closer to that offered in the US. But the US has, itself, moved on. In *State Street Bank & Trust v Signature Financial Group* (1998), the software in question embodied a method for determining the apportioned value of pooled mutual funds. It was held by the US Court of Appeals for the Federal Circuit that mathematic algorithms, provided they were reduced to a practical application, and business methods might be patentable provided that they were useful, novel, non-obvious, based on a written description which enabled an individual skilled in the art to make and use the invention and provided the patent sets forth the best mode contemplated by the inventor for carrying it out. Following *State Street*, the US Patent Office has shown a general willingness to allow the patenting of software and business methods involved in e-commerce, for instance payment methods, electronic shopping carts and a technique for analysing how shoppers browse web content, raising concerns that the development of e-commerce will be hampered by the need to pay royalties on certain of its basic functions. Finally, Art 27(1) of TRIPS does not, in principle, exclude the patenting of computer programs which are also protectable by copyright. However, in their decision in *IBM*, the EBA made it clear that since TRIPS is not directly binding on the EPO, it would continue to rely on the EPC to determine the law in this area. There are now moves among signatories to the EPT and by the EU to seek to harmonise the position in Europe and bring it closer to that of its major international competitors.

The invention 'as such'

2.24 A more general meaning of the phrase, 'as such', beyond its relation to computer programs, has been set out in a number of judgments, including *Gales Application*. In *Gales Application,* it was held that, in so far as a patent claims as an invention the practical application of a discovery, the patent does not relate only to the discovery 'as such', even though the practical application may be obvious once the discovery has been made and even though it is unachievable in the absence of the discovery (*Gales Application; Genentech*).

Inventions which encourage offensive, immoral or anti-social behaviour are not patentable (s 1(3)(a))

2.24A These may have all the attributes of a patentable invention but will be excluded on other grounds, as being unconducive to public order and morality. An invention will not necessarily come within this prohibition only because it is illegal (s 1(4)). For instance, the EC Directive on Biological Inventions and the UK Regulations state that the following are not patentable on the basis that their commercial exploitation would be contrary to public order and morality:

* processes for cloning human beings

* processes for modifying the germ line genetic identity of human beings

* uses of human embryos for commercial purposes

* processes for modifying the genetic identity of animals which are likely to cause them suffering without any substantial benefit to man or animal, and also animals resulting from such processes.

A prominent example of the moral issues involved in this exclusion has been the attempt to secure an EP for a transgenic animal, the 'Harvard onco-mouse', which, as a result of germ cell manipulation, contained human cancer causing genes (*HARVARD/Onco-mouse* (1991)). The onco-

34

mouse was granted a patent in the US. The EPO also granted a patent. In the process, the EPO considered the 'public order' objection. It concluded that the suffering of the animal and possible environmental risks should be weighed against the usefulness of the invention to mankind, and in this case the EPO concluded the latter outweighed the former. This 'balancing' test has now been written into the EC Directive on Biological Inventions and the Implementing Regulations (see **2.18** above). The grant of a patent to the onco-mouse has been heavily criticised, not least, on the grounds that causing animal suffering can never be justified, even if it may also have other positive by-products.

Any variety of animal or plant or any essentially biological process for the production of animals or plants not being a microbiological process or the product of such a process (s 1(3)(b))

2.25   These are excluded inventions. Living material may be patented, provided it is not produced by a biological process. For instance, microbiological processes and their products, such as viruses, may be patented. This exclusion has been interpreted narrowly by the EPO. In the case of the onco-mouse, the EPO held that the application claimed an animal, not an animal variety, referring as it did to 'a transgenic non-human mammalian animal', and so did not fall under the exclusion. The onco-mouse case also presents an example of an animal which was not produced biologically. The process by which the onco-mouse was produced was accomplished, not through natural means, but through the insertion of the onco-gene into the animal. The Directive and the UK Implementing Regulations also make it clear that products and processes involving gene sequences are patentable, if they are divorced by means of an inventive process involving a new technical solution, from how they exist in nature (see **2.18** above). Plant varieties are protected, in the UK, by the Plant Varieties and Seeds Act 1964, as amended by the Plant Varieties Act 1983 and generally by the International Convention for the Protection of New Varieties of Plants. In the context of the patenting of plants, the 'variety' exclusion has also been given a narrow interpretation by the EPO since the exclusion exists merely to take into account other intellectual property rights for the protection of plant varieties provided by the contracting states (for example, *CIBA-GEIGY/ Propagating material* (1984); Llewelyn 'The Patentability of Biological Material: Continuing Contradiction and Confusion' [2000] EIPR 191).

Patentable inventions II: Novelty (s 2)

2.26 An invention is novel if it does not form part of the state of the art (s 2(1)). An invention which already forms part of the state of the art is said to have been 'anticipated'. If an invention has been anticipated it is not a patentable invention.

The state of the art

2.27 This comprises all matter (whether a product, process or any information relating to either) which has been made available to the public, whether in the UK or elsewhere, before the priority date of the invention. Information is made available not just by written or oral description, but 'by use or in any other way' (s 2(2)). 'Elsewhere' in s 2(2) means matter made available worldwide. The state of the art includes matter contained in applications for patents which, although published after the invention in question, nonetheless have an earlier priority date (s 2(3)). It is necessary to consider first how novelty, or its absence, is assessed, before going on to look at the circumstances in which a prior invention is considered to have been 'made available to the public'.

Anticipation

2.28 For the subject matter of a later patent to have been anticipated, the earlier invention must coincide with it exactly. According to Sachs LJ in *General Tyre v Firestone* (1972), 'A signpost, however clear, upon the road to the [later] patentee's invention will not suffice. The prior inventor must be clearly shown to have planted his flag at the precise destination before the patentee.' Anticipation may be based on the prior publication of an invention or its prior use (for the latter see **2.34**). *General Tyre* concerned anticipation by earlier publication of the invention, in this case, by two earlier patents and two journal articles. It was held in *General Tyre* that to determine whether an invention has been anticipated, the prior publication and the later claim are to be construed as at their 'respective relevant dates' (that is their dates of publication) by a reader skilled in the art. (The definition of a reader skilled in the art is looked at below, **2.41**.) This means that when construing the earlier document, the 'reader skilled in the art' will be assumed to be skilled in the art as it was at the time of its publication, and any later technical advances are irrelevant. Similarly, the later claim will be construed in light of the state of the art at its own publication date. The construction of the documents is the job of the court, which assumes the role of 'the reader skilled in the art', often with the help of expert witnesses, since it is unlikely to have the relevant expertise, itself. The court decides as a matter of fact whether the patentee's claim is new or whether it has been anticipated.

The tests in General Tyre

2.29   The general test for anticipation was set out in *General Tyre*. Two situations were considered. In both, it is supposed that the later claim 'A' has patent protection. In the first relatively straightforward situation, the earlier publication is considered and the question is asked whether it contains 'a clear description of' or 'clear instructions to do or make' something which if carried out would infringe Patent 'A'. If it does, then Patent 'A' has been anticipated. The second, more complicated, situation arises when the earlier inventor and the later patentee (of Patent 'A') have approached the invention from different starting points, and have described their inventions so that it would not be immediately apparent from reading the two documents that they have discovered the same device. If, by carrying out the directions contained in the earlier publication, the *inevitable* result is that something will be made or done which would infringe Patent 'A', then Patent 'A' will similarly have been anticipated. In *General Tyre*, the broad claim of General Tyre's patent was to make a tyre tread from tough synthetic rubber which would be softened with oil instead of mastication to produce high abrasion resistance. The defendant alleged it had been anticipated by an earlier patented invention, Semperit. The CA held, inter alia, that it was not possible to conclude that an experienced compounder who carried out the instructions contained in the Semperit patent immediately before the priority date of General Tyre's patent would inevitably achieve the result claimed in the latter. In other words, here the earlier publication contained a direction which could be carried out in a way which would infringe General Tyre's patent, but equally could be carried out in a way which would not. The plaintiff's patent was not anticipated. In *Merrell Dow v Norton* (1996), the HL held that there is disclosure if the invention would inevitably be made if the prior art instructions were followed, whether or not the skilled reader realised he was working in the area of the patent.

Clear and unmistakable directions

2.30   To anticipate a later invention, the earlier publication must contain clear and unmistakable directions to do what the patentee claims to have invented (*General Tyre*). In *Hill v Evans* (1862), it was held that the earlier publication, in order to invalidate a subsequent patent, must be such that a person of ordinary knowledge of the subject would at once perceive and understand and be able practically to apply the discovery without the necessity of making further experiments, because something essential was not disclosed (cited in *General Tyre* and explained in *Van der Lely v Bamfords* (1963) and *Bristol-Meyers Squibb v Baker Norton* (1999) per Aldous LJ). Or, to put it more succinctly, the earlier publication must provide an enabling disclosure (*Asahi*). It must enable a person skilled in the art to perform the invention.

Ordinary knowledge

2.31 The patent is anticipated if someone with ordinary knowledge of the subject can look at the earlier publication, and can understand and replicate the steps which led to the invention. Such a person would have the common general knowledge attributable to a notional skilled person with a background technical knowledge. What constitutes 'common general knowledge' will be looked at below in the section on the inventive step (see **2.43**).

Disclosure

2.32 A claim may have been anticipated by the prior art, but in order for it to be invalid for anticipation the prior art must have been made available to the public. The disclosure must be an enabling disclosure (see **2.10** above). To determine if it has been disclosed, it is necessary to ask two separate questions. First, has the invention been disclosed through written or oral description, by prior use or in any other way? Second, has it, as a result, been made available to the public?

Disclosure by prior use

2.33 In the case of prior use, the question of whether there is an enabling disclosure is equally pertinent. A product which embodies an invention may already be in public use. Does this constitute a disclosure of that invention? Since the passage of the PA 1977, the answer has turned upon whether it is possible, by means of analysis (such as 'reverse engineering') to uncover the invention, embodied in that product. If the product cannot be analysed or examined to disclose the invention, prior use will not invalidate a patent (*Merrell Dow Pharmaceuticals v Norton*). In *Merrell Dow*, the plaintiff held a patent for a method of making the drug terfenadine, an anti-histamine. It then patented a second compound, metabolite, which was found to be produced in the human body when the terfenadine was taken. The second patent was revoked. The HL found that there was no invalidity for prior use, since the patients were ingesting the terfenadine, not the metabolite. Nonetheless, the second patent was still invalidated by prior disclosure in that the first patent already disclosed the way of making the second compound even if it was not known about at the time. Further, it is enough for a finding of anticipation that a product, which has been sold prior to patenting, can be analysed to establish its composition by any purchaser, without establishing that it had been done (*WL Gore v Kimal Scientific Products* (1988)).

Made available to the public

2.34 'Made available to the public' has been understood to have the same meaning as 'published' in the PA 1949 (*PLG Research Ltd v Ardon International* (1993)). However, unlike under the PA 1949, information disclosed secretly is not a disclosure for the purposes of the PA 1977 since it is not made available to the public. To constitute prior art, the information given must have been communicated to any member of the public 'who was free in law and equity to use it as he pleased' (*Humpherson v Syer* (1887) per Bowen LJ). According to Purchas LJ in *Genentech* the public is the 'community of research workers skilled in the art in general.' An invention is not made available to the public if the disclosure is by someone under a duty of confidentiality, for instance, by a researcher to a fellow employee, while both are under a duty of confidentiality to their employer. Indeed, the PA 1977 makes specific provision to protect the novelty of an invention in certain situations when disclosure has been obtained unlawfully or in breach of confidence (s 2(4)). So in *Pall v Commercial Hydraulics* (1990) sending out examples of filter cartridges under confidence to recipients who knew that they were experimental and secret was not making available to the public. Nor is it made available to the public if it is merely known to one or two individual research workers pursuing their own experiments in private (*Genentech* per Purchas LJ). In *Bristol-Meyers Squibb (BMS) v Baker Norton* (1999), the invention was made available to the public through a lecture by the Director of Research and Development of BMS to an audience of 500 at a 'major symposium' in Amsterdam before the priority date of the patent. The patent concerned a drug, Taxol. The drug was used to combat cancer but was in short supply and if taken over an extended period of 24 hours often caused serious side-effects in patients. Through research, BMS 'discovered' that taken for a three-hour period with different dosages the drug might still be effective while reducing the incidence of neutropenia, one of its side effects. This discovery constituted the subject matter of the patent. BMS sued Baker Norton for patent infringement. In response, Baker Norton argued that the patent was invalid, inter alia, because the lecture had made the invention available to the public. The HC held the patent invalid, BBS appealed and the CA came to a similar conclusion. In the CA, Aldous LJ said that anyone listening to the lecture would realise that Taxol was suitable for trying to treat cancer using a three-hour 'infusion'. It was true that in the lecture the issue of reduced neutropenia was not mentioned. However, the HC found and the CA agreed that reduced neutropenia was an inevitable result of the three-hour dose, and that the public could, using the information from the lecture, carry out the three-hour infusion without the need of any information from the patent thus inevitably finding that a reduced amount of neutropenia had occurred. It followed that the lecture contained clear and unmistakable directions to carry out such a three-hour infusion and the result would inevitably be that which was claimed. The patent was invalid for lack of novelty (see also the EPO decision *American Cyanamid/ Melamine derivatives* (1999) with which this decision is consistent).

Available through use

2.35   An invention may be made available to the public through a published document or even a lecture. Use of an invention has also been held to fulfil the requirements of disclosure to the public. An invention relating to the heads of ballpoint pens was held to have been anticipated by the circulation of a 'few' ballpoint pens embodying this invention (*Fomento v Mentmore (1956); see also Humpherson*). In another case, use was public and therefore anticipatory because a boy had used a sailboard (embodying the claimed invention) in a public park (*Windsurfing v Tabur Marine* (1985)).

The medical exception (s 2(6))

2.36   A substance or composition which already forms part of the state of the art may still be novel if the claimed invention is for its first use in a method of human or animal medical treatment. The question of whether second medical uses are patentable is looked at below, under industrial applicability (see **2.58**).

Patentable inventions III: The inventive step (s 3)

2.37   In order to decide whether an invention is a patentable invention, it must be novel. If the invention is novel, next it is necessary to consider whether it required any inventive step. An invention shall be taken to involve an inventive step, if the invention is not obvious to a person skilled in the art, having regard to any matter which forms part of the state of the art (at the priority date of the invention) (s 3) (what constitutes the state of the art is defined in s 2(2) (**2.27** above)). Just as a claim which lacks novelty is said to be anticipated, so a claim which lacks an inventive step is said to be obvious. It has been suggested that while it is comparatively easy to decide whether a claim falls strictly within the wording of an earlier disclosure and so has been anticipated, the question of whether the same invention is obvious because of its proximity to the existing field of knowledge is a more difficult one because of the elusive nature of the inventive step. Indeed, the inventive step may represent 'a very small advance.' (*Killick v Pye* (1958) per Omerod J.)

The Windsurfing Test

2.38   The test for obviousness most likely to be followed by the courts was set out by Oliver LJ in *Windsurfing*. It has four steps:

1.   identify the inventive concept embodied in the patent;

2.   assume the mantle of the normally skilled but unimaginative addressee in the art at the priority date and impute to him what was, at that date, common general knowledge in the art in question;

3.   identify what, if any, differences exist between the matters cited as being known or used and the alleged invention;

4.   ask whether, viewed without any knowledge of the alleged invention, those differences constituted steps which would have been obvious to the skilled man or whether they required any degree of invention.

An objective approach

2.39 *Windsurfing* sets out an objective test. It asks not what is in the mind of the actual inventor, but whether the step would be obvious to the notional person skilled in the art having regard to any matter which forms part of the state of the art. The test for obviousness is essentially a 'jury question'. The *Windsurfing* test has been widely followed (eg *Minnesota Mining v Rennicks* (1992); *Beloit Technologies v Valmet Paper Machinery* (1997); *Union Carbide v BP Chemicals* (1999)). However, it has never been explicitly endorsed by the HL as the only test for obviousness. As a result, it is, in principle, still only one of a number of approaches which, depending on the particular facts of the case, the court might take in assessing obviousness (Griffiths 'Windsurfing and the Inventive Step' [1999] IPQ 160).

Applying Windsurfing

2.40 In *Windsurfing*, the invention claimed was a sailboard with an unstayed spar connected through a universal joint and a sail attached along one edge to the spar and held taut between a pair of curved booms mounted on the spar at one end and jointed together at the other (what is known as a Bermuda rig with a wishbone spar). The advantage of this combination was that the free sail could be used to steer and could also be easily jettisoned in case of trouble. The defendants claimed that the invention was obvious in view of prior use by C and because of the existence of a prior publication by D. C had, when a twelve-year-old boy, built a sailboard which he had used in public over two summers. This had a sail held between straight booms, but they were flexible enough to assume a curved shape on use. D had written an article, 'Sailboarding— Exciting New Water Sport' describing the same basic concept as the patent but the sailboard was fitted with a square-rigged sail. The question was whether the plaintiff's patent involved an inventive step beyond the sail arrangements employed by C and described by D. The CA held that the inventive concept was the free sail. Anyone familiar with sailing would have known as part of his common general knowledge the difference between square sails and Bermuda rigs and the disadvantages as regards manoeuvrability presented by the former and would also have been familiar with twin booms, curved in shape, known as a 'wishbone booms'. The skilled man must be assumed to appreciate and understand the free sail concept taught by D and to consider in light of his knowledge and experience whether it will work and how it will work. He would know

42

the disadvantages from which the kite rig, suggested by D, would suffer and therefore be led to the plaintiff's solution. Similarly, the step from the replacement of the primitive straight boom of C's craft to the wishbone boom of the patent would be an obvious one to take for the notional skilled man with common general knowledge. The plaintiff's patent was, therefore, invalid for obviousness.

The person skilled in the art

2.41   This is the person against whose knowledge the obviousness of the patent will be judged. He is assumed to be the notional addressee of the patent. The patent is addressed to such a man. It must have sufficient detail for him to understand and apply the invention. The invention will lack an inventive step if it is obvious to such a man. Descriptions of him abound in patent law. He is said to lack inventive capacity, but is deemed to have the common general knowledge in the field to which the invention relates (*Beloit*). He is assumed to be sufficiently interested to address his mind to the subject and to consider the practical application of the information which he is deemed to have (*Windsurfing*). He is the sort of man, good at his job, that could be found in real life (*General Tyre*). He is neither a 'mechanical genius', nor is he a 'mechanical idiot' (*Gillette Safety Razor v Anglo-American Trading* (1913) per Lord Moulton). There can be more than one addressee. The directions for the invention may need to be carried out through co-operation of a number of individuals with diverse skills. For instance, where the field of the patent is one of advanced technology, such as genetic engineering, the notional addressee may not be a single person but a team whose combined knowledge would allow them to carry out the instructions contained in the patent (*Genentech* per Mustill LJ).

2.42   The person skilled in the art must have skill in the field in which the invention is concerned. In *Richardson-Vicks Patent* (1997), the proprietor had obtained a patent for a new cough mixture which mixed a well-known NSAID ibrufen with three well-known decongestants. This combination had no synergistic effect, but was still more effective than previous combinations of other NSAID's and decongestants. The proprietor accepted that it would have been obvious to the notional skilled man to consider this combination, but he would have rejected it because it would not have gained drug regulatory approval. The proprietor claimed that the notional skilled man in the case of a

43

pharmaceutical company would have been a team which included an expert on drug regulatory affairs and he would have advised that the combination was not obvious to try because it would not have got approval. The CA was asked whether the skilled addressee comprised a team which included a person who was an expert on drug regulatory affairs. Aldous J held that it did not. A person skilled in the art of obtaining regulatory approval was not a person skilled in the art of producing new combination drugs. To be part of a team, he must be someone who is directly involved in the product described in the patent.

Common general knowledge

2.43 The obviousness of an invention is measured against what will be obvious to a person skilled in the art. This person skilled in the art is deemed to have the common knowledge in the field to which the invention relates. This has come to be called the 'common general knowledge' of the art. Common general knowledge should not be confused with the 'state of the art', against which the novelty of an invention is measured and which comprises, more or less, all the relevant knowledge which is in the public domain. The notional skilled man is not assumed to know everything which comprises the state of the art, some of which may, of course, be extremely esoteric. In a recent case, common general knowledge was summed up by Jacob J as the background technical knowledge attributed to the notional skilled man. Such knowledge forms part of his mental attitude and is generally regarded as a good basis for further action (*Union Carbide Corpn v BP Chemicals* (1998)). In assessing what is common general knowledge, the court will look at the sources from which the skilled man may have acquired his information. If he works for a large company, he may have ready access to advanced information technology which facilitates the retrieval and circulation of information. In fact, the ordinary skilled man is not assumed to be the employee of a large company or to have such advantages and it is assumed that he may not be aware of such information until it is accepted generally and put into practice (*Beloit*). Evidence may be adduced in court as to what is the common general knowledge. But evidence that a fact is known or even well known to a particular witness, who may of course have been chosen precisely because he is an expert in the field, does not establish that it is part of the common general knowledge for the notional skilled man (*Beloit*). Nor will a fact form part of the common general knowledge simply because it is recorded on a document. Widely read publications, such as *Popular Science Monthly,* the journal in *Windsurfing,* form part of the common general knowledge; but, earlier patent specifications, for instance, normally do not (*General Tyre;* but see, anticipation, where a previously published patent application will form part of the state of the art (**2.21** et seq)). Disclosures in scientific publications may form part of the common general knowledge, if the disclosure is accepted generally by those engaged in the art to which the disclosure relates or, in other words, if it becomes part of their common stock of knowledge relating to the art (*British Acoustic Films v Nettlefold Productions* (1935) per Luxmore J).

Other tests for obviousness

2.44   At present, the *Windsurfing* test is certainly the courts' preferred standard for assessing obviousness. There are other tests which have developed through the case law which may still be relevant in assessing obviousness, the most important of which are considered below.

An obvious step

2.45   A person skilled in the art given the state of the art might well find the step leading to the invention obvious. If so, the invention would not be a patentable invention (*Olin Matheson Chemical v Biorex* (1970)). *Olin Matheson* concerned the invention of a tranquilizer through experimentation on a sub-group of a large class of organic substances, phenothiaziens. Another sub-group was already known to produce the tranquilizer chlorpromazine, and an extensive literature and various patents had been generated around it. Graham J asked, 'Would the notional research group at the relevant date, in all the circumstances, which include a knowledge of all the relevant prior art and of the facts of the nature and success of chlorpromazine directly be led as a matter of course' to try the substitution of one sub-group for another, 'in the expectation that it might well produce a useful alternative to or better drug than chlorpromazine or a body useful for any other purpose.' He answered that it would not, and there was an inventive step. In this case, the invention may be said to have resided in the very idea that taking the step in question would have a useful result, even though once the idea was taken seriously it was obvious how to achieve the result. An opposite result was reached by the CA in *John Manville's Patent* (1967). The claimed invention was the addition of polyacrylamide, a flocculating agent, during the process of filtration of asbestos cement slurry, in the

45

manufacture of shaped asbestos cement articles. The idea that flocculating agents might aid filtration was well known, but until the invention of polyacrylamide none had been effective. A research worker for the alleged infringer had himself tried using polyacrylamide as a flocculating agent but had abandoned his experiments when he had found the result was the formation of a thicker skin for asbestos cement, which had its own disadvantages. Later on, returning to the problem, he discovered that a simple technical adjustment to the equipment would overcome this problem. The CA held that the invention would have been obvious to the 'notional' man skilled in the art even though, for the research worker in this case, his 'glimpse of the obvious was spasmodic.' The appellants could not rely on the research worker's failure to complete the initial experiment as evidence of an inventive step, since they had not included the necessary technical adjustment in their original claim. Conversely, even if it had been included, since the adjustment was obvious once the thicker skin resulted, the claim would have been invalid for obviousness.

A step worth taking

2.46 An alternative approach to assessing obviousness lies in asking whether it would be obvious to the man skilled in the art that the inventive step was worth trying. In *Beecham Group (Amoxycillin) Application* (1980)), which concerned successive patent applications for forms of penicillin, Buckley LJ described the measure of obviousness thus:

> Where, however, the skilled man has no particular problem or need in mind but merely regards some part of the known art as giving a good lead for further research, which may result in the discovery of some useful further knowledge, can the result of that research and its ascertainment by carrying out the research be obvious in the relevant sense? I think not, although this also may be a question of degree. By selecting the research, the researcher is, in my view, demonstrating that he is not wholly devoid of inventive capacity. He is not merely employing an obvious technique to get around an awkward corner; he is seeking to extend the field of human knowledge. The distinction is between a mere exercise of ingenuity and a voyage of discovery.

In *Genentech*, it was suggested that where there are many research teams working towards a particular goal, it is necessary to undertake both a surprising course of action and to achieve a surprising result for there to be an inventive step.

The test in Biogen

2.47 An application of the 'worthwhile to try' test occurred in *Biogen*. The plaintiff's claim was for a product, a recombinant DNA molecule made by rDNA techniques and expressed to produce a polypetide displaying HBV antigen specificity in certain circumstances. The priority date for the invention was 1979. The manner in which the antigen was produced was by expressing random pieces of DNA, in a hit and miss way, rather than by identifying the antigen as part of a complete sequence of HBV DNA, which would first have to be described. In fact, it was described by another scientist in 1979 before Biogen's priority date and Medeva used the sequence, after the priority date, to produce the antigen. The question before the HL was whether Biogen's hit and miss approach involved an inventive step. Biogen argued that the inventive step consisted in doing something a skilled person might not have thought worth doing. The CA, following the decision in *Genentech*, had earlier held that there was no inventive step. There had merely been a business decision to pursue an identified goal by known means. The CA offered the analogy of putting a bet on a horse hoping it would come in first. This was not an inventive step. Meanwhile in Europe, where simultaneous opposition hearings were proceeding, the TBA of the EPO found there was an inventive step based in particular on the fact that many others were also seeking to reach the same invention. The HL took a third view. It said that anything inventive done for the first time was the result of adding a new idea to the existing stock of knowledge. If it was the idea of using established techniques to do something which no one had previously thought of doing, the inventive idea would be doing the new thing. If it was finding a way of doing something which people had wanted to do but could not think how, the inventive idea would be the way of achieving the goal. If many people might have had a general idea of how they might achieve a goal but not know how to solve a particular problem which stood in their way, and someone devised a way of solving the problem, the inventive step would be that solution, but not the goal itself or the general method of achieving it. The HL declined to overturn the trial judge's decision that there had been an inventive step. It found that the trial judge had made a reasonable evaluation on the facts. If the inventive step in this case was looked at as the idea of *trying* (author's emphasis) to express unsequenced eukaryotic DNA in a prokaryotic host then it was reasonable for the judge to conclude this was not obvious.

Self-evident extension of prior art

2.48 This would be obvious. In *Hallen v Brabantia* (1991), the plaintiffs had a patent for a 'self-pulling corkscrew' coated with a non-stick polymer, 'PTFE', which they claimed not only eased the penetration of the corkscrew but also, less predictably, helped with the removal of the cork. The same polymer had already been used with 'twin-lever' cork screws to facilitate penetration. The CA found that it was an obvious extension of the prior art to coat the self-pulling corkscrew or any other type of corkscrew with polymer once it had been shown to be useful on one type of corkscrew. Could the patent be saved by the surprising effect the polymer had on removal? The CA accepted that it was not obvious that the polymer would have this additional effect. Although this was 'a golden bonus', the CA held that it was common ground that an added benefit, however great, will not found a valid patent if the claimed innovation is obvious for another purpose. An opposite result was reached in the earlier EPO case of *BAYERC (Baatz et al)/carbonless copying paper) Application* (1981). The application concerned a carbonless copying paper. On the paper's surface was a dye contained in micro-capsules. An earlier published German specification revealed that the walls of the capsules could be made of a particular class of chemicals, polyureas. The claimed invention was said to lie in the selection of diisocyanates, a sub-group of this class. The Examining Division at the EPO said that the selection was obvious. On appeal, the applicant produced comparative tests showing an advantage of the selection to be that the paper did not lose its copying capacity so readily. The application was held to involve an inventive step.

Hindsight

2.49 Sometimes an invention seems obvious in hindsight. It may be easy to retrace the steps leading from the invention to the prior art, and to show that since each step was an simple one, there was no inventive step. This is particularly the case where the problem solved is obvious or the technology involved is not particularly difficult. The court will be careful not to be wise after the event. Obviousness in hindsight will not lead to a finding of invalidity (*Beloit*; *Fichera v Flogates* (1984)).

An original step

2.50 A patentee whose claimed invention is challenged for obviousness by an alleged infringer, may ask, 'Why had nobody taken the inventive step before?' This is a question that the courts have themselves posed in the past when assessing obviousness, as in the much cited comment of Tomlin J in *S Parkes & Co Ltd v Cocker Bros Ltd* (1929):

> The truth is that when once it has been found, as I find here, that the problem had waited solution for many years, and that the device is in fact novel and superior to what has gone before, and has been widely used, and used in preference to alternative devices, it is, I think, practically impossible to say that there is not present that scintilla of invention necessary to support the Patent.

However, the approach of asking whether 'the patent discloses something sufficiently useful to deserve the grant of a monopoly' was disapproved in *Mölnlycke v Proctor & Gamble* (1994) as being too subjective, and the courts are now unlikely to raise the question of why it was not done before in assessing obviousness (see also *Beloit*).

A successful step

2.51   The courts have used evidence of commercial success as an indication that there may be an inventive step. For instance, commercial success might suggest there has been a long-standing need for the successful product that others have tried but failed to supply. The highly-successful anti-impotence drug, Viagra, might be an apt example. But commercial success is not to be used as primary evidence that there is an inventive step (*Mölnlycke*). Commercial success may be due to other factors such as the way the product is marketed. In *Haberman v Jackel* (1999), the inventive concept was the use of a simple slit valve to prevent leakage from a training cup for babies. Laddie J found that the invention had been cheap, simple and effective and also a commercial success. The inventive step had been one many people in the trade would have taken during the past decade if they had come up with it. It was not obvious. The fact that a particular line of research is adopted for commercial, rather than purely scientific, reasons does not mean that there is no inventive step. As Lord Hoffman realistically observed in *Biogen*, 'Most patents were the result of research programmes undertaken on the basis of hard-headed cost-benefit analysis.'

The new use of old things

2.52   This is an area where English case law appears to diverge from the view taken by the EPO. English authorities hold that the new use of a known thing, where there is no additional ingenuity, is not a patentable invention. Conversely, an invention involving the new use of a known thing is patentable, if the new use overcomes practical difficulties which the patentee was the first to identify (*Parks-Cramer Co v Thornton & Sons Ltd* (1966); *Gadd and Mason v Manchester Corpn* (1892)). By contrast, in the EPO case concerning a new use of an old thing, *BASF/Triaazole derivatives* (1989), the claim was for compounds for controlling fungi and the patent application contained teaching as to how to carry this out so as to achieve the desired effect. It was held by the EBA:

> With respect to a claim to a new use of a known compound, such new use many reflect a newly discovered technical effect described in the patent. The attaining of such a technical effect should then be considered as a functional technical feature of the claim (for example, the achievement in a particular context of that technical effect). If that technical feature has not been previously made available to the public by any of the means as set out in the EPC Act 54(2), then the claimed invention is novel, even though such technical effect may have inherently taken place in the course of carrying out what has previously been made available to the public.

The later EPO case, *MOBIL/Friction-reducing additive* (1990) confirmed that it was possible to patent an invention which involved the new use of a known thing. The claim was for use of a friction-reducing additive in a lubricating oil. This same additive was already known to be rust-reducing. No new means were employed to produce the lubricating effect. The question was whether the claim lacked novelty. The Enlarged Board of Appeal (EBA), following *BASF/Triaazole derivates* (1989) found that if the friction-reducing effect had not previously been made available to the public the claimed invention was novel, even though it may inherently have taken place in the course of carrying out the rust-reducing effect (see also, second pharmaceutical use, **2.58**). The EBA acknowledged that this finding might contradict national patent law. However, neither the HL in *Merrell Dow* nor the CA in *B-MS v Baker Norton* concluded that the *MOBIL* decision had been wrongly decided. By contrast, it has been suggested that the EPO has been taking a narrower approach to what may be patented as a new use (see for example, *ROBERTET/Deodorant compositions* (1999)).

Collocations

2.53 If the invention simply combines into one apparatus two machines which had formerly been used separately, each of which performs its normal function, it is not patentable. This is true even if the resulting combination is novel. In the famous sausage machine case, a filling machine was combined with a mincing machine to produce a machine for mincing meat and putting it into skins to make sausages. Since both the original machines were already known and were combined 'in the simplest possible manner', it was held not to be a patentable invention (*Williams v Nye* (1890)). Similarly, in *Merrell Dow*, the combination of ibrufen with a decongestant was not an inventive step even though the product was a more effective drug, because each ingredient was performing its usual and known function. If there had been a synergy between them which had produced a wholly new effect, it may well have been a patentable invention.

Analogy

2.54   According to Lord Herschell in *Morgan v Windover* (1890):

> ... the mere adaptation to a new purpose of a known material or appliance, if that purpose is analogous to a purpose to which it has already been applied, and if the method of application is also analogous so that no inventive faculty is required and no invention is displayed in the manner in which it is applied, is not the subject matter of a patent.

In this case, the invention was the use of springs normally used in the rear part of a carriage in the front of the carriage.

Patentable inventions IV: industrial applicability (s 4)

2.55   The third attribute of a patentable invention is industrial applicability. An invention shall be taken to be of industrial application if it can be made or used in any kind of industry, including agriculture (s 4(1)). An invention is not capable of industrial application if it is a method of treatment of the human or animal body by surgery or therapy or of diagnosis practised on the human or animal body (s 4(2)). Industry has been widely construed to include almost any commercial enterprise. The treatment exclusion covers both product and process claims and methods of testing.

The method of treatment exclusion

2.56   These cannot be patented. This exception reflects a concern not to allow the patent system to constrain the freedom of doctors in how they treat patients, rather from any intention to proscribe the patenting of pharmaceuticals (*John Wyeth & Brother's Application/Schering 's Application* (1985)). It applies to animal as well as human treatment. It does not cover an invention of any substance, composition (or apparatus) which is used in the treatment (s 4(3)). Therapy has been interpreted to mean any medical treatment of a disease whether preventative or curative (*Unilever (Davis's) Application* (1983)). This section is one of those specified in s 130(7) of the PA 1977 to be interpreted as nearly as practicable in the same way as the corresponding Articles of the EPO. Relevant EPO decisions have interpreted the exception narrowly (*EISAI/Second medical indication* (1985)), an approach that was confirmed by the CA in *BMS v Baker Norton*.

First medical use

2.57   When discussing anticipation, it was noted that the first medical use of a known product was patentable (s 2(6)) (see **2.36**). If the product is state of art, the first medical use can be new if that use does not form the state of the art.

Second medical use

2.58   What if the substance already has a known medical use and a second novel use is uncovered? Unless it is a claim for a method of treatment, it can, in principle, be patented. This so-called 'Swiss style claim' was approved by the EPO in *Eisia* (1985) and subsequently confirmed by the UK courts in *John Wyeth's Application*. An example of a 'Swiss style' claim was at issue in *Monsanto v Merck* (2000) which concerned patents relating to anti-inflammatory compounds (NSAIDS). The 'Swiss style' claim was framed as follows: 'Use of a compound of claim 1 for preparing a medicament for treating inflammation or an inflammation associated disorder,' where claim 1 was an earlier patent claim. Crucially, the claim is for the 'preparation' of the substance rather than its new use in a method of treatment. In *Eisia*, the EBA allowed the patenting of second medical uses of known substances. It stated that,

> the Enlarged Board considers that it is legitimate in principle to allow claims directed to the use of a substance or composition for the manufacture of a medicament for a specified new and inventive

52

therapeutic application, even in a case in which the process of manufacture as such does not differ from known processes using the same ingredients.

2.59 It can be argued that the 'Swiss style' claim allows the patenting of medical treatments by other means. However, the decision by the CA in *BMS v Baker Norton* made clear that the two are not equivalent. It may be recalled that BMS claimed as the invention the fact that Taxol administered in three-hour doses might still be effective against cancer and cause fewer side effects than if administered over 24 hours (see **2.34** above). Aldous LJ held that the form of claim was to a medical treatment rather than a claim for a new use for a known substance. He pointed out that the invention was the discovery that by changing treatment from 24 hours to three hours a similar effect was attained with less neutropenia. He said, 'This was a discovery that a change in the method of treatment provided the result. The claim is an unsuccessful attempt to monopolise the new method of treatment by drafting it along the lines of the Swiss-type claim' (Horton 'Methods of Treatment and Second Medical Use: Patents After the Taxol Appeal' [2000] PW 9).

Sufficiency (s 14)

2.60 A patentable invention must be novel, involve an inventive step, have industrial applicability and not fall into any of the excluded categories. These are external criteria against which the patentability of an invention will be judged. But a patent application may fail or a patent be revoked not because of any objective shortcomings of the invention which forms the subject matter of the patent. Instead, there may be shortcomings in the way the specification is drafted which will defeat the application or lead to the later revocation of a patent. The patent may fail for insufficiency. In effect, whether an invention is a patentable invention turns not simply upon the nature of the invention but also upon how it is described. Compare this with registered trade marks, where the subject matter of registration is clear and the question is simply whether the mark meets the external criteria set out by the TMA 1994 for registration.

The need for sufficient disclosure (s 14(3))

2.61 The specification for an application must disclose the invention in a manner which is clear enough and complete enough for the invention to be performed by a person skilled in the art (s 14(3)). In other words, the application must contain an enabling disclosure (*Biogen*; *Asahi*). This is the same enabling disclosure which is necessary to fix a patent's priority date (**2.10**). The courts have made clear that the need for an enabling disclosure is not simply a formal requirement (such as the need to include an abstract in the application) but a substantive one which goes to the heart of the patent regime (*Biogen*). The limited monopoly granted by a patent can be justified only if, when it expires, the specification provides sufficient information to enable the invention to be exploited more generally.

2.62 The importance of the enabling disclosure is also crucial because, for a patent to be valid, the claim or claims must be supported by the description (s 14(5)(c)). A description of an invention will not 'support' the claims for the purpose of s 14(5)(c) unless it contains sufficient material to enable the specification to constitute the enabling disclosure required to satisfy s 14(3) (*Asahi* applied in *Biogen*). This had been the approach of the TBA at the EPO in *Genentech I/Polypeptide*, who were quoted with approval by Lord Hoffman in *Biogen*. The TBA said:

> Furthermore, Article 84 EPC also requires that the claims must be supported by the description, in other words, it is the definition of the invention in the claims that needs support. In the Board's judgment, this requirement reflects the general legal principle that the extent of the patent monopoly, as defined by the claims, should correspond to the technical contribution to the art in order to be justified.

It is for this reason, that failure to satisfy s 14(5)(c) not only leads to a patent application being rejected for insufficiency but also constitutes later grounds for revocation under s 72(1)(c) (*Biogen*).

Assessing sufficiency

2.63 Essentially, a man skilled in the art must be able to perform the claimed invention across the full width of the claims and not just a single embodiment (*Biogen*). Generally, the man skilled in the art is the same individual who appears in the test for obviousness. He is prepared 'to display a reasonable degree of skill and a common knowledge of the art in making trials or to correct obvious errors in the specification if a means of correcting them can be readily found.' If correction of such errors involves prolonged study or an inventive step then there is insufficiency (*Valensi v British Radio Corpn* (1973); *Chiron*). If the art is highly technical then the person skilled in the art must have a degree of inventiveness (*Genentech*). If a team is involved, then it should be credited with sufficient time and the best available equipment to carry out the work (*Genentech*). The performance required is not the production of a commercial product but rather of a workable prototype (*Chiron* per Morritt LJ). However, there is no enabling disclosure if the instructions lead a second notional addressee to arrive at different results to the first, some of which are within and some of which are outside the claimed invention (*Chiron*).

The claim/specification balance

2.64   The breadth of the claim must not exceed the technical contribution to the art embodied in the invention (*Exxon/Fuel oils* (1994) EPO). In *Biogen*, Lord Hoffman, following the TBA's decision in *Genentech I/Polypeptide*, said that,

> the specification must enable the invention to be performed to the full extent of the monopoly claimed. If the invention discloses a principle capable of general application, the claims may be in correspondingly general terms. The patentee need not show that he has proved its application in every individual instance. On the other hand, if the claims include a number of discrete methods or products the patentee must enable the invention to be performed in respect of each of them.

The technical contribution of the claim in Biogen I was to show that recombinant techniques could be used to make HBV antigens in a prokaryotic host cell. But this did not, according to Lord Hoffman, justify a claim to a monopoly of any recombinant method of making the antigens. The claim was too broad. It did not establish any new principle that *must* (author's emphasis) be followed to achieve the same results. Other means could be used to reach the same result which owed nothing to the invention. The patent was invalid for insufficiency (*Biogen*).

Selection patents

2.65   If the inventive step lies in the discovery that one or more members of a class have some special advantage for some particular purpose, it is necessary to define the nature of the special characteristics possessed by the selection for which the patent claims a monopoly. Furthermore, all the selected must possess the advantage claimed (*IG Farbenindustrie's Patents* (1930)).

Infringement

2.66 The PA 1977 sets out those acts which will infringe a patent if they are done without the patentee's consent (s 60(1)). These will be considered below. However, an act will only be infringing if it falls within the scope of the patent's claims. To determine whether an act is an infringing act, the court must first determine the extent of the monopoly claimed by the patent. How does the court construe the claim for the purposes of finding infringement?

The 'fence post' approach

2.67 This was the traditional approach to construction taken by the UK courts. The 'fence post' approach takes the literal wording of the claim as marking off the boundaries of the monopoly. In the famous words of Lord Russell: 'What is not claimed is disclaimed' (*EMI v Lissen* (1939)). Alongside, this literal approach, the courts developed the somewhat less narrow 'pith and marrow doctrine', which ignored immaterial deviations by the alleged infringer from the exact wording of the claim. For example, if the alleged infringer substituted one non-essential 'integer' of a claim with a 'mechanical equivalent', ie one that made no essential difference, there would still be infringement if all the essential 'integers' were reproduced. In *Rodi & Weinenberger v Henry Showell* (1969), which concerned an expandable watch strap, the 'integer' substituted by the alleged infringer was a c-shaped bow for a u-shaped bow in the strap's links. The court held the u-shape to be an essential feature of the invention and there was no infringement (*Cornish*, pp 602-609) .

The purposive approach

2.68 The break with the strict fence post approach came with the decision by Lord Diplock in *Catnic v Hill & Smith* (1982). In *Catnic*, Lord Diplock took what has come to be known as a 'purposive approach' when construing the claim in question. Using this approach, the court is less concerned with the literal meaning of the claim, but rather with the intention behind its wording (although intention should be judged objectively). Lord Diplock put it thus:

> A patent specification should be given a purposive construction rather than a purely literal one derived from applying to it the kind of meticulous verbal analysis in which lawyers are all too often tempted by their training to indulge. The question in each case is: whether persons with practical knowledge and experience of the kind of work in which the invention was intended to be used, would understand that strict compliance with a particular descriptive word or phrase appearing in a claim was intended by the patentee to be an essential requirement of the invention so that *any* variant would fall outside the monopoly claimed, even though it could have no material effect upon the way the invention worked.

In *Catnic*, the claim was for a load-bearing lintel with a back plate extending vertically. The alleged infringer had slightly inclined the back plate from the vertical position. The question was whether a builder familiar with ordinary building operations would understand the claim to have excluded back plates which were not strictly vertical. Giving the claim a purposive construction, Lord Diplock concluded that 'it would be obvious to him that the patentee did not intend to make exact verticality in the positioning of the back plate an essential feature of the invention claimed.' On this construction, the patent was infringed.

The Improver test

2.69   The *Catnic* case concerned infringement of a patent granted under the PA 1949. The judgment was followed by Hoffman J in *Improver v Remington* (1990)). In his judgment, he set out the *Catnic* test for infringement in a systematic way. When deciding whether a feature, embodied in an alleged infringement which falls outside the primary, literal or a contextual meaning of a descriptive word or phrase in the claim (a variant) is nonetheless within its language as properly interpreted, the court should ask the following three questions:

1. Does the variant have a material effect upon the way the invention works? If yes, the variant is outside the claim [and there is no infringement]. If no—

2. Would this (ie that the variant had no material effect) have been

57

obvious at the date of publication of the patent to a reader skilled in the art. If no, then the variant is outside the claim [and there is no infringement]. If yes—

3. Would the reader skilled in the art nevertheless have understood from the language of the claim that the patentee intended that strict compliance with the primary meaning was an essential requirement of the invention. If yes, then the variant is outside the claim [and there is no infringement].

Conversely, if the answer to question three is a negative, then it is possible to conclude that the patentee was not intending that word or phrase to have a literal meaning, but rather to denote a class of things which included the literal meaning and the variant. In this case there would be infringement.

Applying the Improver test

2.70 In *Improver*, the claim was for an electric hair remover, the 'Epilady', with a helical spring which caught the hairs. The defendants used a slitted rubber rod in its place. The claim included an 'equivalence' clause which stated 'that all variations which come within the meaning and range of equivalency of the claims are therefore intended to be embraced therein.' The question for the court was whether the claim should be construed widely enough to include the defendant's variant. The court found that the defendant's variant did not have a material effect upon the way the invention worked (question 1 of the test) and that this would have been obvious to a skilled reader (question 2). It found that the 'helical coil' should not be given a wide general meaning, and a skilled man would not understand it to have had one (question 3). There was no infringement, since the equivalence clause did not change the outcome.

Statutory provisions

2.71 Under the PA 1977, the extent of an invention is taken to be that specified in the claim (s 125(1)). The construction of a patent claim must be in accordance with the Protocol on the Interpretation of Art 69 of the EPC (s 125(3)). The Protocol states that Art 69 (of which s 125(1) is the equivalent) should be interpreted to mean that the extent of protection occupies the middle ground between the two extremes of a strictly literal meaning of the wording of the claim or seeing the claim only as a guideline. It reads:

> Article 69 should not be interpreted in the sense that the extent of the protection conferred by a European Patent is to be understood as that defined by the strict, literal meaning of the wording used in the claim, the description and the drawings being employed only for the purpose of resolving an ambiguity found in the claims. Neither should it be interpreted in the sense that the claims serve only as a guideline and that the actual protection conferred may extend to what, from a consideration of the description and drawings by a person skilled in the art, the patentee has contemplated. On the contrary, it is to be interpreted as defining a position between these two extremes which combines a fair protection for the patentee with a reasonable degree of certainty for third parties.

2.72 A line of English cases have held that the purposive approach to construction set out by Lord Diplock in *Catnic* and explained by Hoffman J in *Improver* is the correct one (*Beloit; Kastner v Rizla* (1995)). Recently, in *Hoechst v BP* (1999), Aldous LJ said that it was 'the correct means of navigating between Scylla, the rock of literal construction; and Charybidis, the whirlpool of guided freedom as required by the Protocol. It enables the court to arrive at a result which gives fair protection to the patentee with a reasonable degree of certainty for third parties.' In *Hoechst*, the defendants appealed from a HC decision that they had infringed the plaintiff's patent by the use of certain resins employed in a process of water purification. The essential ingredient used in the process was the 'ion exchange resin'. A requirement of the plaintiff's claim was that the resin be 'stable in the organic medium'. 'Stable' was defined in the patent as meaning 'that the resin will not chemically decompose or change more than 50% of its dry physical dimension'. The plaintiff maintained that the 50% change meant a change in diameter and that this was the 'dimension' referred to. The defendants submitted the word 'dimension' meant size and any resin that swelled more than 50% 'in volume' was not 'stable' and therefore did not infringe. If the latter reading was correct there would have been no infringement. It was a fact that a 50% change in the diameter meant a change in volume of 240%. The sole issue for the CA was to decide whether the claim referred to the diameter or to volume. The HC had held that the claim referred to the diameter. The plaintiff produced expert evidence to argue that the word 'dimension' had a technical meaning which accorded with its own interpretation.

The defendants produced expert evidence that certain words or phrases in the specification supported their claim that 'dimension' meant volume. The CA first held that there was no rebuttable assumption, as argued by the plaintiff, that words in a specification that could have a technical meaning did have such a meaning. The court had to decide the meaning of the words from their context. The CA went on to hold that the approach to construction taken by the parties was wrong. According to Aldous LJ, 'The close analysis of words in the specification carried out by the parties was, in my view, the literal analysis rejected by Lord Diplock.' The purposive approach to construction as set out in *Catnic* was the correct one. The result of a purposive approach in this case was that there was infringement. If the dimension was understood to mean volume rather than diameter then the result would be the exclusion from the claim of a significant number of resins which were inherently stable and would be seen to be so by a notional skilled man. Such a construction would not achieve the purpose of the definition of 'stable' which was to include those resins which were inherently stable and exclude those which were not.

Construction and infringement

2.73 The general rule is that it is wrong to construe a claim' with one eye on the alleged infringement' (*Consafe v Emtunga* (1999) per Pumfrey J). However, the nature of the alleged infringement may be relevant to how the claim is constructed. This is so because it may be necessary to describe the infringing act in order to ascertain whether it is a variant which falls within the claim (*Minnesota Mining's* Patent (1999)). Without the infringing act, the identity of that variant may not be apparent. In *Consafe*, Pumfrey J, following *Catnic*, held that the court could not ascertain the correct construction of the claim until its literal meaning had been arrived at and any variants from the strict literal meaning that were present in the alleged infringement had been identified.

An alternative European approach

2.74 Despite the UK view that the *Catnic* test coincides with the Protocol, other signatories to the EPC have not taken a similar approach to the construction of claims. In actions between Improver and Remington in Germany and Holland, on similar facts, the courts reached an opposite conclusion. They found infringement by asking only the first two *Catnic* questions, which they answered in the same way as Hoffman J, but by not asking the third. The European approach may be described as a doctrine of equivalents: the function of the elliptical coil and the slitted rod were the same and so the defendant's variant fell within the claim.

Evidence

2.75   It is acceptable to use expert evidence to establish the meaning of words or phrases in the claim. However in *Hoechst*, the CA held that while the court was entitled to hear evidence as to the meaning of technical words, it had thereafter to decide the meaning of those words from the context in which they were used (see **2.73** above).

Infringing acts

2.76   A person infringes a patent for an invention if, but only if, while the patent is in force, he does any of the infringing acts in the UK in relation to the invention without the consent of the proprietor (s 60(1)). There are two types of infringement, primary and contributory. Whether the infringement falls into one category or another depends upon the acts in question.

Primary infringement

2.77   Acts which constitute primary infringement are divided between those done in relation to product and those done in relation to process inventions. Where the invention is a product, the infringing acts are making, disposing of, offering to dispose of, using or importing, or keeping the product whether for disposal or otherwise (s 60(1)(a)). Keeping a product in the capacity of a 'mere warehouseman' is not an infringing act (*Smith Kline & French Laboratories v Harbottle* (1980)). Where the invention is a process, the infringing acts are using or offering the process for use in the UK, where the person knows or where it is obvious to a reasonable person in the circumstances, that its use without the consent of the proprietor would be an infringement, disposing of, offering to dispose of, using or importing any product obtained directly by means of the process or keeping any such product whether for disposal or otherwise (s 60(1)(b)-(c)).

Contributory infringement

2.78 A person (other than the proprietor of the patent) also infringes a patent for an invention if, while the patent is in force and without the consent of the proprietor, he supplies or offers to supply in the UK a person other than a licensee or other person entitled to work the invention with any of the means, relating to an essential element of the invention, for putting the invention into effect when he knows or it is obvious to a reasonable person in the circumstances, that those means are suitable for putting, and are intended to put, the invention into effect in the UK (s 60(2)).

Defences (s 60(5)(a)-(f))

2.79 An act which would constitute an infringement of a patent will not do so if it falls within a limited number of exemptions set out by the PA 1977. The most noteworthy are private and non-commercial use of the invention (s 60(5)(a)) and use for experimental purposes (s 60(5)(b)). Experiment, in this context, carries its ordinary English meaning. In *Smith Kline & French v Evans Medical* (1989), Aldous J held that 'if an act is to fall within sub-s (5)(b) it must be done for purposes relating to the subject matter of the invention found in the claims alleged to be infringed.' The exemption does not cover experiments which are carried out for commercial purposes which do not relate to the subject matter of the invention. However, in *Monsanto Co v Stauffer Chemical Co* (1985), the CA recognised that the two might overlap. In *Monsanto*, the act carried out was field trials of a herbicide in order to obtain clearance from a regulatory body. This was held to be outside the exemption. But Dillon LJ also noted that the purposes for which tests or trials are carried out 'may in some cases be mixed and may in some cases be difficult to discern'. This broad approach was followed in the German case, *Klinische Versuche (Clinical Trials)* (1998). In this case, the German court held that research may have a commercial orientation, but it was exempted as long as it related to the subject matter of the invention. For instance, the court noted that in cases which related to genetic engineering, such as in *Klinische Versuche*, it was highly likely that the experimentation would be based on commercial considerations because of the high cost of undertaking such research but this did not necessarily mean it would fall outside the exemption. Recently in *Auchinloss v Agricultural & Veterinary Supplies* (1999), the CA held, following the approach in *Monsanto*, that trials which had been undertaken, using the patented composition, to obtain official approval for the product from MAFF did not fall within the exemption because they were not undertaken to discover something unknown or to test a hypothesis relating to the invention. Prescriptions made up by pharmacists are also exempted (s 60(5)(c)). Finally, if a person has used the invention before its priority date, he may continue to do so, provided that use is in good faith (eg not in the result of a breach of confidence) (s 64).

Repair

2.80 Are repairs to a patented article exempted from the infringement provisions of the PA 1977? This was the issue before the CA in *United Wire v Screen Repair Services* (2000). The early case of *Dunlop v Neal* (1899) had recognised that the mere repair of a patented article did not amount to infringement. In *British Leyland v Armstrong* (1986), according to Lord Templeman, 'A patent for an invention is only infringed ... where the invention is a product, by a person who 'makes' or 'uses' the product without the consent of the proprietor of the patent. Where therefore a patented product is sold for use with the consent of the proprietor, repair of the patented product will not constitute an infringement; repair amounting to reconstruction will constitute the manufacture of a new and infringing article'. More recently, in *Canon v Green* (1997), Lord Hoffman observed that, 'Because repair is by definition something which does not amount to the manufacture of the patented article, it is not an infringement of the monopoly conferred by the patent. It cannot therefore be an infringing act and needs no special licence to make it lawful.' (Furthermore Lord Hoffman suggested that the doctrine of exhaustion of patent rights (see below **2.96**) allows the owner of an article to make repairs.) In *United Wire*, the repair was to screens used in sifting or filtering machines used in oil exploration. The patents related to the filter meshes and their interaction and the frames to which they attached. The filters had a short life, but the frames were routinely sent to the defendants for 'repair'. Repair involved supplying new meshes at the correct tension. Following *British Leyland* and *Canon*, the CA held that genuine repair did not infringe the patent. Nonetheless, although a patentee exhausted his patent rights on sale, allowing the owner to make repairs, this did not mean that the owner also had a licence to perform any of the infringing acts. Acts prohibited by s 60 were infringing acts whether or not they could be categorised as repairs. What constituted a repair was an objective question. In this case, the defendants were making a product of the invention. They had infringed the patents. (Both *British Leyland* and *Canon* are considered in greater detail in Chapter 4, 'Industrial Designs', **4.2** and **4.3**.)

Losing the patent: revocation (s 72)

2.81   A patent may be surrendered (s 29). It may also be revoked. There are four grounds for revocation. The first is that it is not a patentable invention (s 72(1)(a)). It follows, a patent may be revoked on the grounds of anticipation, obviousness, or because the invention is not capable of industrial application or it fits one of the excluded categories. Second, a patent may be revoked on grounds of insufficiency if the specification does not disclose the invention in a manner clearly enough and completely enough for the invention to be performed by a person skilled in the art (s 72(c)). This ground is identical to that which would lead to an application being rejected for insufficiency (s 14(3)). In addition, since, sufficiency calls for an enabling disclosure, and since a description will only support a claim if it has an enabling disclosure, then a patent may be revoked if the description does not support the claim (*Biogen;* this is also a ground for the application to be rejected, see **2.9** above). When considering whether a patent should be revoked, sufficiency will be judged at the date of filing of the patent application and not later, to avoid an insufficient application becoming sufficient because of developments in the state of the art since (*Biogen*). Thirdly, a patent may be revoked for non-entitlement (s 72(1)(b)). Entitlement to a patent has been considered above (see **2.7** above). Finally, a patent may be revoked because it has been amended impermissibly. For instance, an amendment that leads to the matter disclosed on the specification extending beyond disclosure on the application can lead to revocation (s 72(1)(d)). Nor, following the grant, are amendments allowed which extend the protection conferred by the patent (s 72(e)), although, such amendments are, in certain circumstances, allowed before (*Palmaz's European Patents* (1999)).

Revocation proceedings

2.82   Applications to revoke a patent can be made to the PO (UK) or to the courts at any time during the life of a patent. In fact, an application to revoke a patent is most likely to be made as a counterclaim to an allegation of infringement (together with the defence that the patent is invalid). Anyone can petition for a patent to be revoked, unless it is on the grounds of non-entitlement, where only the person who has the right to the patent can apply. Applications for the revocation of an EP(UK) are brought in the UK courts. It is worth remembering that unlike the EPO, there is no opposition procedure in the UK. As a result an EP may be the subject of opposition proceedings at the EPO and an application for revocation in the UK simultaneously. Until recently, the UK courts had refused to stay revocation proceedings in these circumstances, in part because the inordinate amount of time it took to complete opposition proceedings in the EPO (as long as 6-8 years) might have inflicted injustice on the UK applicant (*Beloit*). In the case of *Biogen*, this led to a situation where the CA found the patent invalid for obviousness while the EPO found the invention to have involved an inventive step (although the CA's decision was subsequently reversed by the HL: see **2.47** above). However, in *Kimberley-Clark v Proctor & Gamble* (2000), Aldous LJ observed that 'the preferred option' when there are opposition proceedings before the EPO is to stay the UK proceedings, provided such a stay does not cause injustice.

Patents as property

2.83   A patent or a patent application is personal property. Patents, patent applications or any rights in them may be bequeathed, mortgaged, assigned, or licensed (s 30). There are two types of licences, voluntary licences and compulsory licences. Voluntary licences may or may not be exclusive licences.

Assignments

2.84   These must be in writing (s 30, s 68). It is possible to assign some rights in a patent but not others: for instance, the right to use the product for one purpose but not another, so-called 'field-of-use' provisions such as to use the patented product as a chemical but not as a medicine, or the right to exploit the patent only within a particular locality. Assignments do not have to be registered. However, failure to register may affect the assignee's rights in infringement proceedings. Registration also protects the patentee against a bona fide purchaser without notice (s 33, s 68).

Exclusive licences

2.85   These need not be in writing. Like assignments, they need not be registered but failure to register may affect infringement proceedings (s 33, s 68). Again like assignments, they may be for 'any right' under the patent but not necessarily for all. The exclusive licensee has the same rights as the proprietor of the patent to bring infringement proceedings and to collect damages (s 67).

Void licence provisions

2.86 The PA 1977 prohibited certain conditions being included in licensing agreements. These related to certain 'tie-in' and non-competition' clauses and were set out in s 44. Such prohibitions were designed to limit the ability of a patentee to extend his monopoly beyond that given by the patent itself, or to impose onerous conditions on a less powerful licensee. They illustrated the perceived need to balance the advantages of patent protection against a commitment to free competition which continues to underpin EC and UK economic policy. The Competition Act 1998 (CA 1998) is to repeal s 44 and s 45 of the PA 1977. The intention of the CA 1998 is to bring domestic legislation into line with EU competition law. Chapter I of the CA echoes the prohibition in Art 81 of the Treaty of Rome so that agreements which may affect trade within the UK are prohibited. Chapter 2 prohibits conduct amounting to abuse of a dominant position in the UK (Art 80 of the Treaty of Rome). In judging whether an agreement falls within the prohibitions set out in Chapter I, European case law will be followed. There are exemptions from Chapter I prohibitions however and these include certain patent agreements which might fall within EU block exemption regulations. These are looked at below (see **2.101**) when EU competition law is considered. By contrast, the CA 1998 also identifies contractual terms which will be seen as anti-competitive or an abuse of a dominant position (s 18(2)(a)), and may apply to patent licences, such as, for example, terms which impose obligations on the licensee which are not connected to the subject matter of the patent (*Terrell on the Law of Patents* (14 edn, 2000) pp 317-319).

Licences of right (s 46)

2.87 A patentee may voluntarily make his patent available for licensing to anyone who applies. These are called 'licences of right', and the fact that they are available will be endorsed on the register. Obviously, these licences will not be exclusive. The terms of licences of right may be agreed between the parties, or in default of agreement, by the Comptroller. An endorsement may be useful for a small inventor who lacks the resources to exploit his own invention.

Compulsory licences

2.88   Under certain circumstances, the licence of right endorsement may be compulsory. The Comptroller (or the courts) may compel a patentee to license his invention to a specific licensee or to make a license of right endorsement. The power to issue compulsory licences stems from a fundamental belief, underpinning the patent system, that it is in the public interest for patented inventions to be worked, a reason specifically referred to in the PA 1977. When deciding whether to grant a compulsory licence the Comptroller must take into account a variety of circumstances, which are set out in the PA 1977, and which include the nature of the invention, measures already taken by the patentee to exploit it and the ability of any future licensee to do so (s 50(2)(a)-(c)). Any person may apply for a compulsory licence, but very few applications are made, suggesting that these provisions serve more as an expression of principle than any pressing utilitarian purpose. There are five grounds under which a compulsory licence will be granted. These refer generally to a failure to work the patented invention in the UK or to grant a licence on reasonable terms (s 48(3)(a)-(e)). These grounds are narrowed to three for a WTO proprietor (s 48(5) as amended) who is defined as being a national of or domiciled in a country which a member of the WTO or who has a place of business there. A key difference is that a WTO proprietor may avoid being penalised for not working his invention in the UK if instead it was imported into the UK market. Compulsory licences cannot be applied for until three years after the patent has been granted.

Crown use (ss 55-59)

2.89   The Crown (that is any government department or any person authorised by a government department) has wide powers to exploit a patented invention, without the permission of the proprietor. The purposes for which a patented invention may be exploited include defence, use by the National Health Service and use by the Atomic Energy Commission. The patentee will be compensated by an amount either agreed with the government department or fixed by the courts. In a recent case, crown use of a patent was allowed for building a blast-resistant police station in Northern Ireland (*Henry Bros (Magherafelt) Ltd v Ministry of Defence and Northern Ireland Office* (1999)).

Enforcing a patent

2.90   Patent actions may be brought either in the Patents Court, which is part of the Chancery Division of the HC or the Patents County Court or the PO. In the latter instance, the case will be heard by a specialist Hearing Officer, although the remedies available to the PO are limited (s 61(3)). It is commonly the case that an action for infringement of a patent will provoke both a defence that the patent is invalid as well as a counterclaim for its revocation. As a result, an infringement action may be complicated and expensive to pursue. This reality has been commonly held to undermine the extent to which patents really provide a useful protection for inventors who do not have the backing of corporate funds.

The Patents Court

2.91   The specific rules to be followed in patent actions differ from those of other civil actions in the HC. However, as with other cases of intellectual property infringement, the primary aim of the claimant will be to stop the infringement as quickly as possible through the use of a pre-trial (interim) injunction. Once such an injunction is obtained, this may bring an end to the matter.

The Patents County Court

2.92   This was introduced by the CDPA 1988 and it opened for business in 1990 (ss 287-292). Its purpose is to provide a less costly and speedier forum for patent actions than the HC, and so to give an opportunity for a wider range of patent holders, beyond those with very deep pockets, to bring patent actions. Parties at the Patents County Court may be represented by patent agents as well as solicitors and barristers. The procedure has also been streamlined to make it both quicker and simpler than in the Patents Court. In order to serve as a true alternative to the Patents Court, the normal County Court limitations as to damages do not apply. As in the Patents Court, there are specific procedural rules in the Patents County Court which reflect its specialist nature. In its first decade of existence it has proved to be a popular forum.

68

Remedies

2.93 The successful claimant is normally entitled to an injunction restraining the defendant from further infringement, together with an enquiry as to damages or an account of profits, an order for delivery up or destruction of the infringing articles and a declaration from the defendant that the patent is valid and has been infringed by him (s 61). Damages may be calculated from the date that the application was published provided the court or the Comptroller concludes it was reasonable to expect, on the basis of the application, that a patent would be granted.

Innocent infringement

2.94 If the infringer can establish that he was not aware of the patent, or had no reasonable grounds for supposing it existed, when he committed the infringing act(s), he may avoid liability for damages (s 62(1)). This provision emphasises the importance of marking the patented object with both the word 'patent' or 'patented' and the number of the patent (the word alone is insufficient, under the section, to prove awareness).

Groundless threats (s 70)

2.95 These are prohibited unless they are made against the manufacturer, the importer or the user of the patented invention. A primary purpose of this provision is to prevent the patentee from intimidating the customers of the alleged infringer, when he has no real intention of bringing an action against the latter for infringement. Any aggrieved person may bring an action against the person making the threats. A defence would be to prove that the patent had, in fact, been infringed. It is not considered a groundless threat simply to notify anyone (including, for example, the customer) that a patent exists.

Patents and the EC

2.96 It is a fundamental concern of the EC to ensure the free circulation of goods. Article 28 (formerly Art 30) of the Treaty of Rome prohibits, 'quantitative restrictions on imports and all measures having equivalent effect' between member states. Like other intellectual property rights, patent protection may conflict with this prohibition. National patent law endows a proprietor with a monopoly right to his patent invention in the relevant territory, and may allow him to keep out the goods of others which embody his invention. The existence of patent protection, as with other intellectual property, can nonetheless be justified by public interest considerations which balance, in importance, the benefits of free trade. Thus, Art 30 (formerly Art 36) of the Treaty of Rome recognises that there can be a public interest in the monopoly rights afforded by intellectual property protection, and that prohibitions or restrictions on imports or exports are justified on grounds of the protection of industrial or commercial property, including intellectual property. However, such prohibitions or restrictions must not constitute a means of arbitrary discrimination or disguised restriction on trade between member states. The ECJ has built up a body of case law which has sought to balance the sometimes conflicting imperatives of promoting free competition and protecting the rights of proprietors of intellectual property. In doing so, it has enunciated the principle of 'exhaustion of rights'. Later chapters will consider exhaustion of rights in relation to copyright and trade marks (**3.91**; **6.104** et seq). Below the principle of exhaustion is examined in relation to patents both inside and outside (see **2.102**) the EU.

The exhaustion of rights

2.97　A neat summary of the general principle of exhaustion of rights was offered by Laddie J in the trade mark case, *Zino Davidoff v A & G Imports* (1999) (see **6.118** for details). He said,

> it is well established that a principle of exhaustion applies to all intellectual property rights. So if an article made in accordance with a patent is put upon the market in one Member State by or with the consent of the owner of the patent rights, that owner cannot use those rights to prevent or hinder the importation of goods into a second Member State or to prevent their sale there. The expression 'exhaustion of rights' accurately encapsulates the principle involved. The proprietary rights have been used up. The owner of them has nothing left to deploy against further exploitation of the goods. This principle applies not only to patents and copyright, but to trade marks as well. So, once the rights holder has put protected products on the market or has consented to such marketing, he loses all rights to object to further exploitation. This effect is indefeasible. The rights owner cannot override it by contract. The Member State cannot override it by national legislation.

It is worth noting that in a considerable number of cases involving exhaustion of rights within the EC in relation to both patents and trade marks, the products at issue are pharmaceuticals. This is largely because pharmaceuticals may be subject to government price controls. As a result, there may be a considerable difference between the prices at which pharmaceuticals are sold in different member states, making the 'parallel importation' of such products attractive

2.98 The principle of 'exhaustion of rights' in relation to patents was established by the ECJ in the case *Centrafarm v Sterling* (1974) (see also, *Centrafarm v Winthrop* (1974) on trade marks, **6.104**). In *Centrafarm v Sterling*, Sterling owned patents relating to an anti-infection drug, 'Negram', in both the UK and the Netherlands. Centrafarm acquired supplies of 'Negram' which had been put on the market in the UK and exported them into the Netherlands, where they could be sold at a higher price. In common parlance, Centrafarm was the 'parallel importer' of the drugs. Sterling sued for patent infringement in the Netherlands. In its judgment, the ECJ held that derogation from Art 36 (now Art 30) concerning the free movement of goods was allowed only to safeguard those rights which constitute the specific subject matter of the property. In the case of patents, the specific subject matter protected by the patent is:

> the guarantee that the patentee, to reward the creative effort of the inventor, has the exclusive right to use an invention with a view to manufacturing industrial products and putting them into circulation for the first time, either directly or by the grant of licences to third parties, as well as the right to oppose infringements.

However, it went on to hold that a derogation from the free movement of goods is not justified where the product has been put on the market in 'a legal manner' by the patentee or with his consent, in the member state from which it has been imported. To decide otherwise, would be to 'partition off national markets' and thereby restrict trade between member states in a situation where no such restraint is necessary to safeguard the specific subject matter of the patent.

2.99 Exhaustion of rights and parallel imports were examined once again by the ECJ in *Merck v Stephar* (1981). The difference in this case was that the product in question, a drug for use against hypertension, had originally been put on the market by Merck in a member state, Italy, where it was not patented. It had then been bought up by the parallel importer, Stephar, and sold in the Netherlands, where it was. Merck sued for patent infringement in the Netherlands. The ECJ confirmed its judgment in *Centrafarm*. It said that the substance of a patent is essentially the exclusive right to first placing of the product on the market. This enables the inventor to obtain a reward for his creative effort, 'without however, guaranteeing that he will obtain such a reward in all circumstances'. It was up to the patentee to decide under what conditions he would market his product. If he decided to market it in a member state where there was no patent protection, then he must take the economic consequences, including the possibility that it will be imported into other member states.

The importance of consent

2.100   Key to the decisions in both *Centrafarm v Sterling* and *Merck v Stephar* is the matter of consent. In both cases the patentee had consented to the first sale of his goods in a member state (*Pharmon v Hoechst* (1985)). In *Merck v Primecrown* (1997), the ECJ was asked to reconsider its decision in *Merck v Stephar*. Once again the case involved drugs which were placed on the market by Merck in member states, Spain and Portugal, where there was no patent protection. They were then bought by Primecrown who marketed them in the UK where they were more expensive. Merck alleged infringement of its patents in the UK. The ECJ approved the reasoning in *Merck v Stephar*. It was a case of proprietor beware. If a proprietor chose to market a product in a member state where it was unpatentable, he had to accept the consequences of that choice. Nor was the rule in *Merck v Stephar* affected by the fact that the authorities in the exporting member state had fixed the sale price of the product in question, as is often the case with pharmaceuticals. Although price controls might, in some circumstances, distort competition between member states, it did not justify a derogation from the principle of the free movement of goods. An exception would be where the patentee was under a genuine legal obligation to market his product in the member state or it was marketed under a compulsory licence (*Pharmon*). In these cases, he would not have consented to first sale of the patented goods and his rights would not be exhausted.

Patent rights and competition law in the EC

2.101   Since patents endow the proprietor with a monopoly right, the question arises as to whether the ownership of a patent or dealings with it may be anti-competitive. In *Parke, Davis v Probel* [1968], it was held that the exercise and existence of patent rights per se do not infringe Arts 81 and 82 (formerly Arts 85 and 86) of the Treaty of Rome. They are not an abuse of a dominant position in relation to Art 82 (formerly Art 86). Nor is the refusal to licence the patent on reasonable terms an abuse of a dominant position, unless such refusal involves abusive conduct such as, for example, the arbitrary refusal to supply spare parts or the fixing of prices for spare parts at an unfair level, 'provided that such conduct is liable to effect trade between member states' (*Volvo v Veng* (1989), a case actually involving registered design). In the UK case, *Pitney Bowes v Francotyp-Postalia* (1991), Hoffman J said that bringing or threatening patent proceedings did not constitute an abuse of a dominant position nor did strengthening a dominant position necessarily involve abusing it. In this case, a 'cross licence' between the patentee and another would not abuse Art 86 (now Art 82) unless it was, itself, procured through the abuse of the dominant position. Nonetheless, it has been suggested that the decision in *Pitney Bowes* does allow for the possibility that, in the right circumstances, Art 82 may be raised as a defence against patent infringement.

Patents and EC block exemptions

2.102   Article 81 (formerly Art 85) of the Treaty of Rome prohibits agreements which have as their object or effect the prevention, restriction or distortion of competition within the common market. It is easy to see how exclusive patent licences might fall within this prohibition. Nonetheless, it is also the case that the monopoly afforded by patents offers countervailing benefits such as an encouragement to research and development. In light of this dichotomy, the EC has developed a system by which certain agreements may be exempted from the prohibitions set out in Art 81, either individually or as a block under Art 81(3). In particular, the EC's block exemption regulations confer an automatic exemption on agreements relating to inter alia patents and 'know how', the Technology Transfer Regulation, provided they fall within its terms (Reg 240/96 [1996] OJ L31/2). The aim of the Technology Transfer Regulation as set out in its recital is to simplify and harmonise the rules governing patent and know-how licensing agreements 'in order to encourage the dissemination of technical knowledge in the Community and to promote the manufacture of technically more sophisticated products.' As a result of the Regulation a patent licensing agreement which might be void under Art 81(1) will be acceptable if it falls within the terms of the block exemption. Such agreements must contain only those terms permitted by the Regulation (the so-called white list of clauses, including for example, licensee minimum quality requirements) and must not include any that are prohibited (black listed clauses, such as wide non-compete clauses) (Taylor *EC & UK Competition Law & Compliance* (1999) pp 167-177).

Patents and the rest of the world

2.103   The question arises as to whether patent rights are similarly exhausted if the relevant products are put on the market outside the EU and are imported into the UK without the patentee's consent. The answer to this question has reflected more general rules of contract law. The leading case is *Betts v Willmott* (1871). The principle enunciated in *Betts v Willmott* is that where a patentee sells his goods abroad without reservation or condition, he cannot then prevent the importation of those same goods into the UK. According to Lord Hatherley:

> When a man purchases an article he expects to have control of it and there must be some clear and explicit agreement to the contrary to justify the vendor in saying that he has not given the purchaser his licence to sell the article or to use it wherever he pleases as against himself.

In *National Phonograph v Menck* (1911), the PC held, following *Betts v Willmott*, that, 'a sale having occurred, the presumption is that the full right of ownership was meant to be vested in the purchaser.' However, it was also the case that 'the owner's rights in a patented chattel will be limited if there is brought home to him the knowledge of conditions imposed by the patentee or those representing the patentee, upon him at the time of sale.' According to the CA in *Gillette v Bernstein* (1942), it was essential that any restriction must have been brought home to the defendant at the time of sale. In *Roussel v Hockley* (1996), Jacob J added the further caveat that to avoid exhaustion of his rights, notice of any limitations on a licence of patented article must be 'brought to the attention of every person down the chain.' *Roussel* involved the sale of insecticide in the UK which the defendant had obtained in China. The insecticide had been sold by the French patentee to a Chinese company, and the patentee claimed that it had been sold subject to the restriction that it was to be used only in China and not exported. The plaintiff relied, inter alia, on the fact that the drums bearing the insecticide had been marked with the information, 'Re-export forbidden'. The defendant replied

74

that the drums they obtained through intermediaries carried no such notices and that the insecticide was advertised worldwide by various third parties without restrictions, so a purchaser would not know of the restriction. Jacob J found that the plaintiff had failed to establish that it had brought home to the Chinese company that there should be no re-export. As a consequence, the defendants were free to sell the insecticide in the UK without infringing the plaintiff's patent rights. In particular, Jacob J stated:

> It is the law that where the patentee supplies his product and at the time of the supply informs the person supplied (normally via the contract) that there are limitations as to what may be done with the product supplied then, provided those terms are brought home first to the person originally supplied and second, to subsequent dealers in the product, no licence to carry out or do any act outside the terms of the licence runs with the goods. If no limited licence is imposed on them at the time of the first supply no amount of notice thereafter either to the original supplyee ... or persons who derive title from him can turn the general licence into a limited licence.

The decision in *Roussel* has been criticised not least for imposing an impossible evidential burden on the patentee (Wilkinson 'Breaking the Chain: Parallel Imports and the Missing Link' [1997] EIPR 319). Interestingly, in *Davidoff*, Laddie J employed the contractual principles enunciated in *Betts v Willmott*, to impose international exhaustion on trade marks despite a clear indication from the ECJ that this is not what the present trade mark regime intends (see **6.118** below).

Further reading

P Drahos 'Biotechnology Patents, Markets and Morality' [1999] EIPR 441

Terrell on the Law of Patents (15th edn, 2000)

A Webster and Packer (eds) *Innovation and the Intellectual Property System* (1996)

Self-test questions

1. Axel Ltd has a patent for a fuel derivative, X, which is used to run central heating systems. Axel's Chief Marketing Officer, Ms Y, has

noticed that X is also excellent for cleaning motor engine parts. She plans to announce this during a speech she is giving at an exclusive luncheon for Axel's most prized customers very soon, since Axel is sure that the use of X for cleaning has enormous commercial potential. For instance, it seems that a Mr W, in Milton Keynes, has been using X to clean his own central heating boiler for some time. Also Axel has discovered that its great rival Brim Ltd has been producing X and burning it as part of a testing programme to see whether it passes environmental standards. Advise Axel on whether they can patent X for use as a cleaning product and whether Brim Ltd or Mr W is infringing their present patent for X.

2. The purposive approach to patent construction is certainly the most likely to produce a patent system which both fulfils its basic functions and satisfies the interests of those who use it. Do you agree?

3. Discuss the problems raised by a) the patenting of gene sequences and b) computer software.

CHAPTER THREE

Copyright

SUMMARY

The origin and development of copyright and the Copyright Designs and Patents Act 1988

Copyright works, fixation and originality, and secondary works

Authorship, ownership and duration of copyright

Infringement: the restricted acts, primary infringement, authorisation and secondary infringement

The permitted acts: fair dealing, criticism and review and reporting current events, and the public interest defence

Moral rights

Dealing with copyright

Civil and criminal remedies

Computers and copyright infringement

Copyright and the international context: exhaustion of rights and competition law

Copyright: its origins and development

3.1 Copyright law in the UK is governed by the 1988 Copyright Designs and Patents Act (CDPA 1988). The CDPA 1988 governs copyright dealings in the UK. There is however an important international dimension to UK copyright law. The Berne Convention 1886 set minimum standards of protection internationally among participating countries, such as the UK, by giving authors of works exploited in any participating country

77

other than their own the same rights afforded to nationals of those countries. Further international regulation was achieved through a number of later Acts and Conventions, most notably the Rome Convention 1960 (concerned with neighbouring rights, see **3.25** below) and the Act of Paris 1971, which increased the uniformity of protection between participating states and the range of works to be offered protection. At the same time, there has been an ever-growing convergence in copyright protection among members of the EC as the result of a series of directives, relating, inter alia, to copyright term, software and to databases.

The history of copyright protection

3.2 Changes in copyright protection have had a close relationship with developments in reproduction technologies. Early interest in copyright protection in the UK coincided with the introduction of the printing press. At first, copyright law was designed primarily to protect the economic investment of printers and publishers, rather than the creative efforts of authors. However, the first copyright statute, the Statute of Anne 1710, did recognise the author as owner of copyright, and gave a limited term of protection to works of 28 years. Sixty years later, the famous case of *Donaldson v Beckett* (1774), itself a commercial struggle between London and provincial publishers, established that literary copyright was a statutory right and so of limited term rather than a common law right and therefore of perpetual duration. It has been suggested that this decision stemmed both from the HL's dislike of monopolies and also from its recognition that publishers rather than authors would be the group most likely to benefit from any enhanced protection. It was not until the nineteenth century that authors came to be seen as central to copyright protection, as romantic ideas of the author as a creative and original genius, increasingly took hold. The Copyright Act 1842, for which a number of prominent author's lobbied, increased the term of protection to 42 years from publication, or seven years beyond the death of the author, whichever was the longer. From the late nineteenth century, changes to copyright law reflected the rapid introduction of new technologies of reproduction and a growing impetus for UK law to conform to international standards. This was true of the two major copyright reforms of the twentieth century before the CDPA 1988. The Copyright Act 1911 further increased the term of protection to the life of the author plus 50 years, as well as introducing reforms which brought the UK law into line with the Berne Convention. Furthermore, the CA

1911 also took account of important advances in the technology of music reproduction, introducing protection for the first time to sound recordings. Similarly, the Copyright Act 1956 (CA 1956) allowed the UK to ratify the Brussels Act of the Berne Convention and provided specific protection for films and television recordings, while the CDPA 1988 incorporated, inter alia, changes to international protection under the 1971 Paris Act.

The justification for copyright

3.3   Since the nineteenth century, it is usual to justify the existence of copyright protection by arguing that it protects the creative investment of the author. The justification may be a moral one. In this view, the author has a natural right to ownership of the fruits of his own labour, a stance commonly associated with the philosophical writings of John Locke. Or justification may be more practical. So it is suggested that without such protection, authors will have no economic incentive to create. Perhaps because of its early influences, copyright law in the UK has continued to be more often justified on grounds of commercial utility. By contrast, in Europe, the tradition has been to view copyright in terms of a natural right accruing to the author. A third justification for copyright lies in its perceived social benefit. It is argued that authors will be encouraged to disseminate their works to the public if they are able, through copyright laws, to profit from so doing. Furthermore, the limited term of copyright ensures that at some point these same works will be freely available to enrich both culture, generally, and to provide the foundation for future creation.

3.4   All of these justifications may be challenged. First, how much do authors actually benefit from copyright protection? It has probably always been true that the entrepreneur who produces and markets the work is most likely to reap the financial rewards of copyright. In many cases, the author will have signed away his copyright as a prerequisite for publication. It is certainly the case that whereas, in the nineteenth century, authors were at the forefront of lobbying for increased copyright protection, today that role is more often played by record companies, film studios and publishers. The inclusion of 'moral rights' in the UK copyright regime stems from a recognition that authors, all too often, are not the beneficiaries of copyright protection. Moral rights attach to authors, whether or not they have alienated the copyrights in their works (see **3.73** below). Secondly, just how important is the 'author'? Recent

79

trends in scholarship have called into question the romantic emphasis on the originality of creative output, and have suggested that much of it is either derivative or shaped by popular culture. From this viewpoint, it is common to emphasise the difficulty in determining where the work of one author ends and the original output of another begins, a necessary prerequisite for finding copyright infringement. Further, it is argued that if copyright protection is drawn too broadly, cultural life will be impoverished because authors will have more limited access to other works on which their own creative output depends. This latter view raises urgent questions about whether the copyright term is too long, how much creative output should remain in what is often termed the 'public domain', and how broad exceptions to copyright protection should be. Finally, does copyright offer appropriate protection for the products of new technologies? Perhaps more so than other types of intellectual property, copyright was the creature of a particular technology: the printing press. Since the eighteenth century, the technical means for reproducing works has constantly evolved, and copyright laws have evolved with them. There is now increasing debate as to whether copyright law with its initial foundation in earth-bound works, most notably books, is really sufficiently flexible to offer protection to new categories of work many of which, produced in cyberspace, have no tangible existence at all (see **3.96** below).

The Copyright, Designs and Patents Act 1988

3.5 As its title suggests, the CDPA 1988 is concerned with a number of areas of intellectual property law, not exclusively copyright. Parts III and IV of the CDPA 1988 provided a much needed overhaul of the law governing industrial designs (see Chapter 4). Parts V and VI are concerned with some aspects of patent and trade mark law, including the introduction of Patents County Courts, an important innovation at the time. Part II is concerned entirely with performance rights, which the CDPA 1988 introduced. This chapter is primarily concerned with Part I of the CDPA 1988, which sets out the substantive law of copyright in the UK. It begins, as one might expect, with a definition of copyright works.

Copyright works (s 1)

3.6 The CDPA 1988 identifies three categories of works in which copyright subsists. They are:

- original literary, dramatic, musical or artistic works

- sound recordings, films, broadcasts or cable programmes

- typographical arrangements of published editions.

A 'work' is not defined by the CDPA 1988 except in a circular way. A 'copyright work' means a work of any of those descriptions in which copyright subsists (s 1(2)). In the case of literary, dramatic, musical or artistic works, whether a work is a 'work' for copyright purposes is inseparable from whether it is 'original', since copyright subsists only in original works. What constitutes originality, for copyright purposes, is examined below (**3.15**).

Literary works (s 3(1))

3.7   A literary work means any work, other than a dramatic or musical work, which is written, spoken or sung. It has been held that a literary work should provide some element of either information and instruction, or pleasure in the form of literary enjoyment (*Hollinrake v Truswell* (1894)). But to qualify as a literary work, there is certainly no need for the work to have any intrinsic literary merit, however defined (*University of London Press v University Tutorial Press* (1916)). Examination papers have been held to be original literary works. So too have a list of foxhounds, a trade catalogue and football coupons. Tables, compilations and computer programs (as well as preparatory design material for a computer program) are specifically defined as literary works, although the EC Database Directive shortens the length of protection given to certain compilations (**3.16** below).

De minimis

3.8   For copyright to subsist in a literary work, it must be more than *de minimis*. Single words will not attract copyright protection. The word 'Exxon' was held not to be a literary work by the CA (*Exxon Corpn v Exxon Insurance* (1982)). Since 'Exxon' is both original, being an invented word, and conveys information about the source of the goods to which it applies, it is arguable that the 'Exxon' decision was actually taken on public interest grounds. There has been a long-standing judicial reluctance to endow single words with copyright protection largely because simple words or phrases, as the basic building blocks of language, should be available for public use. Also, if words have commercial value, such as 'Exxon' itself does, they may well be protected as trade marks or by an action in passing-off, and dual protection would be undesirable (Cullabine 'Copyright in Short Phrases and Single Words' [1992] EIPR 205). Similarly, the courts have suggested that the taking of a title alone is very unlikely to infringe copyright (*Francis Day & Hunter v Twentieth Century Fox* (1940)). More recently, it was held to be arguable that copyright might subsist in a newspaper headline (*Shetland Times v Dr Jonathan Wills* (1997)).

Dramatic works (s 3(1))

3.9 These include works of dance or mime, in the sense that acting, dancing or mime must be intrinsic to the presentation of the work. Or, put another way, a dramatic work 'must have sufficient unity to be capable of performance'. Dialogue cannot, on its own, constitute a dramatic work and is, instead, protected by literary copyright, although, a work without dialogue (ie a mime) can. The 'dramatic format' of the quiz show, 'Opportunity Knocks', which included gimmicks such as stock phrases and the use of a 'clapometer', was held to lack the necessary 'unity' to constitute a dramatic work (*Greene v Broadcasting Corpn of New Zealand* (1989)).

3.10 An important question which has only recently been decided by the CA is whether a film can constitute a dramatic work. In *Norowzian v Arks (No 2)* (1999), the plaintiff directed a short film called 'Joy' which consisted of a man dancing to music. The visual impact of the film was the result of the filming and editing techniques used by the plaintiff, which had the effect of allowing the actor to perform a routine which would be physically impossible in 'real life'. The first defendant produced an advertisement for Guinness entitled 'Anticipation' which featured similar dancing and props. Indeed, the defendant had been instructed by Guinness to produce a commercial broadly similar to 'Joy'. The plaintiff alleged copyright infringement. Among the questions for the HC was whether the film 'Joy' was itself a dramatic work or whether it was a recording of a dramatic work. Rattee J held that while a film might record a dramatic work, it cannot be a dramatic work per se. Nor was 'Joy' the recording of a dramatic work. A dramatic work must be something which is capable of being physically performed, in particular a work of dance or mime must be capable of being danced or mimed. In this case, the film, because of the way it is edited, was not a recording of anything that was or could be danced by anyone. Nonetheless, it was argued that 'Joy' was a work of some originality, 'a manifestation of the film marker's art'. The problem accepted by the HC was that the CDPA 1988 appeared to afford no protection to an original work of art which *was* a film, as long as the film itself was not copied, although it would protect an original work which was recorded *by* a film. The plaintiff appealed and the question of whether a film, itself, could be a 'dramatic work' was reconsidered by the CA. Norse LJ held that in his judgment a film can be a dramatic work for the purposes of the CDPA 1988. The definition of a dramatic work must be given its ordinary and natural meaning. His own summary was that a dramatic work is a work of action with or without words or music, which is capable of being performed before an audience. A film would often, although not always, be such a work. Furthermore, a film can be both a recording of a dramatic work and a dramatic work in itself. 'Joy', being original and a work of action capable of being performed before an audience was a dramatic work. However, Nourse, LJ agreed with Rattee J that 'Joy' was not a recording of a dramatic work. Rather, Nourse LJ compared it to a cartoon, that is a dramatic work in itself, without being a recording of one. Nonetheless, in this case there was no copyright infringement because 'Anticipation' was not a copy of a substantial part of 'Joy'. There were indeed similarities between the filming techniques and editing styles of the two films, but no copyright subsisted in 'mere style and technique'.

Musical works (s 3(1))

3.11 These are works consisting of music, exclusive of any words or action intended to be sung, spoken or performed with the music. Song lyrics, like dialogue in a play, are protected as literary works.

Fixation and originality

3.12 For copyright to subsist in a literary, dramatic or musical work it must be original and it must be fixed. To understand both originality and fixation, it is first necessary to consider the dichotomy between ideas and their expression in relation to copyright works. This is a subject which will be discussed at greater length in relation to infringement below (see **3.51**).

The ideas/expression dichotomy

3.13   It is often said that copyright subsists in the expression of an idea and not the idea itself (*Hollinrake*). Like most generalisations, there is some truth in this statement, but the reality is rather more sophisticated. There are numerous judicial decisions where ideas have been held not to have copyright protection. For instance, the idea or 'concept' for the format of 'Opportunity Knocks', taken in isolation, was held not to be the subject of copyright (*Greene*) (se **3.9**). But in other cases, both the idea and its expression converged to make them inseparable. An example of this difficulty arises with computer software and copyright. It is, of course, entirely possible to 'express' an original program in a completely different computer code, yet both the original program and the 'copy' may embody the same ideas as to structure or 'look' and 'feel'. Recent decisions, have seen the court willing to give some protection to the latter (see **3.81** et seq).

Fixation

3.14   Copyright does not subsist in a literary, dramatic or musical work unless or until it is recorded, in writing or otherwise (s 3(2)). Writing includes any form of notation or code, whether by hand or otherwise, and regardless of the method by which, or medium in or on which it is recorded (s 178). Writing includes, for example, computer code recorded on software. The methods of recording covered by the CDPA 1988 remain an open category to cope with technological developments. A copyright work comes into existence at the time at which it is recorded. It is immaterial whether the work is recorded with the permission of the author. Where the work is recorded, copyright may subsist both in the recording as well as in the underlying work (s 3(3)). For instance, a sound recording of a speech will be protected as a sound recording and the speech itself as a literary work. In *Walter v Lane* (1900), a *Times* reporter took down in shorthand and verbatim a speech given by Lord Rosebery. The speech was subsequently published. It was held that the reporter had acquired copyright in his report of the speech by virtue of the skill and judgment he had employed in reporting it. It is submitted that Lord Rosebery would also have acquired a copyright in the speech as it had now been recorded, or fixed (see also *Express Newspapers v News (UK)* (1990)).

84

Originality

3.15 Copyright subsists only in *original* literary, dramatic and musical works. 'Original' is not defined in the CDPA 1988, so to understand what it means, it is necessary to consider the case law. It is useful to return to the general rule that there can be no copyright in an idea without its embodiment in a 'work'. Copyright is not concerned with the originality of the underlying idea. It is the form in which the idea is expressed which must be original. Originality in copyright is distinct from 'novelty' or an 'inventive step' in patent law (see **2.26** et seq and **2.37** et seq on patents). To be original in copyright the work must originate with the authors. Moreover, the creation of the work must be deemed to entail the expenditure upon it of the author's own skill, effort and capital (*University of London Press*; also *Walter*). In the formulation of the great American jurist, Learned Hand:

> Borrowed a work must indeed not be, for a plagiarist is not himself *pro tanto* an author; but if by some magic a man who had never known it were to compose anew Keat's Ode on a Grecian Urn, he would be an 'author', and, if he copyrighted it, others might not copy that poem, though they might of course copy Keats. (*Sheldon v Metro-Goldwyn Pictures Corpn* (1936).)

Contrast the standard of originality in copyright with the requirement of patentability (**2.26** et seq) where an invention is not novel if it is described in an earlier publication, even if the subsequent inventor had no knowledge of it.

Compilations

3.16 Following the implementation of the EC Database Directive (96/9/EC) (see **3.17** below), compilations may be treated differently from databases, for the purposes of copyright protection. Copyright in compilations rewards not the originality of the constituent elements of such compilations, which may be nothing more than a collection of facts, but the skill, effort, judgment and experience which was expended in bringing those elements together in a particular way (*Ladbroke v William Hill* (1964)). The amount of effort and skill necessary to create an original 'work' is a matter of fact and degree (*Bookmakers v Wilf Gilbert* (1994)). In *Bookmakers*, copyright was found to subsist in racing cards for greyhound meetings and a formula for forecasting dividends because considerable effort had gone into the preparation of each. On the other hand, there was no copyright in the calculation of the forecast dividends,

85

since using the formula did not require sufficient skill, labour or judgment. Copyright has also been held to subsist in football pools coupons, football fixture lists and television programme schedules (*Ladbroke v Littlewoods* (1959) and *Independent Television v Time Out* (1984)). But in *Cramp v Smythson* (1944), the HL held copyright did not subsist in a series of tables in the front of a pocket diary, since their commonplace contents 'left no room for taste and judgment and their selection did not constitute an original literary work.'

Databases

3.17   The Database Directive was incorporated into UK law by the Copyright and Rights in Database Regulations (SI 1997/3032). A database is defined in s 3A of the CDPA 1988 as a collection of independent works, data or other materials which

• are arranged in a systematic or methodical way, and

• are individually accessible by electronic or other means.

In the UK, these had traditionally been protected as compilations (see **3.16** above). The Regulations introduced a new two-tier system of protection for databases. A database will be protected as an original literary work if the selection or arrangement of the data constitutes the author's own intellectual creation (s 3A). It has been suggested that the criterion of 'originality', for databases, may be harder to meet than the traditional UK test for compilations, where originality has turned simply upon whether sufficient skill, effort and judgment has been expended to attract copyright. An 'original' database will have the full term of copyright protection, which is afforded to literary works, of seventy years from the death of the author (see **3.39** below). The Regulations also introduced a new *sui generis* 'database right' which is based not on originality, but on whether the compilation of the database involved a substantial investment in either obtaining, verification or presentation of its contents. Investment can be financial, human and/or technical and it may be judged qualitatively or quantitatively. The new database right will protect the raw data contained in the database rather than its arrangement. It carries a far shorter 15-year period of protection. However, if the database is 'substantially changed', it may go on to attract a further 15-year term and so on. It is possible for a single database to be protected both by copyright, if it is original, and by the database right if its creation involved a 'substantial investment'. Traditionally, the English courts have been slow to offer protection to the basic information which goes to make up compilations. The introduction of the new database right has raised fears that it could limit the availability of such basic information, necessary for example for scientific or other scholarly research, for very considerable periods indeed.

Adaptations, translations and arrangements

3.18 A separate copyright subsists in adaptations and translations, which use original copyright works as their source. This separate copyright is justified by the fact that such works cannot be produced without the expenditure of additional skill and labour. Copyright did not subsist in a textbook which contained a number of excerpts from Plutarch's *Life of Alexander*, because insufficient skill and labour had been expended in selecting them. The court said, 'it is necessary that labour, skill and capital should be expended sufficiently to impart to the product some quality or character which the raw material did not possess, and which differentiates the product from the raw material' (*Macmillan v Cooper* (1924)). It is important to remember that adaptations, translations and arrangements, provided they have sufficient originality, may carry at least two copyrights, one in the underlying work and the other in the adaptation or arrangement. In *Redwood v Chappell* (1982), the plaintiffs owned copyright in the song, 'Zing'. The defendants had originally been licensed to produce arrangements of the song. The plaintiffs' claim for copyright in all arrangements and adaptations of the song was rejected by the court. According to Goff J:

> All arrangements had been so developed from the original song, decorated, transferred to a different medium or otherwise changed as to make them fall within the description of an original work and so attract an independent copyright. To secure such copyright, it is only necessary that the arranger's mode of expression be sufficiently different from the original not to appear to have been copied from it. There is no requirement that the ideas embodied in the arrangement be novel.

However, the owner of the later copyright (in this case the 'arranger') cannot make the adaptation or exploit it without a license from the owner of the copyright in the underlying work as this would amount to infringement.

Artistic works (s 4)

3.19 Artistic works are defined as:

- a graphic work, photograph, sculpture or collage, irrespective of artistic quality

- a work of architecture being a building or a model for a building

- a work of artistic craftsmanship.

In *Interlego v Tyco Industries* (1988), it was held that artistic copyright lay in the design drawings for a plastic brick and not in the written instructions which accompanied them. To quote Lord Oliver, the 'essence' of artistic copyright is that which is 'visually significant'. Graphic works include:

- any painting, drawing, diagram, map, chart, or plan

- any engraving, etching, lithograph, wood cut or similar work.

Some graphic works, for instance a map or a plan, may also contain material which will attract literary copyright. Collage was new to the CDPA 1988 and is not defined. A sculpture includes a cast or model for the purposes of sculpture, but must, of course, have sufficient originality of its own to qualify for artistic copyright. In *Metix v Maughan* (1997), the plaintiffs claimed copyright in their moulds used for manufacturing cartridges, as sculptures. Laddie J held that the moulds did not qualify as sculptures. Ordinary members of the public would not have considered the designers of the moulds to be artists, nor would the manufacturer. The designers were not concerned with the shape or appearance of the moulds, except for functional reasons. Nonetheless, artistic works are protected regardless of artistic merit. For instance, industrial drawings attract copyright protection (although there are differences in how they may be infringed (s 51) (see Chapter 4 on Industrial Designs)).

Works of architecture (s 4(1)(b))

3.20 A building is defined as including any fixed structure or part of a building or fixed structure (s 4(2)). The definition would include a contemporary addition to an old building, such as the Clore Gallery at

Tate Britain in London. There is no need for these works to have artistic quality. In principle, the same protection is given to a monolithic office block as to the Lloyd's Insurance building in London, although it would of course be more difficult to maintain that the design for the former is original.

Artistic craftsmanship (s 4(1)(c))

3.21 This is the only description of work where courts may be called upon to make an artistic judgment. In *Hensher v Restawile* (1976), a mock-up for a suit of furniture was held not to be a work of artistic craftsmanship. The HL disagreed, however, as to why. Lord Reid suggested that a work was a work of art if it was appreciated as such by the public. Lord Kilbrandon said that it was the author's conscious intention to create a work of art which was the key. In *Merlet v Mothercare* (1986), the court found a cape designed to protect babies was not a work of artistic craftsmanship. The purpose of the design had been to protect the child and not to create a work of art.

Artistic works and originality

3.22 Artistic works must be original to attract copyright (s 1(1)(a)). As with literary works, it is the skill and labour which goes into the making of the artistic work which bestows originality. There is said to be the same ideas/expression dichotomy that applies to literary works. In *Catnic v Hill* (1979), Buckley LJ said:

> What is protected is the skill and labour devoted to making the 'artistic work' itself, not the skill and labour devoted to developing some idea or invention communicated or depicted by the 'artistic work'. The protection afforded by copyright is not in my judgment any broader .... where the 'artistic work' embodies a novel or inventive idea than it is where it represents a commonplace object or theme.

The amount of skill and labour necessary for subsistence of artistic copyright is a matter of fact and degree. Copyright may subsist in very basic works, such as a drawing of a hand pointing to a cross on a ballot paper intended for illiterate voters. However, the subject of the illustration (in essence, the 'idea' behind it) was held not to be capable of copyright infringement. It was open to others to draw hands engaged in similar action for a similar purpose (*Kenrick v Lawrence* (1890)). Similarly, in

Hanfstaengl v Baines (1895), a painting of a courting couple at a style was held not to be infringed by a sketch with the same theme, where the depiction of the couple and the landscape were quite different. In assessing the originality of an artistic work, a distinction is drawn between that which is visually significant, where the skill and labour employed are highly relevant, and that which is not, where the skill and labour employed is irrelevant. In *Drayton v Honeywell* (1992) the court compared two drawings of a valve. Knox J held that the later drawings were original because there was a change of shape which was visually significant. However, a mere scaling down of the original work would not have been visually significant, and therefore not original. The decision in *Drayton* suggests that not all skill and labour can ensure a work is original for the purposes of copyright. A scaled down drawing of an original work or a precise copy of a painting would not be. There must, in addition, be some element of material alteration or embellishment which is sufficient to make the work original (*Interlego*).

The idea/expression dichotomy in artistic works

3.23 It is necessary to exercise the same caution regarding the idea/expression dichotomy in artistic works as when dealing with original literary works. Like computer programs, works of art may embody a number of ideas, which the artist, through skill and effort, has put together in a particular way. The decision in *Kenrick* which concerned the pointing hand, suggests that the more general the idea expressed in the artistic work, the more difficult it will be to find infringement. This principle raises interesting questions in relation to the present vogue for 'conceptual art', where, by definition, the originality of the piece rests almost entirely on the concept (or idea) behind it and not on its execution or expression. Consider, for example, an early work of conceptual art, Marcel Duchamp's 'Fountain'. This was a real urinal which the surrealist signed and exhibited in a gallery. To what extent does copyright subsist in this work? Here the real skill and effort went into the idea of the work, rather than its actual physical embodiment, which, at most, entailed locating the urinal and signing it. What of a pile of bricks or a sheep preserved in formaldehyde both of which have been exhibited in museums? Do these works deserve any less protection than a Rothko or a Bacon? On the one hand, the decision in *Kenrick* suggests such works would have very narrow protection. It is submitted that another urinal signed by a different artist may well not infringe. However revolutionary (as it was as the time), the idea that a urinal may constitute a work of art would presumably merit no greater protection than the banal idea of painting a courting couple at a style. On the other hand, to the extent that copyright subsists at all in such works, what is the law protecting but an idea? It may be that Duchamp's urinal falls into that category of work described by Lord Watson in *Hanfstaengl*, 'in which his [the artist's] design and the idea to which it gives birth, are both of them so novel and exceptional that it would be difficult, if not impossible, for another author to create the same idea without trenching upon his design.' But compare this view with Buckley LJ's comment in *Catnic* (cited in **3.22** above).

Artistic works compared

3.24 Some idea of what may constitute the variety of artistic works is to be found in *Creation v News Group Newspapers* (1997). Noel Gallagher, of the band Oasis, had organised a photo shoot at a hotel for an album cover, which involved a white Rolls Royce submerged in a swimming pool and other props. A newspaper photographer managed to infiltrate the grounds and took a photograph of the scene. The plaintiffs' claim that the scene was itself a copyright work was rejected by the court. It was not a dramatic work since 'there was no movement, story or action in the scene'. It was not an artistic work (a sculpture or collage). The scene had not been carved or modelled. It differed from the film set in *Shelley Films v Rex* (1994). It was simply a collection of objects trouvet and not the result, as the film set had been, of an exercise of artistic craftsmanship. It was not a collage within the definition of the *Oxford English Dictionary*, since it did not include a collection of unrelated things and the items were not stuck together. It differed from other examples of artistic creativity, in particular conceptual works, such as Carl Andre's bricks ('Equivalence 2'), an example which was raised by the plaintiffs. In other words, simply describing the scene as a work of art did not make it so.

Secondary works

3.25 These works are also characteristically described as 'derivative', 'neighbouring' or 'supporting' works. In particular, they include sound recordings, films, broadcasts and cable programmes (ss 5, 6, 7). They differ from primary works, such as literary and artistic works, in that the 'authors' of secondary works are typically the entrepreneurs who invest in their production. It is this investment, rather than any creative endeavour, that is primarily being protected by copyright. In the UK, where the history of copyright law has been as bound up with the interests of entrepreneurs (such as publishers) as it has with those of authors, secondary works have traditionally been treated no differently from primary works.

Sound recordings (s 5A (1)(a) and (b))

3.26   Sound recordings are:

- a recording of sounds, from which the sounds may be reproduced or

- a recording of the whole or any part of a literary work, dramatic or musical work, from which sounds reproducing the work or part may be produced

regardless of the medium on which the recording is made or the method by which the sounds are reproduced or produced.

The definition is considerably broader than under the CA 1956, in order to embrace emerging technologies. Under s 5A(1)(a), sound recordings might encompass a broad range of sounds, including anything from natural sounds such as animal sounds to traffic noise to a conversation overheard and recorded. The definition given in s 5(1)(b) would fit, for example, a recording of a performance. Copyright would certainly subsist in parts of previous recordings which have been incorporated into 'rap' songs through 'sampling'. However, given that such songs are often highly original sound recordings in their own right, they would also have their own copyright, subject to any rights in the sample taken.

Film (s 5B(1))

3.27   Film means a recording on any medium from which a moving image may be produced. Again, this definition is very broad and wider than under the CA 1956, which protected 'cinematographic' films. Film soundtracks are treated as part of the film. There is no necessity for the film or sound recording to be 'original' for copyright to subsist. Instead, copyright does not subsist in a sound recording or film which is, or to the extent that it is, a copy taken from a previous sound recording or film (s 5B(4)). This ensures that there will be no new copyright in a simple re-recording of, for instance, a video rented from a video store. It is important to note that a 'film' for the purposes of the CDPA 1988 is the actual material recording not the subject matter of the recording, that is to say what is recorded on the celluloid or videotape. A film of an original dramatic work, for instance a Mike Leigh film, in which, famously, much of the dialogue and action is wholly improvised, creates two copyrights, one in the film and one in the original dramatic work it records. The first time *Norowazian v Arks* came before the HC in 1988, the court held, on the same facts as the later case, that copyright in the film could be infringed only by a copying of the whole or part of the film in the sense of copying a whole or a part of the particular recording of the film. A reshooting of a film sequence in which not a single still from the original copyright film had been included was not a copy for the purposes of the CDPA 1988. The later decision of the CA took a different view. It held that copyright might subsist in the film, itself, as a dramatic work, even if it is not the recording of a underlying dramatic work.

Broadcasts

3.28   These rights subsist without fixation. A broadcast is defined as a transmission by wireless telegraphy capable of being lawfully received by the public and which was transmitted for presentation to the public. Police radio would not constitute a broadcast because it is not for public consumption. However, a broadcast which can only be received through the use of decoding equipment, such as in pay-per-view, would be a broadcast protected by the CDPA 1988 (s 6(2)). Where the broadcast is made via satellite, the place from which the broadcast is deemed to be made is the place from which the signals are transmitted to the satellite (s 6(4)). A broadcast sent from the UK via satellite and picked up in the Netherlands will be subject to UK copyright law. Copyright does not subsist in a broadcast which infringes, or to the extent that it infringes, the copyright in another broadcast or in a cable programme (s 6(6)).

Cable programmes (s 7)

3.29   As with broadcasts, cable programmes must be intended for public reception and, furthermore, be received at two or more places. The exceptions to the definition of a cable programme include interactive services, and business or domestic services, which might include, for example, closed circuit security systems. In *Shetland Times,* the provision of a newspaper on the internet was held to be a cable programme service. The fact that a caller could contact the newspaper on the internet to make comments, did not mean the service fell within the interactive exception.

Published editions (s 8)

3.30   Essentially, this copyright protects the typographical arrangement (or layout) of a literary, dramatic or musical work against reprographic copying. It protects the way the published edition looks rather than its contents.

Authorship and ownership

3.31   The CDPA 1988 defines the author of a work as the person who creates it (s 9(1)). Authorship and ownership do not necessarily coincide.

Authorship of primary works

3.32   The definition of authorship of primary works is generally straightforward. The author is the individual who has expended the necessary effort, skill and labour in creating the work. In *Walter v Lane,* copyright subsisted in the recording of Lord Rosebery's speech, because the reporter has expended skill and effort in transposing the spoken into the written word. In the same case, the court distinguished an 'amanuensis' who simply takes down words as they are dictated, and has no creative input. This individual, such as a shorthand typist, would not be the author (or indeed the joint author) of the original literary work so produced.

Authorship in secondary works

3.33   The CDPA 1988 is more explicit when the question arises of the authorship in neighbouring works (s 9(2)(a)-(d)). The author is the individual (indeed, it is often a company) who has made the necessary commercial arrangements for their creation. This may seem reasonable in relation to cable programmes (the person providing the cable programme service), broadcasts (the person who transmits the programme, providing he has responsibility for its contents or the person who arranges for its transmission), typographical arrangements of a published edition (the publisher) and computer-generated works (the person making the necessary arrangements). But the rule is perhaps less easily justified in relation to sound recordings, where the author of a sound recording is the producer, although the sound engineer, particularly in relation to 'techno' music may have had a major creative input (s 9(2)(aa)). There have been important recent changes in the ownership of copyright in films following the Copyright Term Directive (93/98/EC) (implemented by Duration of Copyright and Rights in Performance Regulations (SI 1995/3297)). Previously, the author of a film had been the producer. The Directive provides that the principal director will be a joint author with the producer, thus belatedly giving directors in the UK the recognition that they have long received in France and other European countries as 'auteurs' (s 9(2)(ab)).

Joint authors

3.34 It is possible to have two or more joint authors of a copyright work so long as the contribution of each cannot be distinguished from that of the others (s 10(1)). In a book of essays, there will be separate authors of each of the essays published, as well as an author of the compilation of which the essays will form a part. It is a question of fact whether an individual has expended the requisite skill, effort and labour to qualify as joint author of a work (*Fylde Microsystems v Key Radio Systems* (1998)). Generally, he needs to do more than make suggestions which are subsequently incorporated into the work. In *Tate v Thomas* (1921), the contribution of the plaintiff to a play, 'The Lads of the Village', for which he suggested the name, some scenic effects and characters, some 'ideas' and a few 'catch lines or words' was held to be too 'insignificant and negligible' to support his claim for joint authorship (see also *Donoghue v Allied Newspapers* (1938)). The question of who 'pushed the pen' is not always or even decisive. In *Cala Homes v McAlpine Homes* (1995), concerning copyright in architectural drawings, the HC took the view that,

What is protected by copyright in a drawing or a literary work is more than just the skill of making marks on paper or some other medium. It is both the words or lines and skill and effort involved in creating, selecting

95

or gathering together the detailed concepts, data or emotions which those works have fixed in some tangible form which is protected. It is wrong to think that only the person who carries out the mechanical act of fixation is the author.

However, in *Robin Ray v Classic FM* (1998), the HC held that for joint authorship what is required is 'something which approximates penmanship' in that sense that what is essential is a direct responsibility for what actually appears on paper. Situations where the putative joint author merely acts as a 'scribe' for the author are likely to be unusual. Nonetheless, the expenditure of skill and effort in itself is not determinate of authorship. In *Fylde,* the plaintiff developed and manufactured inter alia software which the defendant, who claimed joint authorship, installed in his radios over a number of years. It was held that the expenditure of considerable time and effort by the defendants' employees in, for example, testing the program, making sure it performed well and setting specifications, did not amount to contributions to the 'authoring' of the software. In particular, according to the HC, the expenditure of skill, time and effort in testing a program was analogous to the skill of a proofreader. It was not authorship skill.

Ownership (s 11)

3.35 It is generally the case that the author will be first owner of a copyright work, including works which are commissioned. There are two exceptions. Where a literary, dramatic, musical, artistic work or a film is made by an employee, in the course of his employment, his employer is the first owner subject to any agreement to the contrary. Second, certain works will be Crown or Parliamentary copyright, or will be the copyright of certain international organisations.

Works created by employees (s 11(2))

3.36 To decide whether a work was created in the course of employment, it is necessary to ask whether the author was under a contract *of* service when the work was created, or alternatively whether the author was commissioned to create the work under a contract *for* service. In the latter case, copyright will stay with the author, subject to any contrary agreement. In *Belloff v Pressdram* (1973), the court cited with approval the dictum of Lord Denning that an employee is employed

96

as part of the business and his work is an integral part of the business. *Belloff* concerned a journalist for the *Observer* newspaper. The court found that she was an employee of the *Observer*, although she also wrote books and gave broadcasts which did not fall within the terms of her employment. During the time of her employment, the plaintiff both produced works whose copyright belonged to the newspaper, and works, outside her duties to the newspaper, whose copyright belonged to her.

Commissioned works

3.37 Copyright in a commissioned work belongs to the author, in the absence of an express or implied term to the contrary (*Ray*). Where the contract is unclear as to the rights of the commissioner to use the work, the courts may imply the grant of an appropriate right. If the lacuna can be satisfied by the grant of a licence rather than an assignment of copyright, then the court will imply the former. It follows that the ambit of the licence will also be the minimum required to secure for the commissioner the entitlement which the parties to the contract intended for him (*Ray*). There may however be situations where the court vests equitable ownership in the commissioner. In *Richardson Computers v Flanders* (1993), the defendant merely rewrote and improved a computer program, the copyright in which belonged to the plaintiff. There was no contract explicitly vesting the copyright in the revised software in the commissioner. Nonetheless, the court held that the plaintiff had equitable ownership of the copyright, since without ownership he would fail to benefit from the contract, which was the intention of both parties. The frequent failure of those who commission works to determine who will own copyright in the ensuing product provides intellectual property lawyers with a steady and lucrative flow of business.

Qualifying works (ss 153-156)

3.38 Not all copyright works will be protected in the UK. They must be qualifying works. A work qualifies for copyright protection in the UK if

• the author is a qualifying person

• the work was first published in a qualifying country (or published simultaneously, ie within thirty days of first publication)

97

- in the case of a broadcast or cable programme, the UK was the country from which the broadcast was made or the cable programme was sent.

A qualifying person includes a person who, at the time the work was made, is a British citizen or subject or an individual domiciled or resident in the UK, as well as a citizen of or a person domiciled or resident in any extension country, which is a country which is a party to the Berne Convention or the Universal Copyright Convention. If the work is unpublished, first publication of a literary, dramatic or musical work occurs when the work is made or, if the making of the work extended over a period, a substantial part of the period.

Duration of copyright in primary works (s 12)

3.39 Copyright in a primary work lasts for the life of the author plus 70 years. The present term, which replaced the previous term of life plus 50 years, was the result of the Copyright Term Directive, which was designed to ensure a uniform term throughout the EU. The effect of the Directive was that some works which had previously fallen out of copyright in the UK came back into copyright. Others which were about to fall out of copyright had their copyright extended. The length of protection afforded to copyright works has inexorably increased, over the past two centuries, and there has been considerable debate as to whether the broader public interest has been served by this latest extension to the copyright term. A key justification offered by the EU was that people now live longer and that their increased longevity should be recognised (although, it is of course the author's heirs rather than the author who will benefit). Others have argued that the previous life plus 50 years term was sufficient to ensure that author, descendants and publisher were amply rewarded and that the new longer term will stifle the free circulation of ideas (Laddie 'Copyright: Over-strength, Over-regulated, Over-rated?' [1996] EIPR 253). There are special rules for primary works of an unknown authorship, works which are unpublished at the author's death, works of joint authorship and computer generated works. The copyright in the latter expires 50 years from the end of the calendar year in which the work was made (s 12).

Duration of copyright in secondary works

3.40 Some secondary works, like computer generated works, typically have a shorter term of protection than primary works, recognising that here copyright is protecting financial investment rather than creative endeavour. Broadly, sound recordings, broadcasts and cable programmes are protected for 50 years and typographical arrangements of published editions for 25 years. As a result of the Copyright Term Directive, films have ceased to be protected as secondary works in which the term of protection (since 1989) was 50 years. They are now protected like primary works, the term being 70 years from the death of the last to die of the following: principal director; author of the screenplay; author of the dialogue; composer of the music specifically created for the film (s 13B). It is of course important to remember that there will be a number of rights in any given copyright work, and films are a good example, which will expire at uneven dates.

Infringement

3.41 There are two types of infringement. Primary infringement occurs when a person does, or authorises another to do, any of the restricted acts without the licence of a copyright owner (s 16(2)). Secondary infringement, which is mainly concerned with dealings in infringing works or facilitating their production will be considered below (see **3.63**). This chapter now turns to primary infringement.

Restricted acts

3.42 The owner of the copyright in a work has the exclusive right to do the following acts in the UK (s 16(1)):

- to copy the work

- to issue copies of the work to the public

- to perform, show or play the work in public

- to broadcast the work or include it in a cable programme service

- to make an adaptation of the work or do any of the above in relation to an adaptation.

The CDPA 1988 does not give a copyright owner a positive right to do any of the 'restricted acts', since in so doing it is quite possible he may infringe another's copyright. For instance, Y translates a play into French. Y will own copyright in her translation, but she has no right to copy it or issue copies to the public without the licence of Z, the owner of copyright in the play. Instead, the CDPA 1988 gives the copyright owner the negative right to stop anyone else from doing any of the restricted acts without his permission (or licence). Thus, Z can stop Y from publishing her translation without a licence. The relationship between the restricted acts and different kinds of copyright works are considered below (see **3.57**).

The elements of primary infringement

3.43   There are two defining elements to primary infringement. According to Denning LJ in *Francis Day & Hunter v Bron* (1963), there must be a causal connection between the copyright work and the allegedly infringing work. In other words, the copyright work must be the source of the infringing work. Second, there must be copying of a substantial part of the copyright work.

The causal connection

3.44   For a work to be infringing, it must derive from the copyright work. It must be copied. If two works created independently are substantially the same, the first to be created will not be infringed by the second. The similarity may be coincidence or perhaps result from the authors choosing the same subject, for instance photographs of the Manhattan skyline at night, where it is possible that the composition of resulting works will be similar. Alternatively, the two works may have derived from a common source. A great deal of historical writing depends upon the use of a limited pool of sources. If the second author uses the first author's work to identify the common source, there will be no infringement, since by going back to the primary source, the second author will have expended his own skill and effort on his work (*Pike v Nicholas* (1869).

Indirect copying

3.45   The infringing work need not be copied directly from the original work. Indeed, the infringing author may not even know of its existence.

In *Solar Thomson v Barton* (1977), the defendants asked a designer to design a spare part for its machinery. To avoid infringing copyright in the original design drawings of the spare (which belonged to the plaintiff), they gave the designer detailed instructions and the surrounding hardware, but did not show him the original drawing. He produced a design drawing which closely resembled the plaintiff's. The CA held that the instructions were a sufficient causal link for copyright in the original design drawings to have been infringed. In *Plix v Winstone* (1986), the link between the copyright work and the infringing work was even more tenuous. The New Zealand Kiwifruit Authority (NZKA) had published written specifications for kiwi fruit containers, based on the plaintiffs' designs. At the time, the plaintiffs' packing case was the only one to have been approved by the NZKA, thus giving it an effective monopoly. The defendants, seeking to avoid a copyright challenge at all costs and with legal advice, asked an Italian designer to come up with a container to fit the official specifications, without showing him the plaintiffs' case. The resulting design was held to be infringing. The New Zealand CA held it was possible to copy indirectly through the intermediary verbal instructions, provided the verbal description was sufficiently precise to provide a means whereby the copyist could appropriate the substantial features of the original.

Subconscious copying

3.46 It follows that the infringer need not be aware that he is copying to infringe. The copying may be subconscious. In *Francis*, where the plaintiffs claimed infringement in their song 'A Little Spanish Town', the composer of 'Why' did not remember ever hearing the former and the CA accepted that there had been no conscious copying. But it was said that if he had heard the work and subconsciously copied it, then 'Why' would constitute an infringing work.

A substantial part

3.47 Apart from a causal connection, in order to infringe, copying must be in relation to the work as a whole or any substantial part of it (s 16(3)(a)). A 'substantial part' is defined qualitatively not quantitatively (*Ladbrokes* per Lord Pearce). In *Hawkes v Paramount* (1934), the defendants infringed copyright in 28 bars of the 'Colonel Bogey' march, played during the opening of a school by the Prince of Wales, which the defendants filmed. Although the extract took up only 50 seconds or so of film time, the CA held that these 28 bars, being the highly recognisable, 'essential' air of the march, constituted a substantial part (the CDPA now provides a defence of fair dealing, see **3.66** et seq). At the other extreme, in *Warwick v Eisinger* (1969), the defendant, the author of a film script on the trials of Oscar Wilde, borrowed heavily from a book by H on the same subject, which the plaintiffs had also turned into a film. The borrowed passages were not original since they had, in turn, been copied by H from a third book which was based on shorthand transcripts of the trials. The court held that although the passages may have constituted a substantial part of the script quantitatively, they did not constitute a substantial part of the plaintiffs' work for the purposes of infringement, because they were not original. In *Biotrading v Biohit* (1998), the CA posed a third possibility. What if a person takes an unoriginal part from a work in which copyright subsists and uses that part in a similar context and way as it was used in the copyright work? According to Aldous LJ, the answer is that the person would be taking not only the unoriginal part, but also a part of the work which provided the originality. In such a case the amount taken would be likely to amount to a substantial part. *Biotrading* concerned industrial drawings of the pipettes. Aldous LJ noted that industrial drawings often consist of (unoriginal) shapes copied from earlier drawings and new (original) shapes. Accordingly:

> To decide whether copyright subsists the drawing as a whole must not be dissected. Although the copying of an unoriginal shape may not amount to the copying of a substantial part, is likely to do so when the amount copied includes the context in which the shape is portrayed. In such circumstances, the fact that the part copied includes an unoriginal shape becomes of very little relevance in deciding whether the amount copied was a substantial part of the whole, because the copier has taken not only the original part but also much of the work of the author in deciding how and in what way the unoriginal shape should be combined with the original shape.

It is important when judging substantiality, to assess the importance of the copied material to the original work and not to the allegedly infringing work (Romer LJ, *Bauman v Fussell* (1978)); also Aldous LJ in *Biotrading*).

Originality and infringement

3.48   The result in *Warwick* appears to undermine the universal applicability of Peterson J's oft-repeated dictum in *University of London Press,* that 'as a rough practical test', 'what is worth copying is prima facie worth protecting.' It does, however, emphasise that to constitute a substantial part of a copyright work, the part must be original in its own right, even when abstracted from the whole (*Ladbroke* per Lord Pearce; but also *Biohit* above **3.47**). In *Warwick,* H's book was held to be an original literary work by virtue of the skill and labour he had put into editing the source material. But by simply taking the source material, the defendants had not taken advantage of H's skill and labour. They had not taken a substantial part of the work, because the part they had taken was not original.

Compilations

3.49   The principle that a substantial part must be original is clearly demonstrated in relation to compilations. Their originality lies not in the individual contents of the compilation but in the way the author has selected the contents and chosen to combine them in the work, and it is this skill which is protected by copyright (*Ladbroke*) (see **3.16** and **3.17** above). In *Ladbroke,* the court first decided that the plaintiff's fixed-odds football betting coupons constituted an original literary work, ie a compilation, by virtue of the skill, labour and judgment that had gone into their composition. The defendants copied the selection and arrangement of a list of bets and the types of wagers which appeared on the coupons. The court held these to be the essential feature of the plaintiffs' coupon, and therefore a substantial part of the work. A number of cases suggest infringement will not be avoided simply by rearranging the order of the material in the compilation. The court may feel the effort involved in collecting or actually generating the information contained in the compilation is itself worthy of protection. In *Elanco v Mandops* (1980), the defendants produced a herbicide that the plaintiffs had previously sold exclusively under a patent which had now expired. The plaintiffs sent out a brochure with the herbicide, as did the defendants. Almost all the information in the brochures was in the public domain. Goff LJ held that there was an arguable case of infringement because the defendants had originally used the plaintiffs' leaflet to prepare their own. In addition, Buckley LJ observed that the defendants were fully entitled to make use of any information in the public domain. But they were not entitled to save themselves the trouble and costs of assembling their own information by copying the plaintiffs' trade literature, thereby making use of the plaintiffs' skill and judgment, while avoiding having to make their own selection and assemble their own information. They were not entitled 'to take what another had done'. In *Independent Television v Time Out* (1984), the court held that it was the broadcasters' skill and labour in developing daily programme schedules rather than their subsequent listing in the *TV Times* and *Radio Times* that was worthy of protection (see also *Football League v Littlewoods Pools* (1959) per Upjohn J, in which Football League fixture lists were held to be protected by copyright). The consequence of *Independent Television* was to give the plaintiffs an effective monopoly over publishing the television schedules, since they had generated them (but see below **3.95** on *Magill*).

Databases and infringement

3.50 The copyright in an original database will be infringed by the taking of a substantial part. According to the Regulations, a database right is infringed if, without the consent of the owner, a person extracts or re-utilises all or a substantial part of the contents of the database. Extraction is defined as 'the permanent or temporary transfer of any contents to another medium by any means or in any form' and 're-utilisation' means making its contents available to the public by any means. Repeated and systematic extraction or re-utilisation of insubstantial parts of the database may amount to extraction or re-utilisation of a substantial part and hence be infringing.

The ideas/expression dichotomy and infringement

3.51 It has been suggested that, as a general rule, copyright protects the form in which the idea is expressed rather than the idea itself. In *Ward v Sankey* (1988), the defendant copied from the plaintiff the idea of designing a sleeve to fit around 'nestable' flower pots. The defendant's drawing embodying this idea was the same as the plaintiff's drawing. The HC held that this was not infringement. The defendant had infringed the plaintiff's copyright work neither indirectly through copying the dimensions of the plaintiff's pots (as in *Solar Thomson* (see **3.45**)) nor directly through copying the plaintiffs' drawings. It was simply the idea which had been taken.

Non-literal copying

3.52 It is certainly possible to infringe a copyright work or a substantial part of it even though the infringing work is not an exact copy. For instance, the copy may be an adaptation. Is this tantamount to saying that there is, after all, copyright in ideas? One answer may be that if the originality of a work resides in the way an idea is developed or a number of ideas are combined, then there may still be infringement even if there is no literal copying. Cases involving copyright works which have been adapted for plays or movie scripts clearly demonstrate the problematic relationship between ideas and expression. Typically, a scriptwriter or a dramatist may copy the ideas or the situation in the original copyright work, perhaps a novel, but inevitably the form in which he will express them will be different. It has been held that the working out of these ideas may in themselves constitute a substantial part of the copyright work (eg *Poznanski v London Film Production* (1937)). In *Rees v Melville* (1914), the plaintiff and the defendant had both written plays with the central idea that the hero must marry before his 21st birthday or lose his inheritance. Both featured a villainous cousin seeking to prevent the inheritance, and in both the hero is saved by fortuitously marrying a beggar girl on the eve of his birthday. Other details of the two plays were different. The CA found there was no infringement. The plot of the plaintiff's play was not new. It was peopled by stock characters. The defendant would not have taken a substantial part of the plaintiff's play by copying these aspects of it, for in themselves they were not original. Instead, the plays originality lay in the differences between them. Lord Swinford Eady MR said:

> ... the court must have regard to the dramatic value and importance of what if anything was taken, even although the portion might in fact be small and the actual language not copied. On the other hand, the fundamental idea of two plays might be the same but if worked out separately or on independent lines they might be so different as to bear no real resemblance to each other.

A common source

3.53 Courts are frequently asked to decide whether the similarities between two works arise from their sharing the same general idea or, in the case of historical works, a common set of historical incidents, in which case there would be no infringement. In *Ravenscroft v Herbert* (1980), the defendant wrote a novel, 'The Spear of Destiny', about the fate of a spear said to have pierced the side of Christ. He took the idea from a work of 'non-fiction' by the plaintiff, who based his own book partly on 'orthodox' research and partly on 'mystical meditation'. There was some language copying and the same characters, incidents and interpretation of the significance of the events were found in both works. Brigham J found that by taking not only the plaintiff's language, but also identical incidents of real and occult history, the defendant had appropriated to himself the 'skill and labour' of the author. However, the court did note, obiter, that copyright law will probably allow a wider use to be made of an historical work than a novel.

Artistic work and infringement

3.54   The infringement of artistic works presents similar difficulties for the courts seeking to draw a distinction between a general idea which is not protected and its expression which is. In *Hanfstaengel v Baines*, the plaintiff's painting was of a couple by a stile meant to represent 'Courtship'. The defendant's sketch had a similar theme, but was different in detail. There was no infringement. This particular representation of courtship was of 'great antiquity' and not original to the artist. Less clear cut was the case of *Bauman*. The plaintiff had photographed two cocks fighting. An artist painted a picture the idea for which, he admitted, was taken from the photograph. The position of the cocks was the same in both works, although the colours in the painting were heightened to create, according to the CA, 'a quite different effect.' The CA endorsed the view of Dale J that the 'feeling and artistic character' of the painting were the work of the defendant and there was no infringement. In a dissenting judgment, Romer LJ suggested that the position of the birds was a substantial feature of the photograph which had taken both skill and judgment to capture. By reproducing the position of the birds, he believed that the defendant had copied a substantial part of the photograph. In the case of paintings of well-known views or common place objects, copyright will subsist in the details of the design (*Hanfstaengel v Baines*). The more commonplace the subject, the closer a copy will have to come to infringe (*Kenrick* (see **3.22** above)).

Authorisation

3.55   Copyright is infringed by any person who, without the licence of the copyright owner, authorises another to do any of the restricted acts (s 16(2)). Authorisation is a grant, or purported grant, which may be expressed or implied, of the right to do the restricted act. An example of what constitutes authorisation arose in *Pensher Security v Sunderland* (2000). Sunderland city council wanted a specific design of door to be installed in its council flats. In the course of taking tenders, the council specified a design which had originated with the plaintiffs. The successful tender submitted a design similar to the plaintiff's design. The plaintiff alleged infringement. The CA held, inter alia, that a person who commissioned another to produce an article to a particular design, sanctioned and impliedly purported to grant him the right to make it to that design and thus to authorise its production. In this case, the council was well aware that the design they accepted was similar to the plaintiff's design. Typically, the question of authorisation might also arise in relation to the manufacture and supply of the technological means for reproducing copyright works. In *CBS v Amstrad* (1988), the defendant developed and sold a twin-deck tape recorder. The most obvious use for the recorder, which was underlined by the defendant's advertising, was to copy music cassettes. Nonetheless, it was not its only use and infringement was not the inevitable result of the defendant's action. The HL ruled that since the defendants did not purport to have the authority to justify such taping (and nor would reasonable members of the public suppose that they did), it did not amount to authorisation for the defendants merely to enable, assist or encourage others to infringe by giving them the 'power' to copy. The questions raised by *CBS*, are likely to be asked in other contexts. The computer industry is anxious to promote the use of digital video discs ('DVD') in the video rental market. The film industry is equally anxious to maximise the copyright protection of its products. It has suggested regional coding, so that discs tagged for Brazil, for example, can be played only on Brazilian videos and so on. It follows that sale of a decoder in the UK whose *only* use would be to overcome such protection (for instance, to enable UK machines to play cheaper video discs manufactured in Brazil but not licensed for the UK) would constitute authorisation, because there would be no other use for the de-coder.

The restricted acts applied to copyright works (ss 16-21)

3.56 Different types of copyright work may be infringed in different ways. Examined below will be infringement by:

- copying (s 17)

- issuing copies to the public (s 18)

- performance, broadcasting and inclusion in cable programmes (ss 19-20)

- making an adaptation (s 21).

Copying

3.57 Every description of copyright work may be infringed by unauthorised copying. What constitutes copying may differ depending upon the type of work in question. Copying in relation to literary, dramatic and musical or artistic works means reproducing the work (or, of course, any substantial part of it) in any material form, including storing the work in any medium by electronic means. A photograph of a painting may infringe and so may storing a literary, artistic or musical work in a computer memory. Copying of artistic works includes the making of a three-dimensional copy of a two-dimensional work and the making of a two-dimensional copy of a three dimensional work. A photograph of a statue may infringe (subject to any fair dealing provision, see **3.66** et seq) and so may the making of a statue from a drawing. Unauthorised copies of Popeye, in the shape of brooches, were held to be an indirect infringement of the Popeye cartoon drawings (*King Features v Kleeman* (1941)). An important exception is the making of an article or the copying of an article from a design document or model recording anything other than an artistic work (such as, for instance, an exhaust pipe for a motor vehicle; s 51(1)). This exception is discussed in Chapter 4 on Industrial Designs (see **4.3**). It is also not an infringement to produce a three-dimensional work from a set of instructions. In *Foley v Eliott* (1982), a garment made from a knitting pattern was held not to infringe the pattern, because it was not a reproduction of the work.

Issuing copies to the public and the rental right (s 18)

3.58 Every description of copyright work is protected by the right of the copyright owner to issue copies of his work to the public for the first time. This is often called the 'distribution right'. Put generally, this right is exhausted if authorised copies are put on the market in the EEA.

There are also now lending and rental rights in literary, dramatic, musical works, most artistic works as well as sound recordings and films. These rights enable the copyright owner to profit from the circulation of rental copies (eg videos) beyond their first issue to the public and to benefit from the distribution of works made available by public libraries (s 18A). They derive from the Directive on Rental, Lending and Neighbouring Rights (92/100/EC), which was implemented by the Copyright and Related Rights Regulations (SI 1966/2967).

Performance, broadcasting and inclusion in cable programmes (ss 19-20)

3.59   Literary, dramatic or musical works (but not artistic works) are infringed by their performance in public. Performances include lectures, addresses, speeches, and sermons. Performance may be by any mode of visual or acoustic presentation, including the playing of a sound recording, or the showing of a film, broadcast or cable programme. Where the copyright is infringed by the work being performed, played or shown in public by means of audio-visual apparatus, the person who sends the images or sounds or who performs the work is not responsible for the infringement. It is the person who is in charge of the equipment who infringes (s 19). The broadcasting of all descriptions of copyright work, including broadcasts or cable programmes (except typographical arrangements), or their inclusion in a cable programme service is restricted by copyright (s 20). X, a local publican, plans a 'Spice Girls Nite'. He hires four look-a-likes to perform a selection of their greatest hits, and simultaneously arranges for them to be broadcast on a local radio station, which he owns. The performance is interspersed by a DJ playing Spice Girls records. Unfortunately, he neglects to seek any licences for the event. X will, at the very least, have infringed copyright in the lyrics (literary works), tunes (musical works) and arrangements of the songs, possibly in the choreography which accompanies the performances, and in sound recordings (the records) both by performing and broadcasting the show.

Public performances

3.60   What constitutes a public performance is determined by case law, and is widely defined. What have been termed quasi-domestic situations (such as a performance to a small number of doctors and nurses at Guy's Hospital) are largely excepted (*Duck v Bates* (1884)). The court is usually more concerned with the character of the audience (are they part of the likely paying customers for the copyright work at issue) rather than the context in which the performance takes place. So performances in clubs, shops and in a factory (which relayed the radio show 'Music While You Work' to its luckless employees in order 'to raise productivity') have all been held to be in public (for the latter, see *Turner v Performing Right Society* (1943)).

Making an adaptation (s 21)

3.61 This restricted act relates only to literary, dramatic and musical works. Adaptation means a translation of the work, a dramatic work which is converted into a non-dramatic work or the reverse, a version of the work conveyed by pictures (in essence, a strip cartoon), or the arrangement or transcription of a musical work. An adaptation of a computer program means an arrangement or altered version of the program or a translation, which includes a version of the program which is converted into or out of computer language or code or into a different computer language or code, otherwise than incidentally in the course of running the program. Adaptation thus includes a number of acts already considered in relation to copying in general, such as turning a novel into a screenplay. It must relate to a substantial part of the copyright work to infringe. An unauthorised 'study-note' version of Shaw's play 'St Joan', a detailed scene by scene summary, was an adaptation, and not a synopsis. It reproduced a substantial part of the play and was infringing. A brief description of the play would not have infringed (*Sillitoe v McGraw-Hill* (1983)). It is, of course, possible for copyright to subsist both in the adaptation and the original work, although the copyright in the former cannot be exploited without the license of the owner of the copyright in the latter (*Redwood* (see **3.18** above)).

What is proof of copying?

3.62 To summarise, in order to find infringement there must be copying of a substantial part of the copyright work. There must also be a causal connection between the copyright work and the infringing work. It is a question of fact whether the degree of similarity is sufficient to warrant the inference that there is a causal connection between the two works. The causal connection may be unconscious or indirect. A substantial degree of objective similarity together with proof of access to the original work is prima facie evidence of copying (*Francis*). The evidential burden may then shift to the defendant to show that his work was not copied.

Secondary infringement (ss 22-27)

3.63 Secondary infringement is concerned with dealing in infringing copies or providing the means for their manufacture. It includes possessing, selling, exhibiting or distributing infringing copies, and importing infringing copies into the UK. An article is an infringing copy if its making constituted an infringement of the copyright of the work in question or if it has been or is proposed to be imported into the UK and its making in the UK would have constituted an infringement of the copyright of the work in question, or a breach of an exclusive licence agreement relating to the work. A computer program which has previously been sold in any EEA member state, by or with the consent of the copyright owner, is not an infringing copy for the purposes of the CDPA 1988.

3.64 Secondary infringement differs from primary infringement in that it is necessary to show that the alleged infringer knows or has reason to believe that he is dealing with an infringing copy. This is an objective test. Reason to believe means a knowledge of the facts from which a reasonable man would arrive at the relevant belief (*LA Gear v Hi-Tec Sport* (1992); *Linpac v Eagleton* (1994)). It is no excuse for the defendant, who persists in dealing in the articles, to claim that his legal advisors had wrongly assured him that the articles were not infringing, once he has notice of the facts upon which the claim is based (*Sillitoe*). On the other hand, he should be allowed sufficient time to investigate the facts in order to acquire the reasonable belief (*LA Gear*).

Permitted acts

3.65 Section 28 of the CDPA 1988 sets out a number of permitted acts in relation to copyright works. These cover circumstances in which it is possible to make use of a copyright work, or a substantial part of it, without infringing copyright. The aim of the permitted acts is to set the conditions in which a public interest in using the copyright works overrides the private interests of the copyright owner. Undoubtedly, the most important permitted acts are fair dealing for the purpose of research and private study and fair dealing for the purpose of criticism, review and news reporting.

Fair dealing

3.66   According to Lord Denning MR in *Hubbard v Vosper* (1972), what constitutes fair dealing is 'impossible to define.' Nonetheless, some guidelines have emerged in the case law. The CDPA 1988 does not specify the amount of copyright material which may be taken without falling outside the definition of fair dealing (although there are some specific rules for librarians). However, the amount should be commensurate with the purpose for which it is taken. This is a matter of impression or degree. It might justify the reproduction of the whole work, for instance an epitaph on a tombstone, or a large part of it (*Hubbard* per Megaw LJ). There is some authority for the view that it is not fair dealing for an unpublished work to be the subject of public criticism or review (*British Oxygen v Liquid Air* (1925); *Hyde Park Residence v Yelland* (2000)). However, the courts have also been willing to countenance exceptions. In *Hubbard,* Lord Denning gave the example of a company shareholder circular which may be of general interest and therefore legitimate for the press to criticise. In *Hubbard,* itself, the CA accepted that it was fair dealing for the defendant, a disenchanted member of the Church of Scientology, publicly to circulate bulletins sent by the church to its members, because the latter constituted a 'wide circle'. If a work is unpublished, but it has been 'leaked' by an unidentified source, this will increase the likelihood of the court seeing the dealing as unfair (*Beloff*).

Research and private study (s 29)

3.67   This section applies to literary, dramatic, musical or artistic works and typographical arrangements of published works. Fair dealing with these descriptions of work does not infringe copyright if it is for the purposes of research and private study. Without such a provision, academic research would of course be severely hampered, although the research or private study may also be for commercial purposes. A law student may photocopy an excerpt from a law journal, for example, in the course of his academic research, and so may a lawyer in the course of preparing a case. But it is not fair dealing to reproduce a copyright work for commercial purposes, even if one aim of the commercial enterprise is to facilitate private study for others. In *Sillitoe*, the publisher who was found to have produced infringing study notes of the play 'St Joan' could not rely on the defence of fair dealing. According to the court, the publishers were not engaged in private study or research but were merely facilitating this for others.

Criticism and review (s 30(1))

3.68 This section applies to all copyright works, including a performance of a work. Fair dealing with a work for the purposes of criticism and review will not infringe copyright, provided it is accompanied with a sufficient acknowledgement, that is the title and the author (not the owner) of the work. Criticism may be not just of the work itself, but also of its underlying philosophy, so that in *Hubbard* a disenchanted scientologist might reproduce large chunks of the writings of its founder L Ron Hubbard in a book criticising the movement. The criteria for this defence, were discussed recently by the CA in *Pro Sieben v Carlton UK* (1999). Carlton broadcast a documentary, 'Selling Babies', intended to be a critique of chequebook journalism. The programme featured the example of Mandy Allwood, pregnant with eight children, who had sold exclusive rights to an interview to the plaintiff, a German television company, through a well-known agent. The interview was included in a news report, TAFF, which could be received in the UK. The Carlton documentary featured a 30-second excerpt from the interview. The plaintiff sued and the defendant claimed fair dealing for the purposes of criticism and review and reporting current events. The plaintiff succeeded in the HC, but the decision was overturned on appeal. Walker LJ held that in considering fair dealing for criticism and review, the test of fair dealing was an objective one although the intentions of the user were still 'highly relevant'. Nonetheless, a sincere but misguided belief by a journalist that use was for criticism and review was not enough to support the defence. Walker LJ went on that criticism and review (and reporting current events) are of wide and indefinite scope. Criticism can be not just of style but also of a work's social and moral implications. It can be strongly expressed, even unbalanced. But in deciding whether the defence had been made out, the focus should be on the likely impact on the audience. Based on this criterion, the Carlton programme was made for purpose of criticising cheque book journalism, and the treatment of Allwood's story in particular.

News reporting (s 30(2))

3.69   Fair dealing with any description of work (other than a photograph) for the purpose of reporting current events does not infringe copyright, provided it is accompanied with a sufficient acknowledgement (although this is not necessary for sound recordings, films, broadcasts and cable programmes). It was said by North J in *Walter v Steinkopff* (1892) that there is no copyright in the news, but only in the form in which it is expressed. Certainly, it has been widely accepted by the courts that newspapers and journals will pick up stories from each other, and rewrite them. But North J's maxim was perhaps most appropriate in the days of print journalism. Since the CDPA 1988, fair dealing has also applied to broadcasts, as well as more traditional copyright works. When BSkyB showed excerpts of BBC live broadcasts of the 1990 World Cup finals, there was, of course, no question of changing the form of the presentation, hence the importance of the fair dealing defence (*British Broadcasting Corpn v British Satellite Broadcasting* (1992)). Conflict has also arisen over newsworthy interviews, such as with Lady Ogilvy, a royal single mother, where again much would be lost if the exact words were not reproduced (*Express Newspapers v News (UK) Ltd* (1990)). It may even be necessary to refer to news which is not current in order to report on current events, and this too can be fair dealing (*Associated Newspapers v News Group Newspapers* (1986)). But it is not fair dealing for a competitor to take copyright material simply for its own profit, as in *Walter v Steinkopff* (1892), where the 'St James' Gazette' copied excerpts from a 'Letter from America' by Rudyard Kipling, which had been first published in *The Times* (see also *Associated Newspapers Group*). Nor would it be fair dealing, were Marks & Spencer to circulate to its staff press cuttings relating to the store, since this would be copying material subject to copyright within a commercial organisation for commercial reasons (*Newspaper Licensing Agency Ltd v Marks & Spencer plc* (2000)). *Pro Sieben* also looked at fair dealing for the purpose of news and current events. Walker LJ took the view that the media coverage of the pregnancy and the sale of the interview were current events of real interest to the public, and that, as with fair dealing for the purpose of criticism and review, it was the impact on the audience which was key to deciding if the defence succeeded.

3.70   Recently, the criteria for establishing a defence of fair dealing for the purpose of reporting current events was summarised by the CA in *Hyde Park Residence v Yelland* (2000). *Hyde Park* concerned a security video of Princess Diana and Dodi Fayed. The video, filmed at the Villa Windsor in Paris, the day before the couple were killed, was made under the responsibility of the claimant company, controlled by Dodi Fayed's father, Mr Al Fayed. A year later stills from the video, which had been supplied without authority by M, an employee of the claimant, were published in the *The Sun*. *The Sun* claimed that the purpose of publication was to prove that Mr Al Fayed had misrepresented both the length of the couple's visit and the claim that they were engaged. In a copyright action in the HC, Jacob J accepted that the use was covered by both fair dealing and a public interest defence. In allowing the claimant's appeal, Aldous LJ concurred with the judgment in *Pro Sieben* that it is appropriate take into account the motives of the alleged infringer, the extent and purpose of the use, and whether the extent was necessary for the purpose of reporting current events. Furthermore, if the work had not been published or circulated to the public that was also an important indication that the dealing was not fair. It followed that the court must judge fair dealing by the objective standard of whether a fair minded and honest person would have dealt with the copyright work, in the manner, for example, of the defendant, for the purposes of reporting current events. In this case, Aldous LJ believed that to view *The Sun*'s publication of the photographs as fair dealing would be to 'honour dishonour', not least because the information about the length of the stay at the Villa was neither relevant to whether the couple were engaged, nor did its circulation require the publication of the stills. The fair dealing defence failed. The CA then went on to consider the public interest defence.

Public interest

3.71   The public interest defence is recognised by s 171(3) of the CDPA 1988. A public interest defence was first developed in respect of breach of confidence, and gives an exception to the right of the confider to insist on confidence, if the breach is to disclose an iniquity (*Initial Services v Putterill* (1967); for confidential information see **7.47** et seq). In *Lion Laboratories v Evans* (1985), the CA held the public interest defence might also be applied to claims of breach of copyright. In breach of confidence actions, the criterion for a public interest defence is 'exacting' (*Belloff*). It does not apply to information that 'may be of interest' for the public to know, but rather to information which, in the public interest, 'should be known.' Furthermore, once the information is aired in public, it would be difficult to defend further publication (*Express Newspapers v News (UK)* (1990)).

3.72   In *A-G v Guardian Newspapers*, 'the Spycatcher' case (which is discussed at length at **7.52** et seq), Lords Griffiths and Jauncey suggested that it would be right to withhold copyright protection from Peter Wright's memoirs because publication of the memoirs of a former member of MI5 was against the public interest. This was not to say that there was no copyright in the work, but rather that it was against the public interest to permit it to be enforced (*A-G v Guardian Newspapers* (1990)). The HL's opinion in *Spycatcher*, suggests that the basis for a public interest defence in an action for copyright infringement is not the same as for a breach of confidence action. The CA made this plain in the *Hyde Park Residence* case. It is not that the CDPA 1988 gives courts the power to enable an infringer to use another's copyright in the public interest. It does not. Rather, the courts have an inherent jurisdiction to refuse to enforce an action for copyright infringement where enforcement would offend against the public interest, or as put by Aldous LJ, against the 'policy of the law'. Although Aldous LJ said it was impossible to define the circumstances in which a court would be entitled to follow this course, they might arise if the work was immoral, scandalous or contrary to family life or was injurious to public life, public health and safety or the administration of justice or incited or encouraged others to act in such a way. In the *Hyde Park Residence* case, any relevant information could be given to the public without infringing copyright in the stills and the public interest defence also failed. It has been suggested that the CA's decision in *Hype Park Residence* narrows the scope of the public interest defence in relation to copyright infringement, and arose, perhaps, from a desire to curb the perceived excesses of the tabloid press (Browes 'Copyright: Court of Appeal Considers Fair Dealing Defence and Rejects Common Law Defence of Public Interest' [2000] EIPR 289)).

Moral rights (ss 77-89)

3.73   In the UK, it is fair to say copyright law is primarily concerned with protecting the rights of the owner (not always the creator) to exploit a work economically. Moral rights recognise that the creator of a work also has a continuing interest in ensuring that his work is treated with respectfully, even if, by transferring copyright to another, he may no longer have an economic interest in it. Unlike copyright, moral rights are personal to the author of a work and may only transfer on death. They are quite distinct from copyright, and their breach leads to an action for breach of statutory duty and not for infringement. There are four moral rights recognised by the CDPA 1988. The first is the right to be identified as the author of a literary, dramatic, musical or artistic work or the director of a film (ss 77-79). This is sometimes called the 'paternity right'. The second applies to the same description of works, and is the right to object to derogatory treatment of the work, where derogatory treatment amounts to distortion or mutilation of the work or is otherwise prejudicial to the honour or reputation of the author or director (ss 80-83). This is the so-called right of integrity. The third also applies to the same description of works, and is the right against false attribution (s 84). The fourth is the right to privacy of photographs and films and belongs to a person who has commissioned such a work for private or domestic purposes (s 85). It gives the commissioner the right not to have the work issued to the public, exhibited or shown in public or broadcast. This right might prevent tabloid newspapers from publishing say a wedding photograph of an individual who later becomes famous. But it would have no effect on the printing of controversial paparazzi photographs of celebrities in perhaps even more private moments.

The weakness of moral rights

3.74 Moral rights have been criticised for leaning too far in the direction of protecting the economic interests of the copyright owner where these may conflict with the moral rights of the creator (Marino 'R-E-S-P-E-C-T — that' s what moral rights mean to me' [1992] NLJ 1084; Cornish 'Moral Rights under the 1988 Act' [1989] EIPR 449). The paternity right must be specifically asserted by the author or director to have effect. All of these rights may be waived by consent. Understandably, many authors are ignorant of their moral rights, or have little bargaining strength if the copyright owner asks for them to be waived. Moral rights may be expensive to enforce, and the outcome of such an action may be uncertain. For the holder of moral rights in a copyright work, it may still be easier to seek redress through an action for passing-off or defamation (for an example where the claimant was successful in both passing-off (**5.62**) and breach of moral rights, see *Clark v Associated Newspapers* (1998)). The CDPA 1988 also sets out numerous and important exceptions where the right does not apply. For instance, in the case of paternity and integrity rights, they do not apply where the works are made for the reporting of current events or for publication in newspapers, magazines or periodicals.

Dealing with copyright (ss 90-93)

3.75 Like other forms of property, copyright is transmissible by assignment, testamentary disposition or by operation of the law as personal or moveable property (s 90(1)). Assignments must be in writing (s 90(3)). Exclusive licences must also be in writing (s 92). Assignments or other transmissions of copyright may be partial, limiting, for instance, what the assignee may do with the copyright work or the territory in which he may do it. Future, or prospective, copyrights may also be assigned (s 91). Feature films are frequently financed by the production company selling off a host of different rights before they are even made. One distribution company may buy rights to exhibit the proposed film on terrestrial television in the Benelux countries, another the rights to theatrical exhibition in North American, a third the rights to show the film on airlines and so on. Each licensee will be gambling, of course, that the film will be a success. Remember, however, that moral rights cannot be assigned, emphasising their personal nature (see **3.73** above).

Remedies

3.76 Infringement of copyright is both a civil and, in certain cases only, a criminal wrong. Civil actions may be brought in both the HC and the CC. The copyright owner or an exclusive licensee may sue for copyright infringement, although under certain circumstances the exclusive licensee may have to join the copyright owner to the action, and his damages may be limited to reflect the extent of his exclusive rights under the licence (ss 101-102).

Civil remedies

3.77 Plaintiffs may seek interim injunctions, and at trial, damages or an account of profits. The CDPA 1988 specifies that damages are not available if the defendant did not know or had no reason to believe that copyright subsisted in the work. However, once copying is proved this is unlikely to become an issue. On the other hand, the court may, unless the claimant has opted for an account of profits as the main remedy, order additional damages if the infringement is particularly flagrant and the benefit accruing to the defendant substantial (*Redrow v Betts* (1998)). The court may also order the delivery up of infringing copies and articles specifically designed or adapted for making copies of a particular work (although in the latter case, the person in possession must know or have reason to believe this was its purpose) (s 99). As with most cases involving intellectual property, the copyright owner will typically be as concerned with stopping dealings in infringing works as with collecting damages, and the interlocutory stage can be the most crucial period. Perhaps the most powerful, and controversial weapon in his lawyer's armoury is the search order (formerly the Anton Piller). The CDPA 1988 introduced the right of seizure (s 100), sometimes called a 'self help search order'. In essence, this right allows an owner to seize, without a court order, infringing copies from public premises (but not the alleged infringer's own place of business), if the copy is exposed or otherwise available for sale or hire and if he would be entitled to apply for a delivery-up order. This allows copyright owners to take speedy action where the dealings may be on an temporary basis. An obvious example might be traders selling pirated CDs outside rock concerts. Proposed amendments to the CDPA 1988 will broaden the scope of this provision, to take in 'occasional sales' such as car boot sales.

3.78 With respect to literary, dramatic, musical or artistic works, where a name purporting to be that of the author appears on copies of the published work or on the work when it was made, then the named person shall be presumed to be the author of the work (s 104). There is a similar provision in relation to films, sound recordings and computer programs (s 105). These presumptions do not apply in criminal proceedings. Lawyers should always alert their clients, who create copyright works, to these presumptions. Similarly, clients should also be encouraged to date and save all working papers. For instance, in the case of computer software, these might include flow charts and earlier discarded programs, supporting the clients' claim, should his works be infringed, that they are original and of his own authorship. The outcome of *Ibcos v Barclays* (1994) (see **3.84** below) also suggests the utility of building deliberate mistakes into software design, which an unwitting infringer may nonetheless copy, or including extraneous pieces of code which a copier may pick up but be unable to justify.

Criminal offences (ss 107-108)

3.79 These may be brought either at the magistrates' court or the Crown Court (although the latter must be brought by the DPP). The primary purpose of the criminal sanctions is to protect copyright owners against commercial piracy of copyright works, such as CDs and software. Sanctions range from fines to up to two years' imprisonment and orders for delivery up may be made. There are also provisions for Customs and Excise to seize allegedly infringing goods upon their entry into the UK (s 111).

Which jurisdiction?

3.80   The advantages of a civil action include the possibility of recovering damages and the speed at which injunctive relief can be obtained. On the other hand, criminal prosecutions may involve no cost to the copyright owner and their resolution can be quicker than going to a full trial in a civil court. The threat of a criminal sanction may be an effective deterrent or negotiating counter with a recalcitrant infringer. Where copying is widespread within the industry, associations have grown up to help their members to combat copying. For instance, FAST (the Federation Against Software Theft) is an association of computer software suppliers, which takes civil action against infringers, and also co-ordinates action by trading standards officers and the police. Another is the Mechanical Copyright Protection Society, a collecting society for music publishers, which also brings criminal prosecutions. Organisations such as FAST will mount campaigns to raise public awareness of copyright infringement and its consequences, perhaps offering rewards to individuals who provide information leading to successful civil or criminal proceedings.

Computers and copyright

3.81   In order to understand the relationship between copyright and computer programs, it may be useful to set out, very generally, the basic technology and technical terms involved. A programmer writes a program in higher level language, eg BASIC, FORTRAN, COBOL. These languages are in human readable form. This program is the source code. But computers work in binary code (a series of 0's and 1's) and computer programs—which tell the processor what to do —must be in binary form. A compiler, which is itself a computer program, converts the source code into binary code which is machine readable. This is the machine code or object code. Computers are programmed with a computer operating system. In order to carry out specific functions an application program must be loaded into the computer, which tells the operating system what to do. Application programs may consist of a number of individual programs. Each program itself consists of a number of routines or sub-routines, in effect a set of instructions written in code, which the computer will execute. Usually, the programmer will begin by creating a flow-chart of the routines which will make up the program. He will then convert these routines into source code. Consumers of computer software will not normally have access to source code.

Software and the CDPA 1988

3.82   Computer programs and preparatory design material for computer programs, for example flow-charts, are defined as literary works (s 3(a) and (b)). The Software Directive (implemented by the Copyright (Computer Programs) Regulations (SI 1992/3233) sought to harmonise EU copyright law in relation to computer programs. For instance, it is pursuant to the Directive that computer programs are specifically designated as literary works. The Directive also gives a limited right to reverse engineering, in essence to decompile a computer program to achieve interoperability (s 50B). Computer-generated works are also protected (see definition, s 178). Protection lasts for 50 years from when it was made and is owned by the person who 'arranged for its creation' (s 12(7); s 9(3)). Finally, it is important to remember that like other 'literary' works computer programs are frequently 'updated' or modified over time. This may create a fresh copyright in the modified program (*Ibcos*).

Infringement

3.83   Like other literary works, a computer program is infringed by the taking of the whole or substantial part of it. The CDPA 1988 also specifies that infringement by making an adaptation, in this case making an altered version or a translation, applies to computer programs (s 21(3)(ab)). A translation includes a version of the program in which it is converted into or out of a computer language or code or into a different computer language or code otherwise than incidentally in the course of running the program (s 21(4)). Copying of computer programs is, of course, extremely easy as the presence of pirated software in many British homes and businesses makes clear. Infringement may occur when the program is reproduced in any material form, including storage in any medium by electronic means, and this can include unlicensed storage on a floppy disc or a magnetic hard drive or taking it out of storage (*Ocular Sciences v Aspect Vision Care* (1997)). The CDPA 1988 specifies that copying includes the making of copies which are transient or are incidental to some other use of the work (s 17(6)). As a result, merely running a program without putting it into the computer memory can itself constitute infringement. However, pursuant to the Software Directive, it is not an infringement for a lawful user of a copy of a computer program to make a back-up copy where it is necessary for use (s 50A).

Literal copying

3.84   Obviously, unlicensed copying of a computer program line by line, or disc to disc will infringe, so long as a substantial part is taken. An important case involving literal copying is *Ibcos*. The defendant P, a freelance programmer, wrote an applications program, ADS, for keeping track of agricultural machinery. This was marketed by PK Ltd (later Ibcos) by whom P was subsequently employed. When P left PK Ltd he wrote a suite of programs, 'Unicorn' designed to compete with ADS. P wrote some file transfer programs to enable each customer's data to be rearranged from files with the ADS format to files with the Unicorn format without the need to rekey it. In *Ibcos*, the court took a straightforward approach in testing for infringement by asking four questions:

- what are the work or works in which the plaintiff claims copyright?

- is each such work original?

- was there copying from such work?

- if there was copying, has a substantial part of that work been reproduced?

Jacob J said that not only did each individual program in the suite have copyright (and perhaps several, because each had been modified and updated), but also that the whole package, 'the program of all programs', had a separate copyright—as an original compilation, in the same way as any other original compilation. The question of whether there was infringement turned not just upon whether P took literal bits of code and program structure within an individual program, but also whether P took the program structure and the design features as a whole, as these would be integral to the work as compilation. Jacob J affirmed that there was copyright in the source code and also found there had been disc to disc copying (in part because of spelling mistakes and redundant and unexplained code common to both programs). He was not persuaded by P's argument that the commonality between the two programs might be ascribed to P's 'style' as programmer. He concluded that a substantial part of the ADS suite had been infringed as a compilation, by the taking of the program structure. He also found literal copying of a substantial part of the separate programs, as well as of the file transfer programs.

Non-literal copying/the American precedent

3.85 In *Ibcos,* the court also considered the question of non-literal copying. Non-literal copying occurs when what is copied is not the actual code (either source or object) of the program but rather its function, structure or 'look and feel', for instance, the screen displays or menus. As usual, where literal copying is not at issue, the problem for the court is to decide whether what is copied is the idea behind the program or its expression. There have been a number of influential American cases considering this problem. The judgment in *Computer Associates International v Altai* (1992) introduced what became known as the 'abstraction and filtration test'. First, identify the levels of abstraction in a work from the object code itself to discover the general idea behind the work. Next, filter these abstractions in order to discover a 'core of protectable material'. So exclude from consideration elements dictated by efficiency, elements dictated by external factors and elements taken from the public domain. These are not protectable. What is left is the 'core protectable material'. Then compare this to the allegedly infringing program. *Computer Associates* was widely criticised for weakening the copyright protection given to computer programs, because once the filtration process has been followed, there may be little left to protect.

Non-literal copying/the English approach

3.86 The abstraction and filtration approach was adopted in the English case of *Richardson v Flanders* (1993). R produced a BBC stock-taking program for pharmacists, and engaged F to develop the program first as an employee and then as a consultant for JRC. F adapted the BBC program for IBM computers (Chemtech) and when no agreement could be reached with R planned to market Chemtech independently. F did not have access to the source code when creating Chemtech and had not copied it. The court decided that it was possible to infringe a program by copying its structure and 'look and feel'. In order to discover if there had been copying, it posed three questions: first, is the program as a whole entitled to copyright protection; second are the similarities between the programs a result of copying; and third, does any copying identified at the second stage amount to the copying of a substantial part. The court then applied the abstraction/filtration test to answer the third question, concluding, inter alia, that the parts of the original program which related purely to function. and which were similar in Chemtech, could not be infringed. Indeed, although there were 17 similarities between the two programs, using this criteria, only three were found to infringe. Many have taken this result as confirmation that judgments based on the abstraction/filtration test may weaken protection.

3.87 In *Ibcos*, the court, without explicitly disapproving *Richardson*, nonetheless took a divergent approach to non-literal copying. First, it overcame some of the problems posed by non-literal copying by treating the overall program in *Ibcos* as a compilation. The question was then simpler: had the structure and look and feel of the program been copied. If it had, there might be infringement if a substantial part had been taken. The court followed *Richardson* in saying that a substantial part of the program need not be restricted to the text of the code. But it held that the abstraction/filtration test of the core of protectable expression, which it condemned as overcomplicated, was not helpful in English law. In particular, it did not agree that if there was only one way to express an idea then that expression was not subject to copyright. Jacob J stated: 'The true position is that where an 'idea' is sufficiently general, then even if the original work embodies it, the mere taking of the idea will not infringe. But if the 'idea' is detailed, then there may be infringement. It is a question of degree.' It is necessary to see if there has been an 'overborrowing' of skill, labour and judgment which went into the copyright work and this should be left to judgment of the court.

3.88 The general approach of *Ibcos* to both literal and non-literal copying was followed in *Cantor Fitzgerald v Tradition* (2000). The plaintiffs (CFT) and Tradition carried on business as financial brokers. H, the third defendant, was dismissed as the plaintiff's managing director. He was then employed by Tradition, together with other ex-employees of the plaintiff, to set up a computer system for bond-trading. The resulting system had similarities to CTF's own system, for which they had also had some responsibility. The defendants admitted having had a copy of the plaintiff's system which they used for reference when they produced Tradition's system. CTF sued for copyright infringement and breach of confidentiality. In his judgment, Pumfrey J approved the four questions posed in *Ibcos*. He then went on to consider the relationship between the originality of a work and the substantiality of the copying in relation to computer software. He warned that it is not possible simply to apply those principles developed in relation to literary works 'addressed to humans' to software programs whose purpose is to make a machine function. Since a software program which contains any errors will not run, this might suggest that every part of a computer program is essential to its performance, and so every part is a substantial part. In fact, like other literary works, a program was infringed if the alleged infringer took a part of the work upon which a substantial part of the author's skill and labour had been expended. The court then compared the algorithms or sequences of operations in a computer program to the plot of a novel or a play, and suggested that taking a plot without taking the exact mode of expression might amount to infringement. Similarly, the copying of algorithms or sequences of operations from a computer program might be sufficient to amount to infringement of copyright in the program. Further, it was now generally accepted that the 'architecture' of a computer program, a 'vague' term which may refer to the overall structure of the system at a very high level of abstraction or, as in *Ibcos*, the program structure, is also capable of protection, if a substantial part of the programmer's skill labour and judgment went into it. In *Cantor*, what was alleged to have been copied was not the system at such a high level of abstraction, but individual modules of the system. The court assessed the substantiality of copying against the collection of modules viewed as a whole. Substantiality was to be judged in light of the skill and labour in design and coding which went into the piece of code which it was alleged was copied. It was not determined by whether the system would work without the code or by the amount of use the system made of the code. On that basis, the court found that the defendants had infringed in some areas and not others. The judgments in *Ibcos* and *Cantor* suggest that the copyright law may be sufficiently flexible to encompass the protection of computer programs as well as more traditional copyright works. But in stretching copyright law in this way, the ensuing decisions may help to change the way more traditional copyright works are treated. Furthermore, for a variety of reasons, computer software is also increasingly falling under patent protection (on patents, see **2.21** et seq).

Reverse engineering (s 50B)

3.89   The decompilation (or reverse engineering) of software in order to achieve interoperability will not infringe copyright in the software. Interoperability means the ability of one computer program to interface with another program so that they may work together. However, decompilation may only be undertaken for the purpose of interoperability and for no other reason (*Mars UK Ltd v Teknowledge Ltd* (1999)).

Copyright in its international context

3.90   Secondary infringement is concerned with dealings in infringing copies. It can occur when infringing copies are imported into the UK. This raises the question of parallel imports. In relation to copyright works, parallel imports are copyright works which have been placed on the market in one country (X) with the rights holders consent, but are subsequently imported into a second country (Y) without the rights holder's express consent. Often this will happen because these goods are available more cheaply in Country X than in Country Y. Suppose Z imports 100 *Star Wars* videos into the UK which were made in a Chinese factory without the licence of any rights holder in the UK or abroad. These would be infringing copies and X, provided he had the requisite knowledge, would be a secondary infringer. But what if the same videos were produced under licence from the rights holder for the Far East, including China and imported into the UK as parallel imports. These would not be infringing copies in China, because they were produced with the consent of the relevant rights holder. Could the separate rights holder for *Star Wars* in England, nonetheless, prevent their importation as infringing copies? The CDPA 1988 provides that an article is an infringing copy if it has been or is proposed to be imported into the UK and its making in the UK would have constituted an infringement of copyright in the work in question, or a breach of an exclusive licence agreement relating to the work (s 27(3)). It is submitted that, under these circumstances, the *Star Wars* videos produced under licence in China are infringing copies in the UK and their importation constitutes an act of secondary infringement (for a case involving the importation of

BeeGees' records from Portugal on similar facts, see *Polydor v Harlequin* (1980)).

Parallel imports and the EC (s 27)

3.91 Once goods have been placed on the market with the copyright owners consent in one EEA country, they can be freely imported into another EEA country (*Deutsche Grammophon v Metro-SB-Grossmarkte* (1971)). The rights attached to copyright have been exhausted. The CDPA 1988 applies the exhaustion of rights principle expressly to computer programs, but it applies equally to other copyright works. (The antithesis is also true. If a computer program has not been put on the market in the EEA with the consent of the proprietor, importation from outside the EEA will result in infringement of copyright.) As with trade marks (see **6.102**) and patents (see **2.97**), in dealing with the exhaustion of rights in relation to copyright, the ECJ differentiates between the specific subject matter of copyright which is protected and cannot be exhausted, and the exercise of those rights which can, because they may stand in the way of the free movement of goods within the EC. The specific subject matter of copyright works has been held to be the right to reproduce the protected work. In fact, a copyright work often has a bundle of rights attached to it, which may include not only the reproduction right but also the performance right and the rental right, and not all these rights may be exhausted on first sale by the copyright owner. In *Warner Bros Inc v Christiansen*, C brought videos of a James Bond film in the UK and imported them into Denmark for video hire. In Denmark, there was a rental right but there was not, at the time, a similar rental right in the UK. It was held that Danish licensee had the right to collect royalties from C for the rental of the video in Denmark.

EC and competition law

3.92 The same concerns of the EC to balance the protection of industrial and commercial property (which includes intellectual property), whose extent is generally territorial, with the free movement of goods within the EEA arises in relation to competition law.

Article 81

3.93 Exclusive licenses will not necessarily fall under this umbrella of

Art 81. In *Coditel v Cine Vog Films* (1982), the ECJ recognised that it is in the nature of the film industry that there may well be a division of rights by way of exclusive licences in order to finance films, and this was not likely to prevent, restrict or distort competition.

Article 82

3.94   The general approach which has been taken is that protection of the specific subject matter of the copyright, for instance, in *Volvo v Veng* (1988) (see in relation to patents, **2.100**), a refusal by Volvo to license the production of spare parts, would not, in itself, be an abuse of a dominant position under Art 82. There would need to be some particular abusive behaviour such as, in the case of car parts supply, overcharging or refusing to supply spare parts to non-franchise dealers.

3.95   The relationship between Article 82 and copyright was clarified in the *Magill* case (*Radio Telefis Eireann v EC Commission.* (1995)). Magill sought to publish a weekly TV listing magazine in the Irish Republic and Northern Ireland. Copyright in the information was owned by the BBC and other English and Irish television companies, who published their own listings and also gave listings to newspapers on the basis that they were only published 24 hours in advance of broadcast. The television companies refused to licence the information to Magill, in effect preventing Magill's listings magazine competing with theirs. It should be remembered from the earlier case of *Independent Television Publications* (see **3.49**) that such listings were protected in the UK (although not in other EC countries) as compilations, and that since the information contained in the compilations was generated by the television companies, copyright protection gave them a de facto monopoly over that information and, therefore, television listings in general. The EC found the television companies in breach of Art 86 (now Art 82), a decision which was confirmed by the CFI. Eventually, *Magill* reached the ECJ. The ECJ ruled that the television companies were abusing their dominant position by using their monopoly to prevent competition in the market for weekly television listings. The ECJ confirmed that while refusal to licence per se did not represent an abuse, in the particular facts of this case, it did. The essential subject matter of the copyright was not at issue, rather they were using their copyright in the listings to prevent competition in the market for television listings. The ECJ took a similar approach in a recent case, *Micro Leader Business v EC Commission* (2000). This case concerned the refusal by Microsoft to allow its French language software, which was marketed in Canada more cheaply, to be imported and sold in France. The ECJ held that whilst, as a rule, the enforcement of copyright by its holder, as in the case of prohibiting the importation of products from outside the EEC into a member state, is not a breach of Article 82, such enforcement could in certain 'exceptional' circumstances involve abusive conduct.

The future

3.96   The Draft Directive on Copyright and Related Rights in the Information Society is intended to update the EU copyright regime. It reflects new developments in reproductive technology, most notably digital technology and the internet, by which all manner of copyright works can now be circulated in a non-material format. Characteristic of this new technology is that copying is frequently inexpensive, quick and easy and the copied works are of high quality, as is the case with MP3 technology and DVDs. Second, much of this technology is interactive, allowing the consumer enormous leeway as to when and where to access the copyright works. Thirdly, it operates across national boundaries. In the case of music search engines like 'Napster', now the subject of copyright litigation in the US, these characteristics are often combined, posing new and possibly intractable problems for rights holders.

3.97   The Directive is an attempt to strengthen author's rights in light of these technological changes and also to harmonise the common market in copyright and related rights. It will also implement or prepare to implement both present and (future) WIPO obligations. It will give authors, film and record producers, performers and broadcasters exclusive reproduction and communication rights in relation to their works. The reproduction right will cover all acts of direct or indirect reproduction, whether permanent or temporary, on or off line. There will also be an exclusive right to authorise or prohibit the making available to the public of originals or copies of works by 'wire or wireless means' in such a way that members of the public may access them from a place or time individually chosen by them. The Draft Directive will also introduce a distribution right which gives authors an exclusive right to any form of distribution of their works. It stipulates that this right shall not be exhausted within the EU except where the work or copies thereof are put first on the market by the right holder or with his consent. Not surprisingly, the Directive also has provisions for strengthening protection against unauthorised circumvention of anti-copying devices by placing a duty on EU states to provide legal protection against activities intended to circumvent effective technological measures designed to protect any copyright or any rights related to copyright. It is expected that the Directive will be implemented by 2001.

3.98 The Directive has been criticised for being too protective of rights holders. There are exemptions to the restricted acts in the Draft Directive, most notably for temporary acts of reproduction such 'as transient and incidental acts of reproduction' which are an integral and essential part of the technological process, including 'effective functioning of transmissions systems whose sole purpose is to enable use to be made of a work or other subject matter as long as they have no independent economic significance'. This exemption would protect, for example, 'cache copies' held for internet transmission. The Draft Directive also proposes a number of optional exemptions which member states can chose to implement. These are quite narrow. Some, such as the reproduction on various formats for 'private and strictly personal use and or non-commercial ends' are contingent upon the right holder receiving 'fair compensation'. There are certainly no obligatory fair dealing exemptions equivalent to those under the CDPA 1988, and it has been argued that following the passage of the Directive the scope of existing fair dealing exemptions may be restricted (Doherty and Griffiths 'The Harmonisation of European Union Copyright Law for the Digital Age' (2000) EIPR 17). The future is unclear. It is both understandable but also ironic that the restrictive nature of the Draft Directive's proposals coincides with the growth of reproduction technologies which are increasingly difficult to control through the use of purely legal sanctions. Some have suggested that emphasis should be not on strengthened copyright laws but on introducing levies on the use of the new technology itself, such as a blank tape levy, to go to rights holders. Others believe that copyright law, no matter how draconian, offers an increasingly ineffective weapon for dealing with new reproduction technologies. They suggest that rights holders should look for new ways to profit from such technology, for instance by using the internet as a powerful marketing tool for their products (such as videos and CDs), rather than searching for the means to police its use. Certainly, the extraordinary pace of development of reproduction technologies suggests that copyright law is facing a turbulent future.

Further reading

D Bainbridge *Software Copyright Law* (4th edn, 1999)

Copinger and Skone James on Copyright (14th edn, 1999)

W M Landes and R A Posner 'An Economic Analysis of Copyright Law' [1989] JLS 325

Self-test questions

1. Jake, a reporter for the *Daily Scoop*, is asked to 'ghost write' the autobiography of the movie star, Maxine. They work closely together. The book, which is published on the internet, incorporates passages from the transcript of Maxine's infamous divorce trial. It is a huge success and Jake decides to adapt the book for the screen. The film is to be produced by XRated Films and Jake will direct. Jake learns that a rival, Greg, is also writing a book about Maxine based in large measure on the internet edition of Jake's book. Cine Corp has produced their own film based on Maxine's life story, but purporting to be about a fictional movie star, Marilyn. Advise Jake about the copyright position of both the book, the screenplay and the film, in light of the activities of Greg and Cine Corp.

2. Is copyright the appropriate means for protecting computer programs and digital works?

3. Do fair dealing and the public interest defence provide a sufficient balance between copyright protection and the public interest in the dissemination of information?

CHAPTER FOUR

Industrial design

SUMMARY

Development and context of the present industrial design regime

The 1988 reforms

The relationship between industrial design and copyright

Design right

Exclusions from protection

The creation, ownership and duration of design rights

Infringement

Registered designs

Exclusions from protection

Infringement

Ownership

Industrial designs in their international context

Development and context

4.1 By the time of the passage of the CDPA 1988, it was generally accepted that there were some troubling anomalies in the law relating to industrial design. In particular, the Copyright Act 1956 gave the same copyright protection to design documents from which functional, mass produced articles were produced as it gave to artistic works, that is for the life of the author plus 50 years. In addition, a three-dimensional object made from the drawing acquired similar copyright protection. Curiously, if the articles had 'eye appeal' and the design was capable of being registered under the Registered Design Act 1949 (RDA 1949), it would be protected for only 15 years. Obviously, the industrial design regime lacked logic. But by the 1980s, the considerable copyright protection given to functional, mass produced articles was also viewed by many to have other unfavourable consequences. Not least of these was the monopoly it gave to manufacturers of industrial articles over the production of spare parts, and their consequent ability to control markets and prices. In the 1980s, as ideas of free trade became more prevalent, this de facto monopoly granted to manufacturers was widely criticised. For instance, in 1985, the Monopolies and Mergers Commission criticised the Ford Motor Company for its policy of monopolising the sales of its car replacement panels, through the use of copyright protection of their design.

4.2   The HL decision in *British Leyland v Armstrong* (1986) also reflected this prevailing view. In *British Leyland*, the question to be answered was whether artistic copyright in the design drawings of functional mass-produced articles, in this case for motor spare parts, was infringed by their three-dimensional reproduction. The HL, in a majority decision, held that it was. However, the HL also went on to hold that the right of a car owner to purchase spare parts at a reasonable price should take precedence over the protection endowed by copyright. It based its decision on a concept which it borrowed from land law, that a person may not derogate from his grant. In other words, a car owner must be allowed to acquire on the open market the spare parts necessary to make his car go. There can be little argument that the decision in *British Leyland* was driven by public policy concerns, as the HL sought to side-step what had come to be seen as the increasingly indefensible monopoly of car manufacturers over the supply of spare parts.

British Leyland criticised

4.3   While the decision in British Leyland arguably reflected the tenor of its time, fourteen years later, its creative approach was criticised and its implications limited by the PC in *Canon v Green Cartridge* (1997). In this case, the plaintiff manufactured printers and photocopiers, containing replaceable cartridges known as Customer Replacement Units (CRUs). These needed to be replaced when the toner ran out. The defendant first began refilling and refurbishing the CRUs, but eventually moved on to manufacturing its own cartridges. The plaintiff sued, inter alia, for

134

copyright infringement. In its judgment, the PC was asked to consider the scope of the 'spare parts exception' which had been formulated by the HL in *British Leyland*. Lord Hoffman was critical of *British Leyland*. He stated that the judgment 'cannot be regarded as truly founded upon any principle of the law of contract or property.' Instead, he saw it as a 'a clear expression of public policy'. He went on to suggest that it was both 'a strong thing' but also 'constitutionally questionable', for the judiciary to treat public policy as overriding an express statutory right (ie copyright). As such, the courts should be cautious in extending the *British Leyland* exception. The PC held that the scope of the decision in *British Leyland* was clearly limited to the spare parts necessary for repair. The PC reasoned that such parts are inexpensive and so will not effect the consumer's decision to buy the article in the first place. However, once the article is purchased, the parts are needed albeit only irregularly, thus leaving the way clear for anti-competitive practices in their production and supply. As a result, there was a risk that manufacturers might exert monopoly control over the market in spare parts. However, the case of replacement cartridges was different. These were needed on a regular and foreseeable basis, and were not a repair as such. Hence, the cost of their replacement might affect the consumer's decision to purchase the printer and so encourage competitors to limit their cost (Rawkins 'British Leyland Spare Part Defence: Canon Kabushiki Kaisha v Green Catridge Company (Hong Kong) Ltd' [1998] EIPR 674).

The 1988 reforms

4.4   The reform of the law relating to industrial design reflected both an attempt to eliminate the anomalies in the law which had grown up over time, and also the new ideological commitment to free trade. The CDPA 1988 took away copyright protection from almost all industrial designs. To replace copyright protection, the CDPA 1988 introduced a new right, the unregistered design right. At the same time, it amended the RDA 1949.

The UK design regime and the EU Directive

4.5   At present the protection afforded to designs in the EU differs between countries. Given that so much production, not least of cars, now takes place across national boundaries, it is scarcely surprising that the EU has sought to harmonise the industrial design regime. A Regulation which will create a community registered design right and a community registered design is currently under consideration. As regards registered designs, an EU Directive on the Legal Protection of Designs (Directive 98/71//EC) has now been enacted and will be incorporated into national law within three years. The Directive proposes a harmonised registered design right regime across the EU. It is envisaged that there will in the future be a registered design regime, based on the Directive and the Regulation, which will be similar to that which now exists for trade marks. This chapter will examine the law of unregistered design right and registered designs as it now stands, although there will be significant changes in the law relating to the latter, at least, in the next few years.

The relationship between design right and copyright (1): s 51

4.6   Under the CDPA 1988, it is not an infringement in copyright in a design document or model recording or embodying a design for anything other than an artistic work or a typeface to make an article to the design or to copy an article made to the design. Note, however, that it will continue to be an infringement of copyright to copy the design document itself. Clearly, the intention of this section is to prevent artistic copyright from stifling the market in spare parts, as it had done previous to the CDPA 1988. X draws a design for a useful new door hinge. Y finds the design document and makes door hinges to that design. He has not infringed X's copyright in the design document. If Y had secretly copied the design document in order to make the hinges, he may have infringed X's copyright in the document, provided the document itself displays sufficient skill to attract copyright. Even if the original design document or model embodies an artistic work, it will not be an infringement of copyright to copy the articles made from these if the design document or model was intended for the production of non-artistic works. If X had first drawn his dog, Fido, and then produced a design document from which mass produced teapots shaped like Fido would be manufactured, it would not infringe X's copyright in the design document if Y also produced the teapots. For the purposes of s 51, a 'design' means any aspect of the shape or configuration *other than* surface decoration. If X had taken a conventionally shaped teapot and imprinted the portrait of Fido on the sides, Y would infringe his copyright by reproducing this portrait on his own teapots. However, as we shall see, protection for the portrait, in this context, would last only 25 years.

136

Section 51 as a defence

4.7   The possibility of using s 51 as defence against copyright infringement was raised in *BBC Worldwide v Pally Screen Printing* (1998). The plaintiff owned the intellectual property and merchandising rights in the popular children's television characters the Teletubbies, who are basically life-sized puppets. The first defendant, a printing company, printed pictures of the Teletubbies onto clothing, including T-shirts, on the instructions of the second and third defendants. It was not possible to identify the particular copyright works which the first defendant had allegedly infringed, although the image on one lot of clothing appeared to have been copied from a photograph of the Teletubbies on a magazine cover. The plaintiff sued, inter alia, for copyright infringement and asked for summary judgment. The first defendant claimed that it did not know the origins of the designs which it had copied onto the clothing. However, if they had been copied, it was most likely to have been from the television, where what was to be seen were three-dimensional Teletubby puppets made to the Teletubby design. Laddie J agreed that there was an arguable defence under s 51. He first assumed that the original drawings which pictured the Teletubbies were created to depict a design for something other than an artistic work and instead were for use in deciding the shape and appearance of the three-dimensional characters. It followed from this assumption that copying the Teletubby articles themselves 'indirectly through the medium of television is for better or for worse, excluded from being an infringement of copyright' under s 51(1). He then turned to the alleged copying from the magazine photograph, to which the plaintiff did not claim copyright. Here again, Laddie J believed that it was possible to argue that copying from the photograph of the puppets was once again copying indirectly from articles made to the design and so presented an arguable defence to copyright infringement.

Section 51 and the meaning of 'design'

4.8   The question of what constitutes a 'design document', for the purposes of s 51 was looked at in *Mackie Designs v Behringer* (1999), which concerned circuit diagrams for an electrical mixer. The plaintiff alleged that the second defendant had obtained an example of its mixer and had analysed its circuits to obtain a 'net list' of the components and their interconnections. From this list, the defendant was alleged to have used a computer program to produce layouts for circuit boards. The questions before the court were whether the plaintiff's circuit diagrams were 'design documents' within the meaning of s 51 and, if so, whether the defendants had a defence to infringement by reason of s 51. The plaintiff argued that the aspects 'configuration' in a design document must mean the 'physical geometry' of the article. By contrast, what made the circuit diagrams special were the particular components present and their interconnection. These could be seen as being in the nature of a market specification for the circuits rather than an aspect of their design. In his judgment, Pumfrey J held that 'configuration' included the relative arrangement of the parts or elements of an article, and in the case of circuit boards, this included the selection of the components and their interconnection. It followed, they were an 'aspect of design'. In answer to the second question, Pumfrey J, following the reasoning in *BBC Worldwide*, found that the defendant's circuit boards were not an infringement of the plaintiff's copyright in the circuit diagrams.

The relationship between design right and copyright (2): s 52

4.9 Copyright protection of course continues to be given to artistic works, including drawings and works of artistic craftsmanship. However, here too the CDPA 1988 introduced changes. Under s 52, if an artistic work is exploited by producing it industrially, the protection afforded to the industrially produced article is reduced to 25 years after the first marketing of the article. Reproduced industrially means making 50 or more articles to the design. After 25 years, Y would be free to copy Fido's portrait onto his own teapots. However, if he reproduced the original Fido portrait to sell in his gallery, he would infringe copyright in the original drawing which lasts the full 70 years plus the life of the author.

Design right

4.10 The design right regime has been described as embodying 'a modified copyright approach'. Like copyright, the right arises automatically and there is no need for the design to be registered to obtain protection. Also like copyright, design right does not confer a 'monopoly right' in the way that a patent or a registered design does (see below **4.28**). Instead, again like copyright, a design right gives its holder more limited protection against copying (or more grandly, 'misappropriation of the effort which is put into the creation of the work'). Unlike copyright, however, design right protection lasts for a far more limited term and the protection given against copying is also more restricted. The new design right regime has been criticised by some for weighting the balance too far in favour of a free market in functional designs, particularly in relation to spare parts, rather than towards protecting the investment of those who produce such designs. For instance, the length of design right protection (see below **4.27)** has been criticised as being too short. It is certainly shorter than that accorded to registered designs which emphasise eye-appeal rather than the functionality of a design. But it has been suggested that a functional design should be no less worthy of protection, since it may well involve the same if not more investment of resources and skill in its creation than a design with eye-appeal. For much the same reason, the compulsory licence of right (below **4.27)** which is granted in the last five years of the design right term has also been criticised. There is no similar provision under patents nor registered design (Bainbridge 'Why the Design Right is Failing Innovators Opinion' [1999] EIPR 423). Whatever the correct balance, it is probably true that the free-market underpinnings of the unregistered design right reflect the prevailing ideology of the time in which it was created.

The definition of a design

4.11 Design right is a property right which subsists in an original design (s 213(1)). Before going on to look at what constitutes originality for the purposes of design right, it is first necessary to consider the definition of a design. A general definition is set out in s 213(2) and states: 'a design means the design of any aspect of the shape or configuration (whether internal or external) of the whole or part of an article.' These may be functional elements of design or configuration. They may also be elements which are aesthetically pleasing. However, it is important to note that design right will not subsist in surface decoration, which is the province of registered design (s 213(3)(c)). The definition of 'design' is a broad one. It can include the shape or configuration of individual parts of an article but it may also cover the article as a whole. To give an example, provided by Laddie J in *Ocular Sciences v Aspect Vision Care* (1997): 'If the right is said to reside in the design of a teapot, this can mean that it resides in the design of the whole pot, or in a part such as the spout, the handle or the lid, or, indeed, part of the lid.'

The relationship between the design and the 'article'

4.12 It follows from the example given by Laddie J that the term 'article' may likewise mean: individual parts, a combination of parts or the parts made up into a whole. According to Mummery LJ in *Farmers Build v Carrier* (1999)(for the facts see below **4.18**): 'these are all 'articles' with a shape or configuration'. The 'article' need not be one which is intended for or is even capable of being reproduced by an industrial process, in contrast to registered designs. Nor will the design or even the article in which it is embodied necessarily be visible to the naked eye. The design may be an aspect of shape and configuration of a larger article, such as a strainer inside a teapot. A design may only be identifiable through the use of specialist equipment. In *Ocular Sciences* which involved the relative dimensions of a contact lens, these dimensions were too small to be seen by the naked eye.

Originality and design right

4.13 Design right subsists if the design is 'original'. According to the CDPA 1988, a design is not original, 'if it is commonplace in the design field in question at the time of its creation' (s 213(4)). *C & H Engineering v Klucznik* (1992) was the first reported decision to consider what was meant by 'original' in this context. The case involved the design of a pig fender, which is a pen outside of a pigpen low enough for a sow to step over, but too high for her piglets. A customer suggested to the plaintiff, who manufactured pig fenders, that the fender be redesigned to avoid the sow injuring her teats when stepping over it. The plaintiff subsequently placed a bar along the top of the fender. In the event, the HC was unable to conclude who had originated this idea. Nonetheless, Aldous J did consider the question of originality. He held that 'original' had the same meaning in design right as it did in relation to copyright in original literary, dramatic, musical and artistic works. As in copyright, an original design is one that has not been copied, but is 'the independent work of the creator'.

4.14 In *Farmers Build*, the CA endorsed the definition of originality given in *C & H Engineering* and summarised the position under the CDPA 1988. Mummery LJ identified two elements to an original design for the purposes of design right protection. First, it must have been originated by the designer in the sense that it is not simply a copy by him of a previous design made by someone else. Second, where it has not been slavishly copied from another design it must in some respect be different from other designs so that it can be fairly and reasonably described as 'not commonplace'. The next paragraph (**4.15** et seq) considers the meaning of 'commonplace'. Mummery LJ also appeared to suggest, in *Farmers Build*, that originality meant that 'sufficient' time labour and skill had been expended in originating the design as would be necessary to attract copyright protection. However, it is submitted that works do not necessarily need to show these qualities to attract copyright.

The relationship between originality and the commonplace in design

4.15 A design is not original if it is 'commonplace' in the design field in question at the time of its creation (s 213(4)). This means that the same design may be original in the copyright sense, that is it was 'originated' by the designer and was not copied, but can still fail to attract design right protection because the design is commonplace (*Farmers Build*). If it is commonplace, then it is not 'original' for the purposes of design right.

When is a design commonplace?

4.16 This question was considered in detail, by the CA, in *Farmers Build*. The specific facts of the case and the subsequent judgment are set out in the paragraph below (**4.18**). This paragraph considers the general definition of commonplace offered by the CA. The CA took the view that 'commonplace' in design right should be interpreted narrowly. Its approach was shaped by its recognition that design right generally afforded narrower protection than copyright, and that it was directed at offering protection to functional articles. By contrast, an opposite approach would risk many designs of functional articles being found to be commonplace simply because they were well known. The CA also held that whether a design is commonplace is an objective fact. It is a question for the court to decide based upon the evidence before it.

4.17 A design which is not commonplace will be one which is not found in other articles in the same field. Conversely, the closer the similarity of designs to each other, the more likely the design is to be commonplace, especially if there is no evidence of copying. Thus, if a number of independent designers produce similar design solutions to the same design problem, the court is entitled to infer that there is only one way of designing the article in question and that the design may be described as commonplace (*Farmers Build*). Commonplace is not however the same as 'well known'. It is possible for a commonplace article to embody aspects of shape and configuration which are not commonplace. In other words, the nature or character of the 'commonplace' article, such as a fork, should not be confused with aspects of shape and configuration of the article which might not be commonplace at all, for instance the design of the handle of said fork. In *Farmers Build*, the CA also endorsed Laddie J's view in *Ocular Sciences* that even if some features of a design are commonplace, the design which combines them may not be.

The Farmers Build case

4.18 The CA's definition of commonplace was applied in *Farmers Build*, which concerned the design of a slurry separator, a machine which separates manure into solid and liquid parts for use as fertiliser. The plaintiff owned the intellectual property rights in a slurry separator, the 'Target', which the defendants had designed for the plaintiff in 1991. The design for the Target had improved upon designs for two earlier separators. In 1992, the defendants started manufacturing and selling their own separator the 'Rotoscreen', which looked different from the Target but was almost identical inside. The plaintiff claimed that the Rotoscreen infringed its design rights in various component parts of the Target, both individually and in combination with other parts and with the insides of the machine as a whole. The defendants argued that the design of the Target was not original but commonplace in the design field in question at the time of its creation. At first instance, the judge held, inter alia, that design right subsisted in the Target as a whole, and in a number of its component parts and the defendants appealed. Among their counter arguments was a claim that the hopper (a chamber within the slurry) had long existed as a part of agricultural machinery in general and that its design variants were strictly limited. They also argued that the Target as a whole was commonplace because it was simply a recombination of parts of the two earlier machines which improved its functionality. In reply, the plaintiff claimed that the design of the Target was original, being significantly better than the earlier machines, that a new machine could be made out of 'trite' ingredients and, in any event, that the relevant field to judge the 'commonplaceness' of the Target was not agricultural implements generally but slurry separators in particular.

4.19 In its judgment, the CA held that while a hopper is a commonplace article, the design of this particular hopper was not commonplace. It then looked at various other parts of the Target, some of which it decided embodied original designs some of which did not. Finally, it concluded that the design of the Target, as a whole, was not commonplace. There were no other machines like the Target in the field of slurry separators. While design right did not subsist in each and every part of the Target machine, it did subsist in the overall shape and configuration of the combination of parts which made it up. In effect, the CA agreed with the plaintiff's argument that a combination of 'trite' or commonplace designs can result in aspects of shape or configuration which are not commonplace.

The field in question

4.20   A design is commonplace if it is commonplace in the design field in question. It is therefore necessary to identify the design field within which its originality should be judged. In *Farmers Build*, the defendants argued the relevant field was that of agricultural implements. The CA disagreed. The relevant field was that of slurry separators and not agricultural machinery generally or other engineering fields. This suggests that courts will take a relatively restrictive view of the relevant field.

Exclusions from protection (s 213(3))

4.21   There are four exclusions to design right protection. The 'must fit' exception and the 'must match' exceptions are sometimes called the 'interface exclusions' and were designed to avoid creating the same impasse over the supply of spare parts which had dogged the old design regime (discussed at **4.2** above). Design right will also not subsist in a method or principle of construction (s 213(3)(a)). This third exception has a rather different purpose. It may be construed as an attempt to avoid protecting an idea in the copyright sense, although under certain circumstances methods or principles of construction might be patentable. In *Baby Dan v Brevi* (1999) (see **4.23**), it was held that the relative positioning of the functional parts of a child safety barrier was a method or principle of construction, and not, as was claimed, an aspect of its configuration. Finally, design right will not subsist in surface decoration (s 213(3)(c)). This includes not only essentially two-dimensional decoration lying on the surface of the article, but also the decorative features of the surface itself, such as the 'cornices' and 'cockbeading' on kitchen cabinets (*Mark Wilkinson v Woodcraft Designs* (1998) (see **4.24** below)).

The must fit exclusion (s 213(b)(i))

4.22 Design right does not subsist in a feature of shape or configuration which enables the article to be connected to, or placed in, around or against, another article so that either article may perform its function. It has been suggested that it need not be the only design which can achieve the proper interface. There may be a number of designs which will allow the articles to be fitted together, but on the basis of this exception, each of these designs would be excluded. In *Ocular Sciences*, the designs were aspects of the shape and configuration of contact lenses. Obviously, contact lenses are designed to fit the eye. The plaintiff had argued that the 'eye' is not an article for the purposes of design right. Laddie J disagreed. He then looked at whether there were any features of the plaintiff's contact lens design which enabled it to be connected to or placed in, around or against the eye or the eyeball so that either article might perform its function. He found that there was no design right in the back radius of the plaintiff's contact lenses because it was designed to enable the lens to fit against eyeball, so as to perform its function of correcting the eye's focus. The same was true of a number of other design features.

4.23 A related question arises if a number of components are designed to fit together in order to make an article. Can there be design right either in the larger article or its components? This was the issue in *Baby Dan*. The plaintiff manufactured child safety barriers, which the first defendant had distributed. When the distributorship came to an end, the first defendant started manufacturing child safety barriers, which the second defendant sold. The plaintiff claimed that design right subsisted in the shape and configuration of various components of its barrier and that the defendant had copied these. The defendants questioned whether design right could subsist in these various components since they were each articles which needed to fit together to form the barrier. The HC gave a purposive construction to the must fit provision, suggesting that its purpose was to deny protection to spare parts. It held that the must fit exception did not exclude the shape or configuration of the various parts which are necessary to enable such parts to be assembled into the article. Alternatively there will also exist separate design rights in each component part, although their shape or configuration is circumscribed by the 'must fit' provision. In this case, design right in the plaintiff's safety barrier subsisted by virtue of the shape and configuration of its components.

Must match exclusion (s 213(b)(ii))

4.24   Design right does not subsist in features of shape or configuration of an article which are dependent upon the appearance of another article of which the article is intended by the designer to form an integral part. As with the must fit exception, the must match exclusion is clearly designed to exclude spare parts from design right protection. In this case, the concern is with the appearance of an article which enables it to match another, for instance the design of the body panel of a car which is an integral part of the overall design of the car. Conversely, the exclusion is generally held not to apply to car components such as wing mirrors whose design can be changed without compromising the integrity of the overall design of the car (see *Ford Motor Company's Design Applications* (1993), which considered the identical provision in the context of Registered Designs (see **4.43** below)). In *Mark Wilkinson*, the plaintiff and the defendant both designed and manufactured fitted kitchens. The defendant's range included a number of design features which were similar to those on the plaintiff's range, including curved cornices and cockbeading (some of which were held to be aspects of surface decoration (see **4.21**)). The plaintiff claimed design right infringement by the defendant of a wall unit in its kitchen range. The defendants responded, inter alia, that the wall unit was excluded from design right protection as it was designed to match the rest of the plaintiff's kitchen range. The HC held that the 'must match' exception did not apply since while the complete fitted kitchen unit was a series of matching articles, none taken on its own formed an integral part of another article (Rosenblatt 'Mark Wilkinson Furniture v Woodcraft Designs (Radcliffe) Ltd' [1998] EIPR 111).

Creation of design right

4.25   The designer is the person who creates the design (s 214(1)). The designer need not be the same individual as the one who records the design. In the case of a computer-generated design, the designer is the individual who makes the arrangements necessary for the creation of the design (s 214(2)). A design right will not subsist unless and until the design has been recorded in a design document or an article has been made to that design (s 213(6)). A design document can range from a drawing to data stored in a computer.

Ownership of design rights

4.26 The designer is the first owner of a design right provided the design was not produced pursuant to a commission or in the course of employment. In the latter two cases the design will belong to the commissioner and the employer respectively (s 215). In certain circumstances, the design may be owned by the person who first markets the design. Furthermore, for design right to subsist the design must be a qualifying design (ss 217-220). Qualification is by reference to the nationality or country of residence of the designer, commissioner or employer, by reference to the country in which the article was made or first marketed, or, in some circumstances, by reference to the nationality or habitual residence of the person who first markets the article. In general, the qualifying nationalities and countries are those which give reciprocal protection to UK designs.

Duration of design right

4.27 The term of unregistered design right protection is either 15 years from when first recorded or if the design is marketed within the first five years, 10 years from when it was first made available for sale (s 216). During the final five years of the ten-year period of protection (that is from the date of first marketing), licences of right may be granted for unregistered designs (s 237). They are obtained through an application to the Patent Office. The Comptroller will settle the terms of the licence if they cannot be agreed directly between the parties. Once granted, the original owner of the design right cannot prevent the licensee from exploiting the right, but the licensee must pay a royalty for its use. It is possible for a single design right to be subject to any number of licenses. If a defendant infringes a design right during its final five years, it is possible for him to give an undertaking to enter into a licence to avoid injunctive relief and minimise damages.

Infringement

4.28   Design right, like copyright, will only protect against copying. In *Farmers Build*, it was suggested that it is possible for two individuals to have design right in the same design as long as each produced it independently (and as long as the design is not commonplace). This contrasts with the law relating to both patents and registered design, where a proprietor has a right against all competitors, even those who originated the subject matter independently

Primary infringement (s 226)

4.29   The owner of the design right has the exclusive right to reproduce the design for commercial purposes by making articles to the design or by making a design document recording the design for the purpose of enabling such articles to be made. Design right is infringed by the making of articles exactly or substantially to that design. Whether the allegedly infringing design is exactly or substantially the same as the original design is determined through the eyes of the person to whom the design is directed (*C & H Engineering*). In the *Baby Dan* case, where the designs at issue were for parts of child safety barriers, the relevant persons included those persons, 'interested in the design of such gates.' If the difference between the original design and earlier designs is a small one, then infringement will be found only if the difference between the infringing design and the original design is even smaller (*Ocular Sciences*). In *Ocular Sciences*, the designs at issue differed from each other only 'in fine dimensional details.' In fact, a member of the public would not be able to gauge the differences through visual inspection. It was held that, in such circumstances, if the dimensions which supported the claimant's claim to the existence of design right were particularly detailed and specific, then there would be infringement if the defendant's designs were extremely close. Design right is infringed by a person who does, or authorises another to do, anything which is the exclusive right of the design right owner without the relevant permission (s 226(3)). Therefore, authorising copying is an infringement (*C&H Engineering*).

Proving infringement

4.30   To prove infringement, the claimant must show that the defendant has copied his design. There will be no infringement if the defendant arrived at the design independently (**4.28**). Copying may be direct or indirect (226(4)). In *Mark Wilkinson*, Parker J stated that to prove infringement, the 'same general principles' apply as apply to copyright (citing *Francis Day v Hunter* (see **3.62** on copyright)). There has to be a sufficient objective similarity (excluding surface decoration) between the two articles or a substantial part thereof. There also has to be a causal connection. However, it is submitted that other cases do not support Parker J's view in relation to 'a substantial part'. In fact, the test for infringement in *C&H Kluznick* was whether the two designs were 'not substantially different' (a test taken from the registered design regime (**4.46** below)). If they were not, there would be infringement. By contrast, to find infringement in copyright, it must be proved that a substantial part of the original work has been copied. In *C&H Engineering*, the court compared the objects as a whole. Because the allegedly infringing copy had sloping side walls which the original did not, the judge found there was no infringement as the designs were substantially different. In fact, it is generally the case that an object might consist of a number of different aspects of shape or configuration each of which might be subject to a separate design right and therefore each of which may be infringed.

Secondary infringement (ss 227-228)

4.31 Design right is infringed by a person who, without the licence of the design right owner, imports into the UK for commercial purposes, or has in his possession for commercial purposes, or sells, lets for hire or offers or exposes for sale or hire, in the course of a business, an article which is, and which he knows or has reason to believe is, an infringing article (s 227). An article is infringing if its making to that design was an infringement of design right in the article (s 228). Further it is also an infringing article if it has been or is proposed to be imported into the UK and its making to that design in the UK would have been an infringement of design right in the design.

Design right and semiconductor topography

4.32 Semiconductor chips are a crucial aspect of computer technology and expensive to develop. Under UK law before 1988, semiconductor chips received uncertain protection. The EC Directive on Semiconductor Topographies (87/54/EEC) was incorporated into UK law by the Design

Right (Semiconductor Topographies) Regulations 1989 (SI 1989/1100). Furthermore, specific protection for semiconductor topographies is now required under the TRIPS agreement. The 1989 regulations amended the 1988 CDPA Act, and essentially extended a modified form of design right protection to semi-conductor products. Protection for semi-conductor chips differs in certain respects from design right. For instance, the definition of the relevant design is different. There are no licences of right. On the other hand, reverse engineering is possible without infringing the design right in the semiconductor topography. Furthermore, because of reciprocal protection offered abroad, the national protection offered to the design of semiconductor topographies is more extensive than with ordinary design right, encompassing, for example, designs originating in the US.

Registered designs

4.33 The law governing registered designs is to be found in the RDA 1949 as amended by the CDPA 1988. Applications to register a design are made to the Designs Registry, a branch of the Patent Office. The Registrar may make searches and object to the registration of a design if it is not new (see below **4.39** on novelty) or he may object to registration because it is excluded by some other statutory provision. If registration is refused, the applicant may appeal first to the Registrar, then to the Registered Designs Appeal Tribunals. Further appeal would be to the HC for judicial review.

Contrast with other rights

4.34 A registered design must have 'eye appeal'. It thus contrasts with design right which will not protect aspects of surface decoration and with copyright which protects original works, without requiring them to be visually pleasing. Like a patent, a registered design is a monopoly right. This means that to prove infringement of a registered design there is no need to show copying, as is the case for infringement of copyright or design right. Unlike copyright or design right, but like patents, it is necessary to go through the registration procedure to obtain protection for the design. Furthermore, again unlike copyright or design right, it is possible to act against infringers only when registration has been granted, although damages will be backdated to the date of application. As a result, registration may often be a cumbersome way of protecting designs whose commercial appeal depends upon immediate and passing fashion (such as some wallpaper or textile design). Certainly, designs with a relatively short shelf life may not need the full 25 year protection offered, and, as a result, the cost of the registration may be disproportionate to the gains.

Definition

4.35   To be registered, a design must be a registrable design as defined in the RDA 1949 as amended (s 1(1)). It must also be new (s 1(2)). According to the RDA 1949, a design means features of shape, configuration, pattern or ornament applied to an article by any industrial process, being features which in the finished article appeal to and are judged by the eye. The design may be for the shape of an object such as a teapot, or a two-dimensional pattern for wallpaper or textiles. There are also some exclusions to registered design. These are:

- a method or principle of construction (s 1(1)(a))

- features of shape or configuration of an article which are either dictated solely by the function which the article has to perform (s 1(1)(b)(i))

- features which are dependent upon the appearance of another article of which the article is intended by the author of the design to form an integral part (s 1(1)(b)(ii)).

These exclusions will be examined below (see **4.42**).

What is meant by eye appeal

4.36   A registrable design must be a design which is capable of being visually appreciated but need not be aesthetically pleasing. According to Lord Oliver, in *Interlego v Tyco* (1989), a registered design must have features which appeal to and are judged solely by the eye. They must have 'eye appeal'. The relevant 'eye' is that of the prospective customer, and the 'appeal' is that created by a distinctiveness of shape, pattern or ornamentation calculated to influence the customer's choice (*Interlego v Tyco*). A design shall not be registered in respect of an article if the appearance of the article is not material, that is if aesthetic considerations are not normally taken into account to a material extent by persons acquiring or using articles of that description and would not be so taken into account if the design were to be applied to the article (s 1(3)). It has been suggested that this provision would exclude from registered design protection mass produced but functional articles like computers, which are judged by consumers solely on their functional capabilities and where eye appeal is irrelevant. However, even if this was ever so, design is now clearly an important factor in the manufacture even of mass produced functional products, computer design being a case in point. It is submitted that there are now few mass-produced consumer goods, however functional, which are not designed to attract customers by appealing to the eye.

Definition of an 'article'

4.37 The RDA 1949 defines an 'article' as any article of manufacture and includes any part of an article, if that part is made and sold separately (s 44(1)). In *Ford Motor Company*, it was held that the key words were 'made and sold separately.' To fall into this category, an article had to have an independent life as an article of commerce and not merely be an adjunct of some larger article of which it formed a part. Thus, in the context of spare parts, it was held in *Ford Motor Company* that the selling of a mere replacement part was not separate from the article as a whole. The relevance of this definition to the 'must match' exception is looked at below (**4.43**).

Relationship between the design and the article

4.38 The subject of an application for design registration is the design as applied to a particular article rather than for a free-standing design. Registration protects not the finished articles but the design which is sought to be registered. The articles themselves are relevant because they form the media through which the designs intended to be registered under the statute will be put into effect (*Interlego v Tyco* per Lord Oliver). It follows that the design and the article are inseparable.

Novelty

4.39 The design must be new. It must not have been registered for any other article or published in relation to any article in the UK. A design will not regarded as new if it is the same as a design, which is registered in respect of the same or any other article or a design which has been published in respect of the same or any other article before the date of application. Nor will it be registered if it differs from an earlier design only in immaterial details or in features which are variants commonly used in the trade (s 1(4)). Published means applying the design to articles made available to the public or publicising it by other means, such as in documents or even orally. There are obvious parallels between novelty in a 'patent' sense and novelty in registered design, although, in the case of registered designs, publication must be within the UK. In terms of registerability, it has been suggested in a number of cases that novelty must be 'substantial'.

4.40 The question of novelty was examined in the recent cases of *Household Articles' Registered Design* (1998). The design at issue was for a coffee pot which operated on a 'piston principle'. The applicant, Bodum, sought to have the respondent's design expunged from the register on the basis of prior art. The salient features, for which the applicant pleaded prior art, included the container which was transparent, beaker shaped and had two surrounding metal bands, the shape of the handle and of the lid. Bodum claimed that these features were generally common or typical of other coffee pots even if they were not all shared with its own registered design. It was held by Laddie J that a design could be valid over prior art, even if individual features were very similar. On the one hand, the impact of small differences could be considerable. On the other, there might be considerable differences between the design and prior art and the visual impact might be similar. Furthermore, a design may be novel even if it is made up 'entirely of blending together a number of old designs provided the resulting combination itself has a sufficiently distinctive appearance.' However, 'where all the features have been used before, and used commonly (or are immaterial) then the Act deems them to be novelty destroying.' He explained 'immaterial designs' as those features which make no visual impact on the design, while 'common trade variants' could be visually significant. In this case, although the applicant's and the respondent's pots had many common features, where the respondent's designer had had a free hand to 'modify and add eye appeal', its design was noticeably different in both detail and overall effect. In essence, although 'hardly radical', it was visually pleasing and distinctive. It was validly registered.

Judging novelty

4.41   Novelty is to be judged by the eye and particularly 'consumer eye appeal' as interpreted by the court (*Isaac Oren v Red Box Toy Factory* (1999)). Expert evidence may be helpful for determining those features which are to be ignored or given less weight as a matter of law (*Household Articles*). However, in *Thermos v Aladdin* (2000), it was held that expert evidence served little purpose in registered design actions concerned with ordinary consumer articles, and should be discouraged. On the other hand, the evidence of the reaction of the public and the trade to the design might prove useful for suggesting whether the design is striking or novel. The court's first impressions of the design are also important (*Household Articles*).

The exclusions

4.42   A design will not be registered if it is dictated solely by the function which the article has to perform (s 1(b)(i)). This contrasts with design right, which protects functional aspects of shape or configuration, although the period of protection is less. In *Interlego v Tyco*, which was concerned, inter alia, with whether the Lego toy brick was a design capable of registration, it was held by the HL that a design which has eye appeal will be excluded from registration only if every feature of it is one which is dictated solely by function. The HL also said that in order to demonstrate that a particular shape is dictated solely by function, there is no need to show that the function could not have been performed by an article in some other shape. Rather, it is necessary to show that the relevant features of the shape were brought about only by, or are attributable only to, the function that the shape must perform, even if the function could equally well be performed by an article of a different shape (following the HL in *Amp v Utilux* (1972)). In the case of the Lego brick, although the presence of knobs and tubes was attributable simply and solely to the functional purpose of providing 'clutch power', the actual shape and dimensions of the particular knobs and tubes employed for that purpose were not dictated solely by the function, but were chosen, at least in part, with a view to the appearance of the article as a whole. As a result the design was registrable. *Lego* is authority for the fact that designs which are partly functional and partly designed to have eye appeal and designs which are both attractive to the eye and designed to achieve a functional purpose will both be registrable. Another example of the latter is to be found in *Cow v Cannon* (1959), where a hot water bottle was designed with diagonal ribs which were believed to be better at spreading the heat, but were also intended to have eye appeal. The design was held to be registrable. Interestingly, when the CA, in *Philips v Remington* (1999), came to interpret the exclusion to registerability of trade marks which consisted of the shapes of goods which were necessary to obtain a technical result, it took the same approach as that taken in relation to registered designs (see **6.30** on trade marks and registrable shapes).

The must match exclusion (s 1(1)(b)(ii))

4.43 Not surprisingly interpretation of this exception has been relevant to debates concerning the market for spare parts. In *Ford Motor Company*, the car manufacturers made some fifty applications for the registration of various motor vehicle components, such as door panels, steering wheels, seats, bonnet tops and wheel covers. The Registrar and the Registered Designs Appeal Tribunal rejected all but three of the applications as falling within the 'must match' exceptions to registerability. Consequently Ford sought judicial review in relation to those designs which had been refused registration. The matter eventually found its way to the HL. One question that faced the court was whether spare parts for other objects are articles within the meaning of the RDA 1949. This was considered above (see **4.37**). The other was how to construe the must match exception. As his starting point, Lord Mustill cited *Sifam v Sangamo Weston* (1973), which held that to be registrable, designs must relate to articles which are intended by the proprietor of the design to be made and sold separately (not as on the facts of *Sifam*, the front of an electric meter). In *Ford*, it was argued by Ford that this definition could be applied to the spare parts. It had been held by the HC that the definition, in the context of cars, can be applied to optional components such as fancy steering wheels or wing mirrors, because these are designed with the intention that some of the sales will be for use with vehicles other than those marketed by the manufacturer. These had not been refused registration and were not the subject of the appeal. Lord Mustill then went on to consider the separate category of spare parts, that is those which are only relevant to the producer's own range but might be sold as replacement goods for the parts which were incorporated into the original vehicle. While they will be sold and bought 'separately', would they fall within the must match exclusion? The HL concluded that they would. According to the HL, to be registrable, a spare part has to have an independent life as an article of commerce and not be merely an adjunct of some larger article of which it forms a part. Ford's appeal was dismissed.

Method and principle of construction

4.44   This exclusion can be relevant to a general method of construction which would result in articles which are shaped or configured in a variety of ways. Or it may apply to a method or principle of construction in a drawing or illustration of a process or operation by which the shape is produced as opposed to the shape itself. In *Isaac Oren*, the registration was in respect of a square foldable mattress with hoops crossing from the corner. Called the 'Gymini 3D Activity Gym', it was a very popular toy for small babies. According to Jacob J, the success of the toy was due to a number of factors including the function as well as the design of the article, specifically, 'its elegant shape'. Among the defendant's designs was, inter alia, also a mattress with two flaps, also designed for small babies. The plaintiffs alleged infringement and the defendants argued, inter alia, that the registered design was invalid in that it covered a method or principle of construction. In particular, it suggested that the principle was that of a baby gym, with two crossing hoops, which can be folded. Jacob J disagreed. It was possible to make a device whose design would be visually very different to the plaintiffs' design, but which worked on the same principle. This latter design would not infringe the plaintiffs' registration. It therefore followed that there was 'no principle monopolised here—only a visual embodiment of a device constructed in accordance with a principle.' The registered design did not fall within the exclusion.

Infringement

4.45   A registered design gives the registered proprietor the exclusive right to make or import for sale or hire, or to use for the purposes of a trade or business, or to sell hire or offer or expose for sale or hire, an article in respect of which the design is registered and to which the design or a design not substantially different from it has been applied (RDA s 7(1) as amended). To be infringing, the acts must take place within the

UK. The test is comparable to that for patent infringement and unlike that for design right and copyright, in that there is no need for copying (*Thermos*). Infringement may be primary or secondary. Infringement actions may be brought in the HC or in the Patents County Court.

The elements of infringement

4.46 First, the article embodying the allegedly infringing design must be the same as that in respect of which the design in registered. Second, the allegedly infringing design must not be substantially different from the registered design. This test was new to the 1949 Act. The comparison should be between those features of the registered design and the allegedly infringing design which have eye appeal and do not fall within any of the statutory exclusions to registration. The test of whether the designs are 'substantially different' for the purposes of infringement was summarised by Aldous J in *Gaskell & Chambers v Measure Master* (1993):

> It must be decided on a comparison of the features which appeal to, and are judged by, the eye. To do this, the court must adopt the mantle of a customer who is interested in the design of the articles in question as it is the eye of such an interested person, the interested addressee, which is relevant. To adopt the mantle it is often helpful [for the court] to look at what was available before the priority date of the registered design as the eye of the interested addressee could be drawn to details if the design of the registered design only differs from the prior art by such details. However, where a design differs radically from previous designs then the interested addressee's eye would be more likely to concentrate on and he would be more likely to remember the general form of the new design rather than the details.

In *Thermos*, Jacob J added the further qualification that an obscure but prior registered design would not cause the ordinary addressee to concentrate on the detail. He would still be left with the impression of a radical new design. In *Isaac Oren*, Jacob J held that there was a infringement of the plaintiffs' registered design by the defendants' mattress. Although the defendants' mattress appeared different when folded, through 'the eyes of the consumer' there was no particular significance attached to the folded article. What mattered was what the article looked like when it was unfolded, since it was this feature of the finished article which has 'eye appeal'. When laid flat, the defendants' mattress was not substantially different from the plaintiffs'.

156

Ownership (s 2)

4.47 The 'author' of a design is the original proprietor of the design. However, if the design is the result of a commission for money or money's worth, the original proprietor is the commissioner. If an employee creates the design in the course of his employment, the owner is the employer. A registered design may be assigned, mortgaged or transmitted by operation of the law, although the change of ownership must be registered with the Design Registry. Only once registered may the new proprietor sue for infringement. A registered design may also be licensed. Registered designs may be the subject of a compulsory licence, which is granted on an application to the Patent Office, if the design has not been applied in the UK.

Duration

4.48 A design may be registered for 25 years, dating from the date of registration which is when the application was filed. The initial registration is for five years, but the registration may be renewed up to the maximum term.

Industrial designs and the EU

4.49 The protection offered to designs in member states is not necessarily uniform. Nonetheless, unregistered designs are covered by the same free movement of goods rules which apply to copyright (s 228(5)). In respect of registered designs, these are similarly subject to such principles although there is no specific statutory provision. In essence, subject to Art 32 of the Treaty of Rome, the principle is that once goods embodying an unregistered or registered design right have been placed on the market by their proprietor in one member state, industrial design rights cannot be invoked to prevent their importation into another member state. In the ECJ patents case, *Merck v Primecrown* (**2.100**), it was held that the principle held true even where the protection offered in the country of first marketing was less than that in the country of export. This principle is held to apply equally to design rights.

Industrial designs and the rest of the world

4.50 The protection afforded to unregistered designs from parallel imports from outside of the EU is also similar to that afforded by copyright (**3.90**). The design right is infringed by a person who without the licence of the proprietor imports into the UK for commercial purposes an 'infringing' article (s 227). An infringing article is, inter alia, infringing if its making to that design in the UK would have been an infringement in design right in the design (s 228). By contrast, in the context, the relationship of registered designs to parallel imports from outside the EU is similar to that of patents and the principle in *Betts v Willmott* (**2.103**). In essence, if the proprietor of a registered design puts an article embodying that design on the market anywhere in the world, he is assumed to have consented to the resale of that article unless there is an express limitation to that resale where notice is given to all possible sellers.

Further reading

Russell-Clarke on Industrial Designs (6th edn, 1998)

K Hodkinson 'Design right licences—a new nightmare for UK manufacturers' [1990] MIP 28

L Bentley and A Coulthard 'From the Commonplace to the Interface: Five Cases on Unregistered Design Right' [1997] EIPR 401

Self-test questions

1. Keith decides to start a business making spare parts for the best selling Grasso Lawnmower. He plans to manufacture new blades which are a particular design feature of the Grasso but which quickly wear out. He also plans to manufacture replacement seats and a rear view mirror especially designed to fit the Grasso, which allows the mower to check that the way behind him is clear, but which Grasso does not supply. The mirror has an attractive engraved grass-like design on its back, and is also cleverly designed so that the concave glass will not cause glare. Grasso is so impressed that it is thinking of making its own mirror. Advise Keith on whether his business risks infringing any of Grasso's rights and of the best way for him to prevent Grasso from selling a similar mirror to his own.

2. Identify and compare the different protection given to industrial designs by copyright, design right and registered designs.

3. Do you think the new industrial regime is overly protective of industrial designs?

CHAPTER FIVE

Passing off

SUMMARY

Development and definitions of passing off

Unfair competition and the relationship with trade marks

The first element of passing off: goodwill

What is not protected by passing off and the definition of a trader

The second element of passing off: misrepresentation

Types of actionable misrepresentation

The definition of distinctiveness

The third element of passing off: damage

Defences to passing off

Character merchandising

Remedies

Passing off: development and definitions

5.1   Passing off may be defined as a misrepresentation in the course of trade by one trader which damages the goodwill of another. The three essential elements of passing off, the 'classical trinity', are: goodwill, a misrepresentation and damage.

The origins of passing off

5.2   Passing off is a common law tort. Its origins lie in the tort of deception. However, passing off does not now depend upon any fraudulent intent by the defendant (see **5.27** below). In *Perry v Truefitt* (1842), the basic underlying principle of a passing off action was stated to be: 'A man is not to sell his own goods under the pretence that they are the goods of another man.... .' Another summation was given by Lord Halsbury in the later case of *Reddaway v Banham* (1896), where he stated that, 'nobody has the right to represent his goods as the goods of somebody else.' Over the past century, passing off has developed on a case by case basis. Different factual situations have led to an expansion of the law. As Lord Oliver observed in *Reckitt & Coleman v Borden* (1990), the 'Jif Lemon' case: 'this is not a branch of the law in which reference to other cases is of any real assistance except analogically.'

The development of passing off

5.3   It is generally accepted that the modern form of passing off was first defined by Lord Parker in *Spalding v Gamage* (1915). He said:

> ...the basis of a passing-off action being a false representation by the defendant, it must be proved in each case as a fact that the false representation was made. It may, of course, have been made in express words, but cases of express misrepresentation of this sort are rare. The more common case is where the representation is implied in the use or imitation of a mark, trade name, or get-up with which the goods of another are associated in the minds of the public, or, of a particular class of the public. In such cases the point to be decided is whether, having regard to all the circumstances of the case, the use by the defendant in connection with the goods of the mark, name, or get-up in question impliedly represents such goods to be the goods of the plaintiff, or the goods of the plaintiff of a particular class or quality, or, as it is sometimes put, whether the defendant's use of the mark, name, or get-up is calculated to deceive. It would, however, be impossible to enumerate or classify all the possible ways in which a man may make the false representation relied on.

Spalding extended passing off to encompass situations beyond the limited nature of the misrepresentation described in *Perry*. In *Spalding*, the plaintiff produced moulded footballs, of an inferior quality, which it abandoned in favour of sewn footballs. The moulded balls were sold to waste rubber merchants. The defendant acquired the moulded balls. It sold them off, with advertising which imitated the plaintiff's own publicity for the sewn balls. In this case, the misrepresentation was not that the defendant's goods were those of the plaintiff. They were. Rather, this was a misrepresentation by the defendant as to the quality of the plaintiff's goods.

The extended form of passing off

5.4   The most important development after *Spalding* came with the so-called 'drinks' cases, of which the 'Champagne' case, *Bollinger v Costa Brava* (1960), was the first. The successful plaintiffs were a number of French champagne producers and importers who objected to the sale in England, by the defendant, of so-called 'Spanish champagne', an alcoholic beverage produced in Spain. Central to this 'extended form of passing off' is that protection is being given to the goodwill in a name or word which has come to mean a particular product, in this case the generic 'Champagne', rather than the product of a particular trader (see **5.35** below). The 'Champagne' case was followed by the 'Sherry' and 'Whisky' cases (*Vine Products v Mackenzie* (1969); *John Walker v Henry Ost* (1970)).

Lord Diplock's definition in Advocaat

5.5   The 'extended' form of passing off in the 'drinks' cases was confirmed in *Warnink v Townend* (1980), the 'Advocaat' case, which also provided the authoritative modern formulation of passing off. In Lord Diplock's words:

> *Spalding v Gamage* and the later cases make it possible to identify five characteristics which must be present in order to create a valid cause of action for passing off: (1) a misrepresentation (2) made by a trader in the course of trade, (3) to prospective customers of his or ultimate consumers of goods or services supplied by him, (4) which is calculated to injure the business or goodwill of another trader (in the sense that it is a reasonably foreseeable consequence) and (5) which causes actual damage to a business or goodwill of the trader by whom the action is brought or (in a *quia timet* action) will probably do so.

Quia timet means an action for an injunction to prevent damage for which money is no remedy. Lord Diplock warned that an action for passing off did not necessarily follow even if all five factors are present (although they would describe a situation which 'morally' might be considered 'dishonest trading'). In his famous phrase, he noted that, 'in seeking to formulate a general proposition of English law, however, one must be particularly careful to beware of the logical fallacy of the undistributed middle.' He explained: 'It does not follow that because all passing-off actions can be shown to present these characteristics, all factual situations which present these characteristics give rise to a cause of action for passing off.' It is Lord Diplock's formulation which has been generally followed. Nonetheless, in the same case Lord Fraser offered his own—less general—definition which did identify three necessary conditions for passing off. These were that goodwill must be in England, misrepresentations must be about the defendant's goods and not the plaintiffs (although see reverse passing-off, **5.40**), and the plaintiff must be a member of clearly identifiable class who are entitled to make the representation about their own goods. Each of these conditions will be examined later in this chapter.

The classic definition of passing off: the 'Jif Lemon' case

5.6   In 'Jif Lemon', Lord Oliver endorsed Lord Diplock's definition and reduced it to three key elements: goodwill, misrepresentation and damage. He said:

> First the plaintiff must establish a goodwill or reputation attached to the goods or services which supplies in the mind of the purchasing public by which the identifying 'get-up' (whether it consists simply of a brand name or a trade description or the individual features of labelling or packaging) under which his particular goods or services are offered to the public, such that the get-up is recognised by the public as distinctive specifically of the plaintiff's goods or services. Secondly, he must demonstrate a misrepresentation by the defendant to the public (whether or not intentional) leading or likely to lead the public to believe that goods or services offered by him are the goods or services of the plaintiff...Thirdly, he must demonstrate that he suffers or, in a quia timet action, is likely to suffer damage by reason of the erroneous belief engendered by the defendant's misrepresentation that the source of the defendant's goods or services is the same as the source of those offered by the plaintiff.

Lord Oliver's 'classic' definition of passing off continues to be authoritative and was even applied in *Consorzio del Prosciutto di Parma v Asda Stores* (1998), the 'Parma Ham' case, whose facts reflect more closely the extended form of passing off. Lord Oliver's formulation was also preferred over that of Lord Diplock by Millett LJ in *Harrods v Harrodian* (1996), the 'Harrods' case, which is considered below (see **5.12**).

Passing off and unfair competition

5.7   There is in English law no general tort of unfair competition. Recently, Laddie J stated in *Chocosuisse v Cadbury* (1998), the 'Swiss Chalet' case, that 'in its current state of development the common law does not recognise a general right in one trader to complain of damaging dishonest practices committed by his competitors.' As a result, over the years, the law of passing off has become an important element in preventing some forms of unfair competition. However, there has been continued debate as to how far it might be stretched and whether passing off can, practically, compensate for the lack of a general law of unfair competition. In 'Advocaat', Lord Diplock warned that it should not be stretched too far, in case it might be used to hamper genuine competition. Passing off should not, for instance, provide a general remedy against damagingly inaccurate statements by rival traders. A similarly cautious approach was taken by Lord Scarman in *Cadbury Schweppes v The Pub Squash* (1981), the Australian 'Pub Squash' case. The plaintiffs launched a lemon-flavoured soft drink, 'Solo', in a yellow can designed to look like a beer can. In a substantial advertising campaign, the plaintiffs emphasised the masculine nature of the drink and its nostalgic similarity to squash 'which pubs used to make'. The defendants launched a similar product, 'Pub Squash', in a yellow can, with a similarly themed, macho and nostalgic, advertising campaign. A novel question in the case was whether confusion which arose as the result of an advertising campaign could amount to passing off. The court held that it could but that there was no passing off because the can and the advertising were easily distinguishable. In his judgment, Lord Scarman noted the need for balance between competition and laws to prevent unfair competition. He stated:

> But competition must remain free; and competition is safeguarded by the necessity for the plaintiff to prove that he has built up an 'intangible property right' in the advertised descriptions of his product, or, in other words, that he has succeeded by such methods in giving his product a distinctive character accepted by the market. A defendant, however, has done no wrong by entering a market created by another and then competing with its creator. The line may be difficult to draw; but, unless it is drawn, competition will be stifled.

Despite these strictures, there is some argument that recent decisions, particularly those concerned with the extended form of passing off, which appear to downplay the importance of actual or likely damage to the plaintiff's goodwill as a necessary element in passing off, demonstrate a trend towards the metamorphosis of passing off into a tort of unfair competition (Murray 'A Distinct Lack of Goodwill' [1997] 7 EIPR 345; see also **5.35** below).

Other remedies against unfair competition

5.8 While England lacks a general law of unfair competition, other torts, such as breach of confidence, injurious falsehood and trade libel, as well as the Trade Marks Act 1994, the Trade Descriptions Act 1967 and Arts 81 and 82 (formerly Arts 85 and 86) of the Treaty of Rome all play a role in combating various forms of unfair competition. In particular, the tort of malicious or injurious falsehood (trade libel) covers some of the ground left vacant by passing off. The difference between these torts is that trade libel relates to false statements about the claimant's goods, whereas passing off is concerned with misrepresentations about the defendant's goods which damage the claimant's goodwill (although reverse passing off, which is discussed below, is a possible exception to this rule, see **5.40**). Unlike passing off, in the case of trade libel, the relevant misrepresentation must be deliberate or reckless.

The relationship with trade marks

5.9 The protection offered to a trader by a passing off action, on the one hand, and by a registered trade mark, on the other, may overlap at many points. The areas of overlap as well as the important contrasts between passing off and registered trade marks are, where relevant, highlighted in this chapter (and also Chapter 6 on trade marks). However, it is worth emphasising at the outset that perhaps the fundamental difference between them is that in passing off there is no property in the relevant name or other indicia, as there is in a registered trade mark. Instead, passing off protects the claimant's ownership of his goodwill or reputation which may be damaged by the defendant's misrepresentation. Nonetheless, passing off will, for all practical purposes, protect identifying insignia that trade marks will not. Recent changes to trade mark law, ushered in by the TMA 1994, have increased the overlap with passing off. These include the possibility of protecting identical or similar registered trade marks with a reputation on dissimilar goods (see **6.48** on trade marks). Also the category of registrable marks was enlarged to include any which may be represented graphically, including, inter alia, shapes. Nonetheless, it is clear that, in some respects, the protection offered by passing off may still be wider than that endowed by trade mark registration. For instance in *United Biscuits v Asda* (1997), the 'Penguin/Puffin' case, where the defendants marketed a biscuit whose packaging was similar in a number of respects to the Penguin biscuit, the plaintiff was able to obtain an injunction to prevent passing off but failed in trade mark infringement because the precise marks, the Penguin and the Puffin, were not sufficiently similar. It is arguable that traditionally judges have been willing to provide more extensive protection to traders under passing off, for instance, in cases involving descriptive names, precisely because the law of passing off does not provide the potentially indefinite monopoly endowed by trade mark registration.

The first element in passing off: goodwill

5.10   Goodwill is the first element in the 'classical' trinity necessary to establish an action for passing off. Goodwill is personal property, and it is the claimant's goodwill which is the property right protected by a passing off action. According to Lord Diplock, in *Star Industrial v Yap Kwee Kor* (1976): 'A passing off action is a remedy for the invasion of a right in property not in the mark, name or get-up improperly used, but in the business or goodwill likely to be injured by the misrepresentation made by the passing off of one person's goods as the goods of another.' (See also *Reddaway* per Lord Herschell; *Spalding* per Lord Parker.) Note the contrast with trade mark law, where the claimant's property is in the 'mark, name or get-up' provided it is properly registered as a trade mark.

The meaning of goodwill

5.11   Goodwill was defined by Lord Macnaghten in *IRC v Muller* (1901) as 'the benefit and advantage of the good name, reputation and connection of a business. It is the attractive force which brings in custom.' In the same case, Lord Lindsey described goodwill thus:

> I understand the word to include whatever adds value to a business by reason of situation, name and reputation, connection, introduction to old customers, and agreed customers, and agreed absence from competition, or and of these things, and there may be others that do not occur to me.

This definition was adopted by Lord Diplock in *Star*.

The difference between goodwill and reputation

5.12 Although goodwill and reputation are often used interchangeably in relation to passing off, there is strong authority for the proposition that the two do not mean the same and that passing off protects the former and not the latter. As Millett LJ put it in 'Harrods': 'Damage to goodwill is not confined to loss of custom, but damage to reputation without damage to goodwill is not sufficient to support an action for passing off.' In the 'Harrods' case, the plaintiff was the proprietor of the 'world famous' department store. It sought to restrain the defendants from running a private preparatory school, named 'The Harrodian School', in premises which had previously housed the 'Harrodian Club', originally established for the store's employees. The plaintiff certainly had a world-wide reputation, but it was held that the defendant's activities would not damage its goodwill, as such. As Millett LJ stated: 'The name 'Harrods' may be universally recognised, but the business with which it is associated in the minds of the public is not all embracing. To be known to everyone is not to be known for everything.' An earlier case where the unsuccessful plaintiff was held to have had a reputation but no goodwill was *Anheuser-Busch v Budejovicky* (1984), the 'Budweiser' case. In 'Budweiser', the plaintiff, an American brewing company, whose beer was sold almost exclusively on American airforce bases, was unable to restrain a Czech company from selling beer under the same name in England. In his judgment Oliver LJ acknowledged the American company had a reputation as brewers of beer among a substantial section of the British public, but in the absence of carrying on a business in England, it did not have the relevant goodwill (for what constitutes the 'relevant' goodwill, see **5.15** et seq). In *Lego Systems v Lemelstrich* (1983), the court took a more expansive view of the overlap between reputation and goodwill. In this case, the plaintiff manufactured and distributed children's construction kits made from coloured plastic. The defendant had for many years sold gardening equipment including sprinklers made from coloured plastic, under the name 'Lego', although not in the UK. It sought to expand its market into the UK and the plaintiff, who alleged passing off, succeeded in obtaining an injunction. The court found that the plaintiff had established a 'high' reputation in the mark 'Lego' which extended beyond the field of toys. Indeed, its reputation was wide enough to extend to goods such as gardening equipment, so there was a real risk that the public would be led to believe that there was a business connection between the parties.

Dealings with goodwill

5.13 Goodwill is a form of property and can be assigned, licensed, bequeathed, etc. However, goodwill cannot be separated from the business that generated it. It cannot, for instance, be assigned alone. In *IRC v Muller*, it was said: 'Goodwill regarded as property has no meaning except in connection with some trade, business or calling. ...In the wide sense, goodwill is inseparable from the business to which it adds value, and, in my opinion, exists where the business is carried on.' By contrast, registered trade marks can be assigned, licensed, etc by their proprietors separately from the business to which they attach, so long as they do not become deceptive (see **6.92 et** seq).

Goodwill must be in England

5.14 Goodwill is local in character and divisible. If the claimant carries on business in a number of countries, then he will have separate goodwill in each country (*Star* per Lord Diplock). Traditionally, it has been the case that to bring an action for passing off in the UK, the claimant must have goodwill in this country. This was made clear in the 'Budweiser' case. Section 56 of the TMA 1994 has, to some extent, altered the situation, since it offers limited protection to 'well-known' trade marks, which are not registered in the UK, whether or not the proprietor of the mark carries on a business or has any goodwill in the UK (see **6.68** below).

What constitutes goodwill

5.15 The courts will decide whether or not a claimant has the relevant goodwill, not on the basis of whether he actually has a place of business in this country, but rather on whether he 'carries on business' in the UK, in the sense of there being a sufficient number of customers for his product ('Budweiser'; also *Athletes' Foot v Cobra Sports* (1980)). Customers do not necessarily mean persons who have a direct relationship with the plaintiff, such as an agent, but also include the ultimate consumers of his goods on the market ('Budweiser'). In *Panhard v Levassor* (1901), the plaintiffs, who produced cars in France, had neither business nor an agency in England. They could not import their cars into England because of certain patent restrictions. However, the cars were bought in France by an importer who re-sold them in England and private individuals also went to Paris to buy the cars. The court held that 'England was one of their markets' and that they had the necessary goodwill to bring a passing off action. An opposite conclusion was reached in *Athlete's Foot*. The plaintiffs franchised shoe shops in the US. They planned to begin franchising in the UK, but had not yet begun to trade. There was evidence that the public knew of the plaintiff's business but no evidence of purchases. The defendants opened the 'Athlete's Foot Bargain Basement' and advertised in sports magazines. The plaintiff failed to gain an injunction to stop the defendants trading under that name because they lacked goodwill in England. In 'Budweiser', the plaintiff's beer was available to the general public only irregularly but was regularly supplied to US bases. This was held to be insufficient to constitute carrying on business in this country.

Goodwill in services

5.16 A trader who supplies goods abroad may prove goodwill in England by showing he has home-grown customers for his goods. However, a plaintiff who supplies his services abroad may have greater difficulty in demonstrating the necessary goodwill. In *Alain Bernardin v Pavilion Properties* (1967), the plaintiffs owned a Paris nightclub, the 'Crazy Horse Saloon', which it advertised in England and from where it also drew customers. In this case the plaintiffs failed to gain an injunction against the defendants who deliberately copied their name and their advertising for their UK business. The more recent case of *Pete Waterman Ltd v CBS* (1993) has thrown doubt on the 'Crazy Horse' decision. The plaintiffs produced hit records and by 1987 were known to the public as 'The Hit Factory'. They did not trade as 'The Hit Factory' but had released some records under that name. The defendants opened a recording studio in London which they proposed to call 'The Hit Factory'. They were in partnership with a New York recording company, trading as 'The Hit Factory' since 1970, who drew large numbers of recording stars and record companies to use their services in the US. Browne-Wilkinson VC held inter alia that the defendants had sufficient goodwill in England to bring an action for passing off. The presence of customers in England was sufficient to constitute carrying on a business with local goodwill even if the service was provided abroad. He suggested that the 'Crazy Horse' case had been wrongly decided. It is certainly true, as Browne-Wilkinson VC pointed out, that markets for both goods and services are becoming increasingly international, as a result of the ease and availability of air travel and of advertising which crosses national boundaries. One might now add the internet. As a consequence, the *Pete Waterman* decision may more closely reflect present-day commercial realities. It remains to be seen how persuasive the courts will find it in the future.

Who owns goodwill

5.17   This is a question of fact in each case. It is not necessary for the public to know which individual or company may own the goodwill. It is enough if they think that the claimant's goods derive from a particular source ('Jif Lemon'). In *Edge v Niccolls* (1911), the plaintiffs had manufactured 'washing blues' and 'tints' for many years, which they had sold on a stick without an identifying label or name on the wrapper. They had also advertised that their 'blues' always had a stick. The defendants who had also sold 'blues' and 'tints' for many years, in a different shape and get-up, began selling their products on a stick, but with 'Niccolls' prominent on the label. The HL found passing off. When the defendants began to sell their products in the same get-up but with their name on the bag, the public would think that they were getting the plaintiffs' goods and that the defendants and the plaintiffs were the same (although, of course, they did not know the plaintiffs' identity).

Goodwill can be local

5.18   A passing off action may protect local goodwill. In *Clock v Clock House Hotel* (1936), a hotel obtained an injunction against the defendant's similarly named 'road house' five miles away, but the injunction was confined to those premises. Conversely, in *Chelsea Man v Chelsea Girl* (1987), the plaintiff who had shops in Leicester, Coventry and London, but was known more widely, sold clothes under the label, 'Chelsea Man'. The defendant who had a nationwide chain of shops, called 'Chelsea Girl', opened 'Chelsea Man' shops. The plaintiff obtained a nationwide injunction in the face of the defendant's argument that it should be confined to the three shop locales. It was held that since the defendant intended to use the name 'Chelsea Man' nationwide, the plaintiff was entitled to a nationwide injunction.

Shared goodwill

5.19   Goodwill may be shared. Shared goodwill might arise in jointly owned partnerships or through the division of a business on the death of the original owner (*Dent v Turpin* (1861)). However, the most obvious example of shared goodwill is to be found in the 'drinks-type' cases and their successors. In these cases, it has been suggested that goodwill attaches both to the product and to each producer individually. In 'Advocaat', it was held obiter that each member of the class must have built up his own goodwill in the product before he could sue. However, in the 'Swiss Chalet' case, Laddie J suggested that although this held true for classic passing off cases, it was unrealistic in the context of the extended form of passing off. Even new producers should be assumed to have a stake in the collective goodwill. The 'Swiss Chalet' case suggests that the class sharing a reputation can be a large one, and the product itself can be broadly (even indefinitely) defined. The plaintiffs, who produced and sold chocolate made in Switzerland, obtained an injunction against the defendant who sold an English chocolate bar, which was marked 'Swiss Chalet' and carried a picture of the Matterhorn mountains and a chalet. In the HC, Laddie J held that the relevant goodwill was shared by the producers of any Swiss-made chocolate, no matter how recent their entry onto the market. Further, it was sufficient that Swiss chocolate was perceived as having a distinctive reputation even though the public may not be agreed as to those qualities which made it so. Indeed, the chocolate may have no common quality apart from its manufacture in Switzerland. In confirming Laddie J's judgment, the CA agreed that it was necessary for the plaintiffs to show that the words 'Swiss chocolate' had been taken by a significant section of the public in England, at the time of the action, to mean only chocolate made in Switzerland and that Swiss-made chocolate had a discrete reputation, distinct from other chocolates, which the manufacturers were entitled to protect. The CA endorsed Laddie J's view that the plaintiffs' chocolate had such a reputation. It will be interesting to see whether this case marks a high-water mark in the protection given by the 'extended' form of passing off.

What is not protected by passing off

5.20   Lord Oliver's formulation in 'Jif Lemon' indicates that what is protected by passing off is the goodwill attached to the goods or services which the claimant supplies by association with the identifying name or get-up, and not the brand name or get-up, itself (see also 'Harrods').

Traditionally, it is has been this principle which differentiates the protection given by passing off from that given by trade mark registration. In 'Jif Lemon', the plaintiff had sold lemon juice in yellow plastic squeeze packs for many years. They were embossed with the word 'Jif' and they also had a green paper label printed with the word 'Jif'. The product had come to be known as 'Jif Lemon'. The defendant began selling lemon juice in yellow lemon-shaped containers which had a green cap (the plaintiff's cap was yellow). The plaintiff obtained an injunction. The point here was not that the plaintiff had a proprietary right to the lemon-shaped container. Instead, it had acquired goodwill in the product, which was known to its buyers by the distinctive get-up in which it was sold. As Lord Oliver put it: 'There is not and cannot be any proprietary right in an idea nor can a trader claim a monopoly in the manufacture or sale of a non-patented article or, in the absence of a registered design, in the configurations of shape in which an article is manufactured.' He went on to cite Lord Cranworth LC in the earlier case of *Farina v Silverlock* (1856):

> I apprehend that the law is perfectly clear, that anyone, who has adopted a particular mode of designating his particular manufacture, has a right to say, not that other persons shall not sell exactly the same article, better or worse, or an article looking exactly like it, but that they shall not sell it in such a way as to steal (so to call it) his trade mark, and make purchasers believe that it is the manufacture to which the mark was originally applied.

Recent decisions have suggested that courts are increasingly willing to protects marks against damage caused by loss of distinctiveness, or dilution, quite apart from actual damage to goodwill. (This trend is discussed in **5.56** below.)

The origin of goodwill

5.21 The length of time it takes to establish goodwill sufficient to bring an action for passing off is a question of fact in each case. Put simply, if the claimant shows that he has the requisite goodwill, then the length of time it has subsisted is irrelevant. In some instances, the courts have considered actions brought before the claimant has begun actual trading, but where he has already acquired sufficient goodwill, for instance through pre-launch advertising (*My Kinda Bones v Dr Pepper* (1984) concerned advertising of The Chicago Rib Shack which had not yet opened). In others, the claimant may have traded for some time but be held not to have the necessary goodwill. This is particularly true where the name at issue is primarily descriptive. For instance, despite using the name 'The Gold AM' for six months for a radio station, the plaintiffs, in *County Sound v Ocean Sound* (1991), were held not to have acquired the requisite goodwill because of the descriptive nature of the name. The station played 'golden oldies'.

The end of goodwill

5.22   Goodwill will not necessarily dissipate when a business closes. Provided the claimant intended and still intends to recommence trading, it may be possible to bring an action for passing off. In *Ad-Lib Club v Granville* (1972), the plaintiff had run a successful night club called the 'Ad-Lib Club', which it had been forced to close, some four years before, because of noise complaints. It was looking for alternative premises when the defendant opened its own club, 'Ad-Lib'. The plaintiff claimed that customers of the latter would be confused. The court held the plaintiff still retained sufficient residual goodwill in the name to be entitled to an injunction. If, however, during the lapse of time, the mark has ceased to be distinctive of the claimant's business, despite the presence of goodwill, the relevant misrepresentation may be lacking.

Who is a trader?

5.23   For the purposes of passing off, 'trader' is given a wide definition. Provided the claimant can show that there are goods and services supplied to customers, that there is trading activity calculated to generate goodwill, and further, that there will prospective loss of income from the damage done to this goodwill by the relevant misrepresentation, then even 'non-trading' organisations such as clubs and charities are entitled to protection from passing off ('Harrods'). Traders have been held to include the late politician and diarist, Alan Clark, ballroom dancers and an association of accountants, whose damage, through the defendant's misrepresentation, would have been loss of subscriptions from present or future members (*Society of Accountants and Auditors v Goodway* (1907)). Conversely, in *Kean v McGivan* (1982), the Social Democratic Party failed to obtain an injunction because, as a political party, it was held to be engaged in 'non-commercial activity'.

174

The second element of passing off: misrepresentation

5.24 Misrepresentation is the second element in passing off. To be actionable in passing off, the misrepresentation must be a material misrepresentation. The deception must be more than momentary and inconsequential ('Pub Squash'). In other words, the claimant must demonstrate that it is a reasonably foreseeable consequence of the defendant's misrepresentation that his business or goodwill will be damaged ('Jif Lemon' per Lord Jauncey). It is worth noting that not all damaging misrepresentations are actionable in passing off. For instance, if trader A dishonestly claims that a rival Trader B's goods are substandard or overpriced, this may be damaging to Trader B, but it is not, on the face of it, a misrepresentation which is relevant to a passing-off action.

The nature of a material misrepresentation

5.25 The misrepresentation may be express or implied, although express misrepresentations are rare (*Spalding* per Lord Parker). The classic misrepresentation, as described by Lord Oliver in 'Jif Lemon', is one by the defendant to the public (whether or not intentional) leading or likely to lead the public to believe that the goods or services offered by him are the goods or services of the claimant. This is an effective elision of Lord Diplock's first and fourth elements of passing off. More generally, a material representation may be any misrepresentation where there is use by the defendant of the claimant's indicia as a result of which the defendant's goods or services are 'associated' in the minds of the public with those of the claimant. As summed up by Buckley LJ in *Bollinger*, a relevant misrepresentation is one calculated to mislead the public into a mistaken belief that 'the goods or services of the defendant or the defendant's business are or is either (a) the goods or services or business of the plaintiff or (b) connected with the plaintiff's business in some way which is likely to damage the plaintiff's goodwill in that business... .'

The difference between confusion and misrepresentation

5.26 Confusion alone does not necessarily amount to a material misrepresentation. According to Lord Green MR in *Marengo v Daily Sketch* (1946):

No one is entitled to be protected against confusion as such. Confusion

175

may result given the collision of two individual rights or liberties and where that is the case neither party can complain; they must put up with confusion as one of the misfortunes which occur in life. The protection to which a man is entitled is protection against passing off which is quite a different thing from mere confusion. ... If all that a trader is doing is to carry on trade in his own name and in disposing of or advertising his goods does no more than make the perfectly true statement that the goods are his goods, no other trader is entitled to complain.

It has already been suggested that the confusion which results from two traders using indicia which are common to the trade is not actionable ('Jif Lemon' per Lord Oliver). Nor is confusion relevant when it does not lead to a sale or when it stems from the purchaser being mistaken rather than misled. For instance, as Lord Oliver noted in 'Jif Lemon',

> If a customer asks for a tin of black shoe polish without specifying any brand and is offered the product of A which he mistakenly believes to be that of B, he may be confused as to what he has got but he has not been deceived into getting it. Misrepresentation has played no part in his purchase.

Indeed, in cases of what is known as 'reverse passing off', there may be a misrepresentation but no confusion (see **5.40** below). However, although the presence of customer confusion may not be sufficient to establish a case in passing off, it has been suggested that evidence of actual confusion is always relevant and may be decisive in judging whether passing off has occurred. Conversely, the absence of confusion may often be readily explained and is rarely decisive ('Harrods'). In the event it is always up to the court to decide, even if there is no evidence of confusion whatever, whether or not passing off has been established (*Electrolux v Electrix* (1954); *Spalding*; per Lord Parker; *HFC Bank plc v Midland Bank plc* (2000)).

Passing off and fraud

5.27 There is no need for a defendant to have deliberately set out to deceive the public, if that is the probable result of his misrepresentation. However, the courts will see the reasons why the defendant chose to adopt a particular indicia as highly relevant. As stated by Kerr LJ in *Sodastream v Thorn Cascade*, '...it is a question which falls to be asked and answered' (cited in 'Harrods' and 'Penguin/Puffin'). In the 'Penguin/

Puffin' case, the defendants consciously designed the get-up of the Puffin biscuit to avoid deception, yet nonetheless with the idea of 'matching', 'challenging' or 'parodying' the Penguin get-up. Walker J concluded that, 'while aiming to avoid what the law would characterise as deception, they were taking a conscious decision to live dangerously', and that was not something the court was bound to disregard.

Instruments of fraud

5.28 A claimant will usually obtain an injunction against a defendant where passing off is established or threatened. It is also possible to obtain an injunction where the defendant equips himself or intends to equip another with an instrument of fraud, in other words, *the means* of passing off by himself or by another. In *BT v One in a Million* (1999), the defendants had registered a large number of internet domain names which were the names or trade marks of well-known commercial enterprises, without their consent. They included BT, Virgin, J Sainsbury and Marks & Spencer. The defendants admitted that they had registered the domain names for profit, planning to sell them to the owners of the goodwill in the names or to others. They advertised the names on the internet. An injunction was granted in the HC on the grounds, inter alia, that the defendants had created an instrument of deception (or fraud). The defendants appealed arguing, inter alia, that there should be no injunction unless they had threatened passing off, themselves. The CA found that the defendants had registered the names because of the value of their goodwill and not because, as the defendants unconvincingly claimed, they could be used in some legitimate way by a third party. The registrations were made with the purpose of appropriating the plaintiffs' goodwill or with the intention of threatening dishonest use by the defendants or another to whom the registrations might be sold. Accordingly the CA found that the domain registrations were instruments of fraud. The CA also found passing off. An internet search for the owner of the domain name 'Marks & Spencer', for example, would reveal the owner to be the defendants, leading the searcher to assume a connection between the two. This misrepresentation would lead to damage, because it would erode the exclusive goodwill in the name Marks & Spencer.

'Customer' deception

5.29 An actionable misrepresentation is made by a trader to prospective customers or ultimate customers of his goods and services

('Advocaat' per Lord Diplock). It is a general rule that customers must be taken as they are found ('Jif Lemon' per Lord Oliver). Customers will not be assumed to be 'morons in a hurry', to quote Foster J in *Morning Star v Express Newspapers* (1979). But, according to Lord Oliver in 'Jif Lemon', it is no defence that the public would not be misled if they were more 'literate, careful, perspicacious or wary'. The amount of attention that a customer might be expected to exercise must be judged in the context of the type of goods or services concerned, the market in which they are sold, and the habits and characteristics of the customers in that market ('Jif Lemon' per Lord Oliver). In other words, as with so much in passing off, it will depend upon the facts of the particular case. In 'Jif Lemon', the defendant had distinguished its goods from those of the plaintiff by a different coloured label. The HL made the assumption that the customer for this particular product, which typically would be sold in the supermarket, would look for the distinctive lemon shape and not read the label. It followed the addition of the label would be insufficient to avoid deception. Conversely, potential customers 'wishing to borrow quite large sums of money from a bank could reasonably be expected to pay rather more attention to the details of the entity with which they are ... seeking to do business' (*HFC Bank*). So too might customers of specialist articles sold to the trade. However, in *Ravenhead Brick v Ruabon Brick* (1937), the court found that it was precisely the knowledgeable purchaser who would most likely to make the connection between the plaintiff's 'Rus' bricks and the defendant's 'Sanrus' bricks, because only he would be aware of both. In *Alan Kenneth Clark v Associated Newspapers* (1998), the 'Alan Clark Diaries' case, the *Evening Standard* produced a weekly parody of the MP's well-known diaries entitled, 'Alan Clark's Secret Political Diaries', which carried a photograph of the plaintiff, followed by a further heading saying, in effect, that the column was how the *Standard*'s journalist imagined the plaintiff would record the events which followed. One question was whether this was sufficient to alert the reader to the fact this was a parody, and not the work of the plaintiff. The court found, inter alia, that the *Evening Standard*, being an evening paper read by many on their journeys home, was not the sort of publication which is 'read word for word'. As a result the defendant's disclaimer was not sufficient to avoid confusion amongst a number of the public.

How many customers must be deceived?

5.30 It is necessary for a substantial number of customers to be misled or to be likely to be misled but not all of the potential public (*Neutrogena v Golden* (1996) per Morritt LJ). There may still be passing off even if many people are not or will not be misled ('Alan Clark Diaries'). In the 'Swiss Chalet' case, Laddie J concluded that the number of people who would be confused into thinking that the defendant's chocolate was Swiss chocolate was less than the number who would not. Since the former group was, nonetheless, substantial in number, this was sufficient.

Evidence of deception

5.31 In passing off cases, either side may produce evidence of actual customer confusion. It also common to produce survey evidence, although the courts are often wary of this. Experts may also be called, but there is conflicting authority as to whether their evidence should cover only the circumstances of the trade and their own likely confusion or whether they may give an opinion on the likelihood of others being confused. The authorities are rehearsed in *Dalgety Spillers Foods v Food Brokers* (1994) (see also *Taittinger SA v Allbev* (1993), the 'Elderflower Champagne' case, at **5.35** below). While such evidence may assist the judge in reaching a conclusion, in the final analysis the question of whether the defendant's conduct is calculated to deceive is a matter for the judge alone. According to Lord McNacghten in *Payton v Snelling* (1900), he 'must not surrender his own independent judgment to any witness whatever.' Thus, if confusion is imputed to arise from a similarity of names, the court must form its own view. As Laddie J pointed out in the 'Swiss Chalet' case, the court will put itself in the place of the relevant public in making such a judgment, but it will do so in circumstances the customer will not share. It may examine the two products at length, and side by side and it will be aware they are the subject of a passing off action. It follows that the court must exercise care to ensure these circumstances do not influence its decision.

Types of actionable misrepresentation

5.32 In *Spalding*, Lord Parker stated that it would be 'impossible to enumerate or classify all the possible ways a man may make the false representation relied on.' Some of the more common types of actionable misrepresentation to be found in the case law are set out below.

The defendant's goods are the claimants

5.33 Probably the most common form of passing off, it is most likely to arise when the name, mark or get-up of the defendant's products or services is the same or similar to that of the claimant. In *McDonald Hamburger v Burgerking* (1987), the defendant ran an advertising campaign for its 'Whopper' hamburger on the London Underground. Its posters declared, 'It's not just Big, Mac'. They also named the 'Whopper' and stated, 'Unlike some burgers, it's 100% pure beef, flame grilled never fried, with a unique choice of toppings.' The plaintiff, whose flagship product was the 'Big Mac', sued for passing off. The CA held that a significant number of people reading the advertisement would find in it a misrepresentation as to the possible source or origin of the 'Big Mac'. There was also a sufficient likelihood of damage for the plaintiff to succeed. A defendant may also deceive the public by adopting the claimant's style of promoting or advertising his products and so lead the public to assume that his product is that of the claimant. This was the position in the 'Pub Squash' case (see **5.7** above), where the defendant adopted the same advertising theme of nostalgia and manly outdoor pursuits, as the unsuccessful plaintiff. In his judgment, Lord Scarman noted that passing off,

> is now wide enough to encompass, not only the name or trade mark of a product or business, but other descriptive material, such as slogans or visual images, which advertising could lead the market to associate with the plaintiff's product provided that such material has become part of the goodwill of the product. The test is whether the product has derived from the advertising a distinctive character which the market recognises.

Misrepresentation as to quality

5.34 The defendant may sell the claimant's goods, but pass off inferior goods as if they were of superior quality, as in *Spalding* (see **5.3** above). In *Revlon v Cripps & Lee* (1980), the defendants imported 'Flex' shampoo which had been put on the market by an associated company of the plaintiff in the US. The imported shampoo was medicated, whereas the 'Flex' shampoo sold in England was not. The CA held that the anti-dandruff shampoo was not of inferior quality, and that a 'reasonably perspicacious' member of the public would understand that it was different from the British version. Passing off also failed because the CA found there had been no misrepresentation as to the origin, class or

180

quality of the goods. A misrepresentation may arise when the defendant sells the claimant's second-hand goods as if they were new (*Gillette v Diamond Edge* (1926)) or goods which have passed their 'sell by' date as if they were fresh (*Wilts United Dairies v Thomas Robinson* (1958)). In both cases, the defendants will have passed off one class of the claimant's goods as if they were another class.

The extended form of passing off

5.35 Often referred to as the 'extended form of passing off', here Trader B misrepresents the quality of his own goods thereby purporting to render them competitive with a class of products of that quality, rather than with the goods of a particular trader. In the first case to recognise the extended form of passing off, *Bollinger*, the 'Champagne' case, the plaintiffs were producers and importers of champagne who sought to restrain the defendant from selling 'Spanish champagne'. The court held that champagne was distinctive of wine produced in the Champagne region of France. As a substantial number of the public would know little about the actual nature of champagne, but view it as a wine with a 'high reputation', they would be misled by the defendant's representation of its product. Other 'drinks' cases followed (see **5.4** above). In 'Advocaat', the plaintiffs had sold the 'Advocaat' drink in the UK since 1911. By 1976, sales totalled 75% of the market. Before 1974, practically all the 'Advocaat' sold in the UK was made in Holland and consisted of eggs, spirit and sugar but no wine. In 1974, the defendant began to market 'Old English Advocaat' which was made from eggs and fortified Cyprus wine. In his judgment, Lord Diplock approved the extended form of passing off, the principles of which, established in the 'Champagne' case, were that 'a person competing in a trade may not attach to his product a name or description with which it has no actual association, so as to make use of the reputation and goodwill which has been gained by a product genuinely indicated by the name or description... .'

5.36 'Advocaat' also made it clear that the extended form of passing off might stretch beyond products whose reputation resides in a particular locality. In 'Advocaat', it was the composition of the product which was at issue. More recently, in the 'Elderflower Champagne' case, the plaintiffs objected to the marketing of a (very inexpensive) non-alcoholic sparkling drink as 'Elderflower Champagne' in a champagne-style bottle. The CA held that while the vast majority of the public would not be confused

181

into thinking the beverage was champagne, they might nonetheless believe it was a product that was associated in some way with the champagne houses (particularly in light of the proliferation of low-alcohol and non-alcohol drinks being introduced by the drinks trade). It has been argued that this decision extends the scope of passing off beyond the traditional 'drinks' cases, where one product might be taken for another (see **5.56** below). There is a further argument that 'Swiss Chalet' also extended the scope of passing off. In this case, Laddie J held that Swiss chocolate manufactured in Switzerland in accordance with Swiss food regulations was sufficiently identifiable as a class of goods with a public reputation, whether or not the public appreciated the identifying characteristics of the class or indeed had quite different views as to what those were. In 'Advocaat', Lord Diplock had stated that,

> the larger the class of traders, the broader must be the range of products to which the descriptive term used by members of the class has been applied, and the more difficult it must be to show that the term at issue had acquired a public reputation and goodwill as denoting a product endowed with recognisable qualities which distinguished it from others of inferior reputation which competed with it in the same market.

'Swiss Chalet' posed the interesting question of what happens when the public perception of what those qualities are and the court's definition of what qualities distinguish the range of products differ. In 'Swiss Chalet', the court held that there was still a material misrepresentation.

A business relationship

5.37 Trader B may deceive the public into thinking there is a business relationship between his goods or services and those of Trader A, with the effect that it damages Trader A's reputation and therefore his goodwill. In *Ewing v Buttercup Margerine* (1917), the plaintiffs had shops which sold margarine under the name 'Buttercup'. The defendants were planning to sell margarine under the same name, but wholesale. As a result it was unlikely that customers of the plaintiffs would also be customers of the defendants. However, according to Lord Cozens Hardy MR:

> I should be very sorry indeed if we were so to limit the jurisdiction of the court.... . I know of no power and can see no principle for holding that a trader may not be injured, and seriously injured, in his business as

a trader by a confusion which will lead people to conclude that the defendants are really connected to the plaintiffs or a brand of the plaintiffs or in any way mixed up with them.

5.38   An operative misrepresentation may arise even when Trader A or Trader B are not competing in the same line of business ('Advocaat'). However, it may be easier to establish a likelihood of confusion when the parties' trading activities are similar or overlap. If they do not, then the likelihood of confusion may depend upon the scope of the 'field of recognition' of the claimant's reputation (*Lego*). However, not all connections which might be drawn by the public are relevant. In 'Harrods', the CA held that it was not enough that the public might think that Harrods sponsored or backed the school. Millett LJ noted that it was common practice for traders to sponsor sporting or artistic events or teams, but the public would not assume that the sponsor controlled or was responsible for the organisation of the event or the performance of the team. The relevant connection must be one by which the plaintiffs would be taken by the public to have made themselves responsible for the quality of the defendant's goods or services. Kerr LJ dissented and said a belief in sponsorship was enough (see also, *British Legion v British Legion Club* (1931)). In the 'Penguin/Puffin' case, where the product as issue was the supermarket's own-brand biscuit, Walker J did not believe that a substantial number of the public would take the Asda Puffin for the McVities' Penguin. It was enough that the general public might be led to 'suppose', 'assume' or 'guess' that the plaintiff was in some way responsible for the defendant's goods, in that the two were made by same manufacturer.

A licensing relationship

5.39   One way the public may be deceived into concluding there is a relevant trade connection between the goods of Trader B and Trader A is if they mistakenly take them to have been made under license. This issue is central to the problem of character merchandising which is looked at below (**5.61** et seq).

Reverse (or inverse) passing off

5.40   In these cases, Trader B misrepresents Trader A's goods or services as his own, reversing the classic misrepresentation that Trader B's goods are those of Trader A. It is generally accepted that reverse passing off is not a separate tort, but would fall within the ambit of passing off as set out by Lord Diplock in 'Advocaat'. This was confirmed in *Bristol Conservatories v Custom Built* (1989). The defendants' salesmen showed prospective customers photographs of conservatories as examples of their own work, which were actually photographs of the plaintiffs' conservatories. The CA held that the defendants, by their misrepresentation, were seeking to induce customers to purchase conservatories from them in the belief that they would actually get a conservatory from the 'commercial source' (ie the plaintiffs) which had designed and constructed the conservatories shown in the photographs. In fact, previous cases had recognised misrepresentations analogous to that in *Bristol Conservatories*, without characterising them as a reversal of the classic misrepresentation. For instance, in *Samuelson v Producers Distributing* (1931), the plaintiffs were the owners of a famous theatrical sketch, 'The New Car'. The defendants were the owners of a film, 'His First Car'. Both starred the comedian, George Clarke. The defendants used the press notices of the plaintiffs' sketch to advertise the film, leading the public to believe that the film was a reproduction of the sketch. The court held that this was an attempt to pass off the film as a version of the plaintiff's sketch. In the later case of *Copydex v Noso* (1952), the defendants' advertised their adhesive 'as shown on television' when in fact it was the plaintiffs' product which had been advertised on television, albeit anonymously. The HC granted an interlocutory injunction, but was unsure whether the defendant's conduct amounted to passing off. It is submitted that the decision in *Bristol Conservatories* confirms that it was. Interestingly, the *Bristol Conservatories* decision recognised that the misrepresentation left no room for customer confusion. Since they were not compared side by side, the prospective customer was unable to judge the difference between two allegedly similar products. Because reverse passing off is, by definition, characterised by an absence of confusion, it has been argued that it approaches a new tort of unfair competition, in that the defendant is not damaging the claimant's goodwill as such but appropriating the value that the claimant has in it. In *Bristol Conservatories*, the court held that the plaintiffs' goodwill arose only when the defendants showed the photographs of their conservatories to prospective customers and was simultaneously misappropriated. The traditional reluctance of UK courts to recognise reverse passing off has been explained as arising from its resemblance to a more general tort of unfair competition (Carty

'Inverse Passing Off: A Suitable Addition to Passing Off?' [1993] EIPR 370).

Common field of activity/competition

5.41   It is now generally accepted that there is no need for a defendant in a passing off action to carry on business which competes with that of the claimant, or which may compete with any 'natural extension' of the claimant's business ('Harrods' per Millett LJ). In other words, there is no need for a common field of activity between the claimant and the defendant. In the early case of *McCulloch v May* (1947), it had been held that a common field of activity was necessary (see **5.61** et seq on character merchandising). However, this case went against the spirit of earlier decisions. For instance, in *Eastman Photographic v John Griffiths* (1898), the plaintiff manufactured Kodak cameras including cameras specifically designed for cyclists and the defendant was enjoined from selling Kodak bicycles. In 'Advocaat', Lord Diplock confirmed that there could be passing off even though 'the plaintiff and the defendant were not competing traders in the same line of business.' In *Mirage Studios v Counter-Feat Clothing* (1991), the 'Ninja Turtles' case, the 'so-called' requirement that a common field of activity is necessary was held to be discredited. Instead, it was necessary for the plaintiff to show not a common field of activity with the defendant but that there is likely to be confusion between common customers of the parties. For instance, in *Lego* (see above **5.12**), the plaintiff made plastic construction kits and the defendant made plastic garden hoses. There was evidence that the public was deceived into thinking that the plaintiff had diversified into garden equipment. Realistically, however, the presence of a common field of activity may assist the claimant in persuading the court that there has been an operative misrepresentation. By contrast, only a slight overlap or its absence will make this far more difficult. In the *Lego* case, Falconer J stated:

> In the law of passing off as it has recently developed, there was no limitation in respect of the parties' fields of activity. Nonetheless, the proximity of the defendants' field of activity to that of the plaintiffs would be relevant as to whether the acts complained of in a particular case amounted to a misrepresentation.

(For another example, see *Stringfellow v McCain* (1984) at **5.64**, concerning a night club and oven chips.) It follows that the absence of a common field of activity will also make it more difficult for a claimant to persuade the court it has suffered or is likely to suffer damage from any confusion that does result (*Stringfellow* per Stephenson LJ).

The definition of distinctiveness

5.42 Passing off involves the use by the defendant of a mark, trade name, a get-up, or any other indicia which are associated in the minds of the public with the claimant's goods or services, or, in other words, which are distinctive of them. It is a matter of fact in each case whether the indicia is sufficiently distinctive of the claimant's goods so that its use by the defendant will lead to confusion in the minds of the public. In principle, any indicia can be distinctive. The following discussion looks at marks (which might include, inter alia, personal names, descriptive and fancy names, titles of books, newspapers or other works), get-up and other distinguishing features (see **5.61** et seq for the related subject of character merchandising).

Distinctiveness in trade marks and passing off

5.43 Until the TMA 1994, there was a wide disparity between indicia which had been held to be distinctive in passing off, and the more limited range of marks which could be protected by registration. For instance, the classic Coca Cola bottle, like other containers, was not capable of trade mark registration but arguably would have been protected in passing off. Since the passage of the TMA 1994, many of these limits have been breached. Nonetheless, trade mark actions are still relatively limited since a registered mark is only infringed by use of an identical or similar sign (see **6.54** et seq), whereas a passing off action may take into account any indicia, alone or in combination, which the claimant claims has become distinctive of his goods or services. A good example of the contrast can be found in the 'Penguin/Puffin' case. The plaintiff had registered the pictorial mark of a penguin for chocolate biscuits and used a picture of penguin together with the word in black lettering on its packaging. The defendant sold chocolate biscuits using both a picture of a puffin and the word 'Puffin' in black lettering. The Penguin and Puffin marks were held to be insufficiently similar for a finding of trade mark infringement. However, taken as a whole, the get-up of the packaging, including the use of the birds, together with other unregistered elements such as colour and materials, was held to be sufficiently similar so that the public would be confused into thinking that the products were associated in some way. An injunction was granted.

Descriptive words

5.44   As is the case with registered trade marks, a fancy or made-up word or an imaginative device will more readily distinguish the goods or services of a trader than a purely descriptive word or a plain get-up (*Cellular Clothing v Maxton* (1899)). Not only is it difficult for a claimant to prove that a descriptive mark has become distinctive, but also, as a matter of public policy, the courts are traditionally reluctant to grant protection in passing off where the mark at issue is descriptive, and therefore one which other traders may wish to use. This is so even if confusion may result from the use of a purely descriptive word or a word which is common to the trade by more than one trader. Of course, in this case there will be no cause of action in passing off, because there will have been no relevant misrepresentation ('Jif Lemon' per Lord Jauncey).

Descriptive marks and secondary meanings

5.45   However, even a purely descriptive name or other indicia may, through use, become associated by the public with the claimant's goods or services, so that it may be said to be descriptive of only the claimant's goods. It will have acquired, in the words of the courts, a 'secondary meaning'. In such circumstances, a passing off action may well succeed. According to Lord Herschell in *Reddeway*:

> To succeed in such a case he [the plaintiff] must demonstrate more than simply the sole use of the descriptive term. He must demonstrate that it has become so closely associated with his goods as to acquire the secondary meaning not simply of goods of that description but specifically of goods of which he and he alone is the source.

In *Reddeway*, the plaintiff manufactured belting with the descriptive name, 'camel hair'. It was found that the words had acquired the secondary meaning of belting manufactured by the plaintiff. By contrast, in *Cellular Clothing*, the plaintiff failed to establish a secondary meaning in the term 'cellular', which was descriptive of its clothing. According to the Lord Chancellor:

187

> It was for the Appellants to establish, if they could, that an ordinary word in the English language and properly applicable to the subject matter of the sale was one which had so acquired a technical and secondary meaning that it could be excluded for the use of everybody else.....the [plaintiffs] have failed in establishing this initial fact.

Where a claimant uses a descriptive mark, the court will accept very small differences in the defendant's own mark as sufficient to avert the relevant confusion. In *Office Cleaning Services v Westminster Window and General Cleaners* (1946), the plaintiff, trading under the name 'Office Cleaning Services' was unable to secure an injunction against the defendant, trading as 'Office Cleaning Association'. The HL believed that a certain amount of confusion was inevitable, but this was a risk the plaintiff ran by choosing a wholly or partly descriptive name. On the other hand, the public might be expected to exercise greater discrimination when faced with a descriptive name on a product. In trade mark law, descriptive marks which acquire distinctiveness through use, may be registered (see **6.22** et seq). By contrast, a fundamental principle in passing off is that the relevant trader has no ownership in the use of a distinctive mark (or get-up), as such, but rather the right to stop its use by other traders in a deceptive way (*Reddaway* per Lord Herschell). Realistically, however, the trader may well end up with a de facto monopoly in his mark ('Jif Lemon' per Lord Jauncey).

Generic names in passing off

5.46   When a trader introduces a new product, there is a risk that the name he gives to it might come to be taken by the public as denoting all similar products, as well as his own. In other words, it may become the product's generic name. A generic name will lack the distinctiveness necessary to a successful passing off action (*British Vacuum Cleaner v New Vacuum Cleaner* (1907)). In *McCain v Country Fair Foods* (1981), the plaintiff introduced a new product, chips that could be cooked in an oven or under a grill, onto the UK market. It sold the product under the name, 'McCain Oven Chips'. About a year later, the defendants marketed their own products under the name 'oven chips', with and without their brand names. The plaintiff obtained an injunction in the HC and the defendants appealed. The CA decided for the defendants. The plaintiff's argument that term 'oven chips' was distinctive of its products was rejected. Instead the CA held it to be a descriptive name. The plaintiff's case was weakened by the fact that it had always advertised its product as 'McCain oven chips', even before its competitors had entered the market. As a result, the CA found that 'oven chips' had not acquired a secondary meaning. The CA noted that where a person introduces a new product to the market, gives it a descriptive name and has a monopoly over the product, he cannot then claim a monopoly on the name. He can only require that other traders who enter the market distinguish their products from his. This the defendants had done. Other examples are 'Chicago Pizza' in *Chicago Pizza (My Kinda Town) v Soll* (1983) and, of course, cellular clothing. It is also possible for 'fancy' or made-up names, which bear no relation to the product itself, to become generic, for example, linoleum (*Linoleum Manufacturing v Nairn* (1878)). A trader who introduces a new product is always well advised to give it both a generic name and a brand name under which it is sold. An example is the brand name 'Librium' for the tranquilliser, chlordiazepoxide. Indeed, pharmaceutical companies routinely give new drugs both a generic name (often difficult to remember and pronounce!) and a brand name, in the expectation that customers will almost certainly refer to the product by its easier, brand name, when ordering the drug.

Generic names and extended passing off

5.47   There is one group of passing off cases where the generic name is given protection, that is in the extended form of passing off. In the 'drinks-type' cases, protection is given to a name or word which has come to mean a particular product, rather than a product from a particular trader. The word is entirely descriptive of the product. However, the drinks-type cases differ from other cases involving the use of generic names. In the drinks-type cases, the defendant uses the name deceptively to describe his goods which are not of the same quality as those of the claimant, and as result damages or potentially damages the claimant's goodwill. In other cases involving generic names, it is precisely because they accurately describe the defendant's goods as well as those of the claimant, as in 'oven chips', that a passing off action will fail. In 'Advocaat', a product of a particular character or composition, had been marketed under a descriptive name, 'Advocaat', under which it had gained a reputation which distinguished it from competing products of a different composition. As such, the goodwill in the name enabled those entitled to make use of it to be protected against deceptive use by competitors.

Get-up

5.48 Get-up may be broadly defined as the visual features which distinguish a trader's goods, most notably, the packaging of goods. It might also include the shape of the goods themselves. As defined by Lord Jauncey in 'Jif Lemon': 'Get-up is the badge of the plaintiff's goodwill, that which associates the goods with the plaintiff in the mind of the public.' Features of get-up which may be imitated include colour, the shape of the product or its container ('Jif Lemon' is an example of the latter), the style of lettering and so on. In *Hoffman-La Roche v DDSA Pharmaceuticals* (1969), the plaintiff, who sold the drug chlordiazepoxide ('Librium'), in distinctive green and black capsules, was granted an injunction against the defendant, who used the same colour combination for the same drug. Often the success of a passing off case will rest on the defendant's using a combination of features which together distinguish the claimant's get-up (as in the 'Penguin/Puffin' case).

Get-up common to the trade

5.49 In 'Jif Lemon', Lord Jauncey observed: 'Any monopoly which a plaintiff may enjoy in get-up will only extend to those parts which are capricious and will not embrace ordinary matters which are in common use' (for a similar approach to registered trade marks, see the CA decision in *Philips v Remington* (1999) at **6.19**). As with names and other marks, passing off will protect only those features of get-up which are distinctive of the plaintiff, and not those which are common to the trade as such. In 'Jif Lemon', the get-up at issue was the yellow plastic lemon-shaped container. This was found not 'to be common to the trade' because the lemon-shaped package was not in general use and so it was capable of protection. Nor was it 'available to the trade', since the HL found that having come to distinguish the plaintiff's goods in the minds of the public, use by the defendants would be deceptive. According to Romer LJ in *Payton*, 'when one person has used certain leading features, though common to the trade, if another person is going to put goods on the market, having the same leading features, he should take extra care by the distinguishing features he is going to put on his goods, to see that the goods can be really distinguished.' Interestingly, Lord Bridge in 'Jif Lemon' expressed his concern that the judgment gave a de facto monopoly to the plaintiff in lemon-shaped containers, which would not have been registrable as trade marks. Since the TMA 1994, of course, it is possible to register shapes.

Get-up and the shape of the goods

5.50   Can the shape of the goods themselves be protected in passing off? In 'Jif Lemon', it was suggested there was nothing in law that would prevent this result, provided the shape of the object had become distinctive of the particular trader. Arguably, the courts will be reluctant to endow a monopoly over the actual shape of a product if it is necessary for the product to function (the CA took this view towards registered trade marks in *Philips v Remington* (1999); see **6.30** below), but it is submitted that such a result would be possible in passing off if the functional shape had become sufficiently distinctive of one trader. However, by adding capricious, decorative or other distinctive features to such a product, a rival trader may be in a position to sell his own version without passing it off as the original ('Jif Lemon' per Lord Jauncey; also *Edge*). In 'Jif Lemon', the product itself was the lemon juice and the lemon-shaped container was the packaging, so the question did not arise.

The name of the trader need not be known

5.51   The distinguishing indicia need not call to the minds of the public the actual name of the trader to whose goods it attaches (*Edge*; 'Jif Lemon'; *Hoffman La-Roche*). But the public must know there is such a person and care that the goods or services come from that person ('Penguin/Puffin' per Parker J). In the 'Penguin/Puffin' case, the public would not know that Penguin biscuits were made by plaintiff, but they would assume that they came from a single, reliable source.

Passing off and brand 'lookalikes'

5.52   It is now common for supermarkets to sell goods under their own brand name or label, alongside the goods of other brand owners. It was certainly true that when this practice began, the supermarket's packaging of its 'own brand' goods was frequently designed to resemble that of famous brand names or a brand leader. Perhaps, the most well-known example of such marketing resulted in dispute between Coca Cola and J Sainsbury over the latter's product, 'Classic Cola' in 1994. The law of passing off does not always provide brand owners with a remedy for such practices, because of the difficulties of proving an actionable misrepresentation. In other words it is necessary to show that consumers are deceived into buying the 'own-brand' product in mistake for original. In fact, there may be no such confusion. Consumers may well be aware that they are buying the supermarket's products, but are nonetheless attracted to it by the similarity of packaging with a brand leader. Many would argue that the supermarkets are taking advantage of the brand owner's goodwill which may be identified with their well-known packaging. Others suggest that a certain uniformity of packaging allows shoppers to make speedy and informed choices in supermarkets. A number of European countries have laws to counter 'misappropriation' of this type. However, there is no comparable law in the UK, despite lobbying by brand owners before the passage of the TMA 1994 (Mills 'Own Label Products and the "Lookalike" Phenomenon: A Lack of Trade Dress and Unfair Competition Protection?' [1995] EIPR 116). As a result, passing off remains the main barrier against such practices. This was made clear in the 'Penguin/Puffin case'. According to Walker J:

> The importance of brands and the emergence of competing own-brands means that the law's tests of what is fair and what is unfair competition have to be applied in new and changing conditions. But the basic tests are the same. I have to apply the non-statutory principles of the law of passing off as they have developed over the years, and the statutory principles of trade mark law now embodied (with significant changes from the earlier law) in the 1994 Act.

In this case, the court accepted there was passing off because a substantial number of the public would assume there was a connection between the two products in that the two were made by the same manufacturer, although they would not suppose that the Asda Puffin was the McVitie's Penguin.

The third element of passing off: damage

5.53 The third element in passing off is damage (or the likelihood of damage). The damage is to the claimant's goodwill, which is the property protected by a passing off action. There is a need to establish a real likelihood of more than minimal damage to the claimant's goodwill. ('Advocaat'; 'Harrods'). In many cases, where the claimant has proved both goodwill and a relevant misrepresentation by the defendant, the court will go on to infer that there will be a real likelihood of damage. However, as with all generalisations in passing off, the courts' willingness to make this assumption will depend upon the facts of a particular case. For example, the court will look to see whether the parties share a common field of activity (see **5.41**). Below are set out some the more common types of damage which have been recognised by the courts.

Damages for lost business

5.54   This is most likely to occur if the parties are in direct competition with each other and the defendant represents his goods as those of the claimant (eg *Reddeway*). It may or may not be the case that the defendant's goods are inferior to those of the claimant. In a number of the drinks cases, the defendant's product was inferior (for example, 'Advocaat' (**5.35**)). However, in 'Swiss Chalet' (see **5.19**), the defendant's chocolate was not necessarily inferior. A related head of damage is where the defendant sells the claimant's inferior goods as if they were superior (*Spalding* (see **5.3**)). In *Gillette v Edenwest* (1994), the plaintiff was entitled to damages where the defendant had unwittingly sold counterfeit Gillette blades.

Damage by association

5.55   Here, damage is caused by the defendant's misrepresentation that there is some connection between the parties. In these cases, the claimant's reputation may be damaged without the defendant's receiving a corresponding gain ('Harrods'). Where the quality of the defendant's reputation is inferior to that of the claimant, the courts may be more ready to assume the likelihood of damage. In *Annabel's v Schock* (1972), the plaintiff, who ran a well-known and 'respectable' night club, won an injunction against the defendant, who had set up an escort agency, also named 'Annabels'. While escort agencies are not illegal, the CA recognised that they had 'an indifferent public image' which might affect the plaintiff's reputation. There are also examples where the defendant's reputation is not necessarily inferior to that of the claimant, but the court has recognised a risk that, as was put by Millett LJ, in 'Harrods', the plaintiff may nonetheless 'lose control over his own reputation' (see also *Warwick Tyre v New Motor & General Rubber* (1910)). One risk might, of course, be that the defendant's reputation will deteriorate in the future because some, at present, unforeseen 'evil might befall' him. For instance, in *British Legion v British Legion Club (Street)* (1931), the defendant opened a British Legion club in Street which was not connected to the national organisation, which ran its own clubs. It was suggested by the court that if 'evil befell' the defendant in the future, for instance if it were in trouble over licensing laws, the plaintiff might suffer damage. In *Lego*, it was suggested that a customer dissatisfied with the defendant's garden equipment may not buy the plaintiff's bricks.

Damage for loss of distinctiveness

5.56 In the extended form of passing off, the damage to the claimant's goodwill may be caused directly through lost sales to the defendant or indirectly through the damage to the reputation of the mark in question. In 'Advocaat', Lord Diplock recognised these two forms of damage. The plaintiffs' trade and goodwill would suffer directly in the loss of sales and indirectly in the debasement of the reputation attaching to the name 'Advocaat'. What is notable about Lord Diplock's formulation is that although the damage may be direct or indirect, it is still damage to the claimants' goodwill which is at issue. The persistent question is whether the extended form of passing off may be said to go further and offer a remedy purely for loss of distinctiveness in the mark itself. In other words, does it protect against 'dilution' of the reputation in the name or other indicia. Key to the dilution approach is that there is no need for public confusion for such damage to occur. In the 'Elderflower champagne' case (see above **5.36**), the CA recognised that the plaintiff would suffer damage both from public confusion that the defendant's product was champagne or that there was some connection between the parties' drinks. However, Gibson LJ went further to state that if defendant was allowed to market Elderflower Champagne, 'there would take place a blurring or erosion of the uniqueness that now attends the word 'champagne' so that the exclusive reputation of the champagne houses would be debased.' In the same case, Sir Thomas Bingham MR appeared to endorse this argument, although it was probably obiter. Some take the view that the decision in 'Elderflower' marked a new departure for passing off (Russell 'The Elderflower Champagne Case: Is This a Further Expansion of the Tort of Passing Off?' (1993) EIPR 379). In 'Harrods', Millet LJ warned that although erosion of a mark's distinctiveness has been recognised as a form of damage to the plaintiff's goodwill in the business to which the name is connected, care should be taken to ensure that it did become an 'unacceptable' extension to passing off. He went on to observe that his discomfort arose from the fact that the degeneration of a distinctive brand name into a generic term is not necessarily dependant upon confusion although the law of passing off which 'insists both upon the presence of confusion and damage'. By contrast, in his dissenting judgment, Sir Michael Kerr suggested that the reputation in a trader's name may be such that it constitutes part of the goodwill of his trade, and may therefore be in the nature of a property interest. A recent CA case to canvas this same territory was *BT v One in Million* (see **5.28**). The CA held that the registration of distinctive names, such as 'Marks & Spencer' made a representation to persons who consulted the register that the registrant was connected or associated with the name registered, and thus to the owner of the goodwill in the name. This amounted to passing off. Damage lay in an erosion of the exclusive goodwill in the name. It is difficult not to see this decision as recognising that passing off actions may protect the goodwill in a name as such, without any obvious evidence of confusion, and it is submitted that it goes beyond the cautious approach to dilution taken, by Millett LJ, in the 'Harrod's' decision. The extent to which trade mark registration is intended to protect against dilution is considered in Chapter 6 (**6.5** et seq).

Defences to passing off

5.57 The three most important defences in a passing off action are:

. use of own name

. honest concurrent use

. delay.

Each of these are looked at below.

Use of own name

5.58 The general rule is that a trader cannot use his own name if the effect would be to pass off his goods as those of another. This is true even if the use is innocent. There is a very limited defence (and exactly how limited is a matter for debate) that a trader may use his own name as a trade name, even if there is confusion as a result (*Rodgers v Rodgers* (1924); also *Parker-Knoll v Knoll International* (1962). Furthermore, use must be of the defendant's full name and not of nicknames or abbreviations (*Biba Group v Biba Boutique* (1980)). Companies are even less likely to succeed with this defence. Interestingly, the TMA 1994 allows a broader defence. Use of by a person of his own name and address will not infringe a registered trade mark, provided the use is in accordance with honest business practices. Such use also extends to companies (on trade marks, see **6.71**).

Honest concurrent use

5.59 Sometimes two traders may use a name or mark concurrently. If the name or mark is distinctive of both traders (rather than having lost its distinctiveness altogether as a result) then a situation may arise in which the law recognises the right of both traders to continue such use. In *Habib Bank v Habib* (1981), the court found that where two traders had concurrently made use of the same name, there may be 'a factual situation in which neither of them can be said to be guilty of any misrepresentation.' Clearly, where concurrent use is long-standing, a claimant may find it difficult to prove either an operative misrepresentation or the likelihood of damage.

Delay

5.60 There is no 'time limit' for bringing a passing off action, as long as the claimant can prove all the elements of passing off. However, if a claimant delays, he may find it more difficult to persuade the court both that there is an operative misrepresentation or that there is the likelihood of damage. In *Bulmer v Bollinger* (1972), the champagne houses failed to prevent the defendant from using the name 'champagne perry' for cider, a name which it had used for 18 years, because the plaintiffs were unable to show that, in all that time, there had been any confusion or that they had suffered any damage because of the defendant's actions. In some circumstances, delay by the claimant may give rise to a defence of acquiescence or estoppel, if the claimant's actions, on the particular facts of the case, are found by the court to have been 'unconscionable' or 'inequitable' *(Habib)*.

Character merchandising

5.61 Character merchandising involves merchandising products by reference to real or fictional characters. Over the past decades, it has become an ever more profitable global activity. A number of countries, including the US, have introduced separate publicity rights for famous individuals. In the UK, however, those who engage in character merchandising have most frequently resorted to the law of passing off to protect their interests. One reason for this has been the limited protection which the Trade Mark Act 1938 (TMA 1938), which preceded the present TMA 1994, offered character merchandisers. Under the TMA 1938, trade mark proprietors were forbidden to traffic in their marks. In effect, this provision prevented merchandisers from registering famous names or characters as trade marks if their intention was to deal in the marks primarily as commodities in their own right, rather than to identify or promote merchandise in which they were interested (*Re American Greetings Corpn's Application* (1984)). There were also stringent restrictions on the licensing of marks. It was assumed, before its passage, that the TMA 1994 would offer more extensive protection to character merchandisers, by sweeping away the anti-trafficking provisions and allowing registration of marks for licensing purposes alone. Although these changes have widened the area of legal protection offered to character merchandising, the *Elvis Presley Trade Marks* (1999) decision suggests that the protection offered under trade mark law remains limited and passing off will continue to play a role (discussed in relation to trade marks at **6.96**).

Character merchandising and passing off: the basis for protection

5.62   It is important to remember that in UK law there is no protection offered to a name or even a fictional character 'as such'. There can be no copyright in a name (*Du Boulay v Du Boulay* (1869)). To succeed in passing off, it is necessary to demonstrate not only that there is a material misrepresentation, but also that there is goodwill, that is an economic interest which will be damaged. It is quite possible for an individual to have a business to which his name is connected and in which his goodwill can be damaged. For instance, cases which involve false attribution of authorship may be placed in this category. In the 'Alan Clark diaries' case, it was his reputation and goodwill as an author which was put at risk by the defendant's parody and so too were prospective sales of his published works and the market value of his rights to exploit his works (see also, *Marengo*). The problem has been that not all famous people or indeed those who create fictional characters can show a business with goodwill, even as they may wish to complain that the use of a name or character, the same or similar to their own, implies a connection or even an endorsement that does not exist.

Character merchandising: the common field of activity

5.63   In passing off cases, until relatively recently, the courts have sought to identify a common field of activity between the real character or the merchandising of a fictional character and the defendant. In the early case of *McCulloch*, Uncle Mac, a children's radio presenter, tried to restrain the defendant from selling a breakfast cereal also named 'Uncle Mac'. He failed because the court could find no common field of activity between the plaintiff and the defendant. In later cases, the need for a common field of activity continued to restrict the protection given in passing off. In *Wombles v Wombles Skips* (1977), the plaintiff owned the copyright in the books and drawings of the Wombles, fictional characters known for their tidiness. The plaintiff's business was to licence copyright reproductions. The defendant leased skips under name 'Wombles Skips Ltd.' The plaintiff unsuccessfully argued that use of the Womble name by the defendant was bound to lead some to believe the defendant was connected to the plaintiff. The HC held that there had to be a common field of activity or one that a reasonable man might assume, and that there was none in this case. An important consideration for the court was that the name only was taken. It has been argued that the court might have taken another line if the Womble image was also used by the defendant. In *Tavener Routledge v Trexapalm* (1977), the defendant company was licensed by the producers of a popular television series featuring the detective, Kojak, well known for his affection for lollipops, to use the name Kojak on merchandise, including Kojak Lollies. It was sued by the plaintiff company which sold 'Kojakpops', in which it had built up considerable goodwill and reputation, but without a licence from the creators. The plaintiffs succeeded. Again it was held that there was no copyright in the name as such, even though it was an invented one. Furthermore, the court could find no common field of activity between the television company which licensed the name and the plaintiff confectioners. The court held that it was not enough to show that the public would think that the television company had given a license to the plaintiff. The public must also assume the licensed goods would be of a certain quality. However, Walton J did suggest that in future, as the public became more familiar with character merchandising, a simple misrepresentation that the plaintiff had licensed the defendant might be sufficient.

Character merchandising: the move away from a common field

5.64   In 'Advocaat', it was made plain that there is no need for a common field of activity to succeed in passing off. Similarly, the trend in character merchandising cases has been to move away from a common field of activity to look instead for an operative misrepresentation. This was the approach taken by the CA in *Stringfellow*. The plaintiff, Peter Stringfellow, owned a famous nightclub, 'Stringfellow'. The defendant manufactured oven-ready chips named 'Stringfellows', advertised by a boy dancing in a kitchen with 'disco' lighting. The CA looked for an operative misrepresentation and held there may have been some members of the public who would think the two were connected. However, because there was no evidence that the plaintiff had been able to exploit any merchandising rights in his name, he was unable to prove damage and the action failed. Here the absence of a common field of activity was still relevant, because its absence meant the court was less likely to find confusion, and therefore damage.

Character merchandising: the 'Ninja Turtles' case

5.65   The *Stringfellow* decision pointed the way to *Mirage Studios v Counter-Feat Clothing* (1991). The plaintiffs licensed the reproduction of fictitious humanoid cartoon characters, the 'Teenage Mutant Ninja Turtles', but manufactured no goods themselves. The unfortunately-named defendant made drawings of humanoid turtle characters using the concept but not copying the plaintiff's drawings, and licensed them for use on clothing. The plaintiff sued for copyright infringement and passing off. The court held there was a case to answer in passing off. Echoing the prediction in the 'Kojak' case, Browne-Wilkinson VC took the view that the public would be aware of the licensing industry and would assume a connection between the plaintiff and the defendant. Accordingly, the operative misrepresentation was that the reproduction on the defendant's goods had been licensed by the plaintiff. However, since they were not, the goods were not 'genuine'. The damage was to the image, which by being placed on inferior goods would the reduce value of the plaintiff's licensing rights. The licensing business in the copyright was held to have the relevant goodwill.

5.66   In his judgment, Browne-Wilkinson VC approved a line of Australian cases, which, as early as 1969, had rejected the need for a common field of activity in passing off cases involving character merchandising. In the Australian cases, it had been sufficient that there had been wrongful appropriation of a plaintiff's reputation by falsely representing that he had endorsed a product. This was the position in *Henderson v Radio Corpn* (1969), where the plaintiffs were well-known ballroom dancers, who had not so far licensed their name or image. The defendant used their picture, without a license, on a gramophone record, 'Strictly Dancing'. In finding for the plaintiffs, who had alleged passing off, the court held that there was no need to show a common field of activity or damage. This principle was extended to fictional characters in *Hogan v Koala Dundee* (1988) and *Pacific Dunlop v Hogan* (1989)) where the character in question was 'Crocodile Dundee'. In the latter case, a television advertisement for shoes caricatured a knife-fight scene from the film, 'Crocodile Dundee'. In its judgment, the court held that there was no need for the public even to assume a licensing relationship for passing off to succeed. Passing off was established, merely because an erroneous belief was created that the plaintiff may have approved the advertisement. It is submitted that the 'Ninja Turtles' decision actually stopped far short of the Australian destination. The operative misrepresentation in the 'Ninja Turtles' case was the public's assumption that there was a licensing arrangement between the parties. The second 'Crocodile Dundee' case jettisoned the need even for such a minimal assumption.

Beyond the 'Ninja Turtles'

5.67   It is possible to distinguish the 'Ninja Turtles' case from earlier passing off decisions involving character merchandising, because the plaintiff's business was licensing not just a name or an image but a piece of intellectual property, that is the copyright in the turtle drawings. In *Elvis Presley,* the CA confirmed that it was this fact that was the distinguishing feature of the 'Ninja Turtles' decision and also the basis for its limited application (see **6.97** for a discussion of the trade marks issue). In *Elvis Presley*, the estate of the late singer sought to register his name for use on toiletries. The CA refused registration on the grounds that the names, Elvis and Elvis Presley, were too descriptive to function as trade marks. It also took the opportunity to comment on the implications of the 'Ninja Turtles' case. In his leading judgment, Walker LJ rejected the idea, advanced by the applicant, that following the 'Ninja

Turtles', it was now a general rule that a trader should not make unauthorised use of the name of a well-known person or character on his merchandise. Walker LJ emphasised that the 'Ninja Turtles' decision was justified only on its particular facts, of which the most important was that the plaintiff had copyright in the drawings and a substantial business in licensing them. Another clear implication of the *Elvis Presley* judgment was that, in character merchandising cases, the claimant will still need to show that the public will assume a licensing connection between the parties. It will not be taken for granted by the courts. The *Elvis Presley* decision confirmed the approach taken in *Halliwell v Panini* (1997), a HC case involving the Spice Girls. The defendant published an 'unofficial' sticker collection, consisting of photographs of the girl band, entitled 'The Fab Five'. The band was unable to obtain an injunction preventing its distribution. According to the court, it did not believe that members of the public would buy the collection believing that it was authorised by the plaintiffs

Remedies

5.68 Passing off actions may be brought in the CC and the HC, although in *McCain*, the CA took the view that the most appropriate forum was the Chancery Division of the HC. As in other actions involving intellectual property, a claimant who brings a passing off action is interested first and foremost in stopping the defendant's activities as quickly as possible. Damages will usually be a secondary consideration. If the claimant is successful in obtaining an interim injunction, it unlikely that the case will continue to trial. Usually, the defendant, whatever his own view about the rights and wrongs of the case, will prefer to change his marketing approach rather than to refrain from marketing the product until the issues are resolved at trial. If passing off is proved, the usual remedies, damages, delivery up, and so on, are available.

Actions for passing off and trade mark infringement

5.69 The protection offered by registered trade marks is generally considered superior to that offered by passing off, particularly now that trade mark protection extends to include shapes, noises, smells (indeed, any sign that can be represented graphically). Trade mark registration endows its proprietor with exclusive use of the mark. By contrast, for a passing-off action to succeed, it is, of course, necessary for Lord Oliver's trilogy to be present. Nonetheless, passing off remains a useful adjunct to an action for trade mark infringement, and the two are often combined. Typically, this is because in trade mark actions, it is open to the defendant to argue in its defence that the trade mark at issue is invalid or should be revoked. If the defendant is successful, it may yet be possible for the claimant to fall back on the claim in passing off.

Further reading

Wadlow *The Law of Passing Off* (2nd edn, 1995)

Murray 'A Distinct Lack of Goodwill' [1997] EIPR 345

Carty 'Character merchandising and the limits of passing off' [1993] LS 289

Jones 'Manipulating the Law Against Misleading Imagery' [1999] EIPR 28

Self-test questions

1. 'Firenzo' is a cheap and cheerful sparkling wine produced in Northern Italy by a number of producers. It is sold in brown glass bottles with a pinched waist, although different producers have different labels. It is very popular in the UK. Three years ago a UK company, X, started selling 'Florenzo' wine, which is also cheap but is it not sparkling. It too is sold in a brown glass bottles with a pinched waist. However the labels are identical on all the bottles, and show the name 'Florenzo' clearly. Over the years the popularity of 'Florenzo' has increased and it is now sold in large numbers. Advise whether the producers of 'Firenzo' can bring an action for passing off against X.

2. To what extent has passing off moved beyond protecting damage to the claimant's goodwill to protect against other forms of 'unfair' competition?

3. Discuss the development of passing off in relation to character merchandising.

CHAPTER SIX

Trade marks

SUMMARY

The Trade Marks Act 1994 and the function of trade marks

Domestic registration and the routes to international protection

The definition of a trade mark

Absolute grounds for refusal of registration

Relative grounds for refusal of registration

Infringement, comparative advertising and exclusions from trade mark protection

Losing the mark: revocation and invalidity

Licensing, assignments and character merchandising

Civil and criminal remedies

Trade marks and the international context: exhaustion of rights, common origin and competition law

Introduction: the law and function of trade marks

6.1   Trade mark law in the UK is governed by the Trade Marks Act 1994 (TMA 1994). Registered trade marks were introduced into the UK by the Trade Marks Act of 1875. The TMA 1994 represented the first major overhaul of trade mark law in almost 50 years, replacing the Trade Marks Act 1938 (TMA 1938). It incorporates into UK law the First Council Directive of 21 December 1989 to approximate the laws of the member states relating to trade marks (89/104/EEC)(the TM Directive). The TMA 1994 is organised into four parts. Part I covers substantive trade mark law and much of its wording is taken verbatim from the

Directive. Part II deals with international matters, including the Community Trade Mark (CTM), the Madrid Protocol and the Paris Convention for the Protection of Industrial Property. Parts III and IV include administrative, supplementary and general provisions relating the Registry's powers, to legal proceedings and definitions.

6.2   Because the TMA 1994 implements the TM Directive, it would be fair to say that it is the protection of trade marks, of all the intellectual property rights, which is now the most uniform across the EU (and the EEA). The move towards a uniform EU trade mark regime has been further encouraged by the introduction of the CTM, since in both the case of the CTM and national laws implementing the TM Directive, the final word in interpretation lies with the ECJ (for instance, see Volker and Schuster 'Community Trade Marks and Absolute Grounds for Refusal [2000] Parts 1 and 2, TMW 24 (No 124) and 22 (No 125)). Furthermore, although there have always been some trade marks whose fame crosses national boundaries, 'Coca Cola' springs to mind, an ever-growing number of trade marks are coming to have broad international recognition. The impact of e-commerce is an important but by no means unique factor behind the internationalisation of brands. Despite these developments, however, trade mark protection remains essentially territorial in extent. UK law applies almost exclusively to trade marks registered in the UK. Furthermore, the UK courts have at times followed a markedly different approach to interpreting the TMA 1994 than their European colleagues have taken with respect to similar legislation. There is thus a growing tension between the increasingly international character of brands and the essentially national character of trade mark protection. This tension has inevitably inflected the way trade mark law has developed since the passage of the TMA 1994, no more so than in the intense debate over which of the trade mark's functions the law should recognise and protect.

The function of trade mark protection: (i) an indictor of origin

6.3   Traditionally, the justification for trade mark protection has been to protect the trade mark's function as an indicator of origin of the goods and services to which it attaches. This means, at its simplest, that the registered trade mark X on a soft drink should reliably tell the consumer that all drinks marked X originate from a single proprietor and not from any other enterprise. This protection is taken to be both for the benefit

204

of the proprietor against his competitors and as a guarantee of quality for the buying public. The essential function of registered trade marks and their specific subject matter (ie the rights conferred on the proprietor by registration) have been confirmed by the ECJ in a number of cases (for example, *Hoffman-La Roche v Centrafarm* (1978) and *IHT v Ideal Standard* (1994)). They were summarised by the Advocate-General in *Bristol-Meyers Squibb v Paranova* (1996):

> In so far as the trade mark protects the interest of its proprietor by enabling him to prevent competitors from taking unfair advantage of his commercial reputation, the exclusive rights conferred on the proprietor are said, in the language of the Court's case law, to constitute the specific subject-matter of the trade mark. In so far as the trade mark protects the interest of consumers by acting as a guarantee that all goods bearing the mark are of the same commercial origin, this is known in the Court's terminology, as the essential function of the trade mark. These two aspects of trade mark protection are of course two sides of the same coin.

6.4   In recent years, the role of the trade marks in the market place has substantially changed. For a number of reasons, the perceived link between many trade marks and the origin of the goods or services to which they attach is becoming increasingly attenuated. For example, the TMA 1994 made licensing of trade marks and assignments substantially easier (**6.94** et seq). For another, the ownership of many well-known brands is becoming concentrated in a relatively small number of companies, many of which operate across national boundaries. For instance, it has been reckoned that just three companies account for the ownership of nearly one third of all branded products sold in UK supermarkets. As a result the trade mark X on a soft drink may not mean it is produced by X Soft Drinks Ltd but by its brand owner, a large multinational, which may also produce a number of competing brands as well as the supermarket's 'own brand' product. Secondly, the role of the trade mark as a guarantor of quality is also arguably less crucial to a wide range of goods and services. One impetus for early trade mark legislation had been to enable the consumer to choose between products of a certain quality which carried a known trade mark and others of more dubious (and in the case of food stuffs, occasionally fatal) attributes. However, consumer legislation has ensured, that, in many countries, the public can expect a certain minimum quality for a wide range of goods and services, whatever mark attaches to them. As a result, the competition

205

between goods and services has increasingly come to reside not in their differing quality but in the relative attractiveness of the trade marks they carry. An obvious example is the competition between different athletic shoes (many of which are made in the same third-world factories) which is based on the wide range of associations which their trade marks carry, beyond the simple message of where they originate.

The function of trade mark protection: (ii) brand attractiveness

6.5   Many insist that it is now common sense to recognise this second and ever more important function of trade marks, that is their publicity value or reputation. They point out that increasingly, trade marks will attract the consumer through these 'extrinsic' qualities, which go beyond their 'intrinsic' function as indicators of origin. Furthermore, marks which have acquired such extrinsic qualities may be extremely valuable, even more so if they are internationally recognised. Indeed, the extrinsic attractiveness of a mark is often acquired only as the result of vast and expensive advertising campaigns, with again the relationship between athletic shoes and major sporting events being a case in point. It is scarcely surprising, therefore, that the most intense debate in relation to the TM Directive has been over the extent to which it intended to give protection to the extrinsic publicity value of trade marks as divorced from their function as indicators of origin. It is a debate that will figure largely in the chapter which follows. But it is perhaps useful to begin with a brief background.

6.6   In the Benelux countries, the Uniform Benelux Trade Mark Law, even before the implementation of the TM Directive, recognised this second function of trade marks. It introduced the concept of 'dilution' into trade mark protection. Registered trade marks would be protected in situations where the public was not confused as to the origins of two identical or similar marks. Under Benelux law, registered trade marks would also be protected where the use of two identical or similar marks created a simple association in the public mind between one mark and another, because such an association might be detrimental to the first registered mark's exclusivity or diminish its attractiveness and hence 'dilute' its reputation and therefore its value. Many commentators insist that it is simply good sense to recognise this altered role for trade marks and to follow the Benelux approach throughout the EEA. Others take the view that this would give far too much opportunity to wealthy owners of famous brands to corner large areas of language and shapes, and that

206

it would be anti-competitive. Unfortunately, the wording of the TM Directive was ambiguous as to the extent to which it was intended to introduce 'dilution' into EU trade mark law, perhaps because member states were and are themselves divided. Hence, the debate as to which way the law will fall has been central to interpreting the TM Directive and, in the UK, the TMA 1994.

Trade marks and the public interest

6.7   Trade mark registration places under private control for an indefinite period certain uses of the mark which would previously have been available to society at large. The monopoly will only bite if the proprietor uses the mark in the course of trade (for instance, a private individual may still use the colour green for his living room wall, even though only BP may have exclusive use of it for service stations). Nonetheless, such use is no longer commonly available. As has been suggested, the creation of trade mark monopolies has been justified by the benefit to the public of knowing the trade origins of the goods they buy and to proprietors (who may have invested a good deal in the promotion of their marks) of being able to prevent others trading on their reputations (*Bristol-Meyers Squibb v Paranova*, **6.3** above). Nonetheless, in the past, successive TM Acts have been based on the assumption that the public interest and trading interests may not always coincide and have sought to hold a balance between them. For instance, under the TMA 1938, the conditions for licensing trade marks were tightly controlled to protect the trade mark's role as an indicator of origin. There were also significant limits to the category of signs which could be registered as trade marks. For example, shapes were excluded from registration on the basis that they should be freely available for public use. In general, the UK courts adopted a similar balancing approach in interpreting the legislation. In *Coca Cola Trademarks* (1985), the CA refused registration of the Coca Cola bottle even though it was clearly acting as an indicator of origin. In part, its decision was based on a conviction that giving indefinite protection to functional objects such as containers was against the public interest. By contrast the TMA 1994, which was framed during a period when free trade and unrestricted competition represented the economic orthodoxy, gives proprietors a largely free hand in dealing with their marks. With very few exceptions, it also allows the registration of any sign, including shapes, so long as it is acting as a trade mark, that is as an indicator of origin, in the market. Some have argued that an increasingly unrestricted trade mark regime will create broad monopolies with little concern for the general public good. Others take the view that it is in the self-interest of proprietors to maintain their marks as indicators of origin, without the prodding of government regulation.

Interpreting the TMA 1994

6.8   The TMA 1938 was a consolidation Act which drew together the fruits of previous legislation and judicial decisions. By contrast, the TMA 1994 introduces new legal principles, many of which were framed at the EU level. The courts have taken a purposive approach to interpreting the TMA 1994, assuming that it must be construed in a manner consistent with its EU origins and purposes (*Procter & Gamble's Trade Mark Applications* (1999)). In interpreting those provisions which incorporate the TM Directive, the courts have generally looked for guidance to the TM Directive, itself, and not to earlier domestic case law nor to evidence of domestic government intent (*Wagamama v City Centre Restaurants* (1995)).

6.9   Nonetheless, cases decided under previous trade mark legislation will continue, in some circumstances, to have relevance if not authority. The TM Directive is a collection of broad statements of substantive law, but individual member states have a relatively free procedural hand. Previous domestic case law will apply when dealing with procedural issues, such as in determining which marks or goods are 'similar'. Previous case law and reference to Parliamentary sources will also be relevant to interpreting provisions of the TMA 1994 which have a purely domestic origin. In *Philips v Remington* (1999), Aldous LJ summarised the general approach to interpretation taken by the UK courts. He observed:

> That new law, drafted with input from representatives of the Member States, should not be assumed to be the same as the old UK law nor to be different from it. The law must be determined from the Act construed in the light of the Directive. Cases decided under the old law are no longer authoritative. However, knowledge of the reasoning in such cases can provide awareness of the types of problems that arise during use of trade marks and a general feel for them.

Registration

6.10   In the case of domestic applications, these are made to the Trade

Mark Registry (TMR). They include a representation of the mark and a list of the goods or services, with which the proprietor intends to use the mark. Goods and services have been classified into classes, periodically updated by WIPO. For example, Class 23 represents yarns and threads for textile use. It is possible to register a mark in respect of goods or services in one or any number of classes, as well as only some of the goods or services within a single class. The filing date of the application is generally that mark's 'priority date'. If the application is successful, the filing date becomes the date of registration and the rights endowed by registration, such as to pursue infringers, backdates to the filing date.

6.11 The TMR will examine the mark to determine whether it falls foul of the absolute grounds for refusal of registration (see **6.18** et seq), or conflicts with any marks with an earlier priority date (see **6.33** et seq). If the mark passes the examination stage, it will be advertised in the 'Trade Mark Journal'. At this stage, an opposition may be entered against it, for instance by a party which, seeing the advertisement, believes that it has a conflicting mark. Conflict will be resolved either at TMR level, or in the HC. If there is no opposition, the trade mark will proceed to registration. Initial registration is for 10 years, but may be renewed an indefinite number of times thereafter.

Collective and certification marks

6.12 The proprietor of the mark is likely to be the intended user of the mark, although he may assign or licence it. There are two exceptions. A certification mark is held by an association that must not trade in the goods or services itself. The mark indicates that the goods or services of the members of the association are certified to be of a certain quality (s 50). Examples are the 'Woolmark' or 'Harris Tweed'. The collective mark (s 49 and Sch 1) is also likely to be held by an association. Its purpose is to distinguish the goods and services of its members from those of other undertakings. It may for instance be held by an association of tradesmen, such as stationers, a professional body with a common field of activity, or traders from a particular area.

International protection

6.13 There are two routes to protecting a trade mark abroad through a single application. First, under the Madrid Protocol, to which the UK acceded in 1996, it is possible to obtain protection for a UK trade mark in any of the 29 or so countries which are parties to the Protocol, and the Madrid Agreement from which it derives, by a single application made through the national trade mark office to WIPO for an International Registration (IR). The examination of the mark, rules for opposition and infringement will be those of the countries to which the IR extends. If the application fails in one country designated by the applicant it may nonetheless be registered in any of the others. The second is the CTM which was introduced in 1996. The CTM is distinct from national registration. It is a separate unitary mark covering all the countries in the EC. An application is made through the national trade mark registry or direct to the Community Trade Marks Office in Alicante (OHIM). However, because the CTM is a unitary mark, if an application is successfully opposed because of a prior mark in one member state, the application will fail. The Council Regulation of 20 December 1993 (40/94/EEC) sets out the terms of the CTM. The conditions of registerability and infringement are in most important respects the same as those of the TM Directive and hence the UK's own trade marks regime. In cases of infringement, a national court is designated to hear cases in the first instance, with appeals going to the ECJ. Since its introduction, the CTM has proved popular and increasingly the ECJ has been called in to settle questions of interpretation, in decisions which will inevitably have an impact on domestic trade mark law.

The definition of a trade mark

6.14   The TMA 1994 defines a trade mark as 'any sign capable of being represented graphically which is capable of distinguishing the goods or services of one undertaking from those of other undertakings' (s 1(1)). To understand this definition, it is useful to break it down into its three constituent parts:

- any sign

- capable of being represented graphically

- capable of distinguishing the goods and services of one undertaking from those of others.

Any sign

6.15   The sign is the subject matter of a registered trade mark. For instance, the word 'Nike' or the 'swoosh' with which that company marks its goods are signs. Any sign may serve as a trade mark provided it can be represented graphically and does not fall foul of the absolute grounds for refusal of registration, which are looked at below (**6.18**). The TMA 1994 continues: 'A trade mark may, in particular, consist of words (including personal names), designs, letters, numerals or the shape of goods or their packaging.' This is an open-ended list. It demonstrates the new, expansive scope of the TMA 1994, since earlier TM Acts had limited what could be registered as a trade mark (for instance, excluding shapes). Applications have been made to register the shapes of containers (the 'Coca Cola' bottle), the shapes of goods ('Toblerone' triangular chocolate), slogans, radio jingles, and sensory marks such as colours, smells, sounds and even gestures. To some, this open-ended definition of what may constitute the subject matter of a trade mark registration represents the unacceptable appropriation of signs into private ownership which have been in common use in the past. Others argue that traders have, anyway, had a de facto monopoly of a multitude of signs (including shapes) through the common law protection offered by passing off. The 'Jif' lemon is an obvious example (*Reckitt & Coleman v Borden*, see **5.20**).

Capable of being represented graphically

6.16   Marks must be capable of graphic representation so that the TMR can easily record and search for them and so that they can be advertised in a two-dimensional form. In *Swizzels Matlow Ltd's Trade Mark Application* (1999), the applicant sought to register a trade mark consisting of a 'a chewy sweet on a stick'. The Registrar held that the application did not comply with acceptable forms of graphical representation, because it did not define what was distinctive about the mark with sufficient precision. Since it would not be possible to understand the mark precisely without reference to a sample of the goods, the mark was not capable of being represented graphically and so did not satisfy s 1(1). By contrast, the OHIM has accepted that the 'smell of freshly cut grass' for tennis balls was sufficient to fulfil the requirement of 'graphic representation' and the scent was registered.

Capable of distinguishing the goods and services of one undertaking from that of other undertakings

6.17 All signs (except a very few absolutely excluded on public interest grounds (**6.29** et seq) are deemed capable in *principle* of distinguishing the goods or services of a particular trader from those of any other trader. Whether or not a sign will actually succeed in being registered depends upon whether it is capable, in *practice*, of being distinctive of a particular trader's goods or services, that is to consumers in the market place. For example, two boxes of soap powder, one red displaying the word 'Soap' in white and one green displaying the word 'Soap' in black will, of course, be distinguishable from each other. But s 1(1) will only be satisfied if the designs of these boxes distinguishes for the public the goods of one particular trader from any other trader. It is up to the applicant to persuade the TMR or the courts that his sign is capable of functioning as a trade mark. The task will be easier with an entirely invented word (a strong mark) such as 'Kodak' but harder with one which is essentially descriptive of the product (a weak mark). In *Philips v Remington* (1998), Jacob J suggested that for certain signs there may be a 'factual' (or practical) bar preventing them from ever really being sufficiently distinctive to satisfy s 1(1). According to Jacob J the test is to ask whether, no matter how much the sign may be used and recognised, can it really serve to convey in substance the message: 'here are a particular trader's goods'. In the case of purely descriptive signs, as in *Philips*, the facts of which are set out below, the answer may always be a negative (see **6.19**). The categories of signs (and marks) for which it is necessary to prove distinctiveness in practice, before they will be registered, are identified in s 3 of the TMA 1994, to which this chapter now turns.

Absolute grounds for refusal of registration (s 3)

6.18 The basic approach of the TM Directive and the TMA 1994 is that any sign which is de facto operating as a trade mark in the market place, that is acting as an indicator of origin, can be registered, although there are some signs which, on public interest grounds, should not be registrable at all or should be registerable only in certain limited circumstances. This latter category of marks is identified in s 3 which sets out the absolute grounds for refusal of registration. They are absolute because it is the nature of the mark itself which renders it inappropriate for registration, not the mark's relationship with other marks (as in the relative grounds for refusal listed in s 5 (**6.33** et seq)). Section 3 covers three categories of marks (and signs):

- signs which do not satisfy the requirements of s 1(1) and so cannot be registered (s 3(1)(a))

- trade marks which shall not be registered unless, according to the proviso, by the date of application they have 'in fact acquired a distinctive character through use' (the proviso) (s 3(1)(b)-(d))

- trade marks which shall not be registered because registration would be against the public interest (s 3(2)-(6)).

Each of these categories is considered below.

Signs which do not satisfy s 1(1)

6.19 Signs which are not capable of distinguishing the goods or services of one undertaking from those of other undertakings or which cannot be represented graphically cannot be registered. The CA addressed the meaning of s 3(1)(a) in *Philips v Remington* (1999). The facts were these. Philips had marketed a three-headed rotary shaver with the heads arranged in an equilateral triangle since 1966. In 1985, it registered a picture of this face for electric shavers. The design is not now protected by patent. Nonetheless, until the defendant began marketing its own rotary shaver with a similar head design, but with the mark 'Remington' prominently displayed, rotary shavers were unique to Philips. Philips sued Remington for trade mark infringement and Remington claimed the Philips' registration was invalid. The parties agreed that the registration should be treated by the court as covering the three-dimensional shape of the head and was not just a pictorial representation of it. In the HC, the mark was held to be invalid because, inter alia, it was not capable of distinguishing the goods of one trader from another and the plaintiff appealed. The CA first considered whether the mark satisfied s 3(1)(a) and held that it did not. In essence, the CA accepted that the public generally associated the three-headed razor shape with Philips. However, since Philips had had an effective monopoly of three-headed shavers for many years, this did not mean that the shape was distinctive in a trade mark sense. Philips still had to establish that the shape had features which would distinguish it from those of a competitor who put similar goods on the market. The CA went on to say that the shape of an article could not be registered in respect of goods of that shape unless it contained some addition or 'capricious alteration' which made it capable of distinguishing those goods from the same sort of goods sold by someone else. It would be that addition which made it distinctive and so capable of registration. In this case, the primary meaning of the trade mark as it stood was a three-headed rotary shaver. There was no distinctive addition to the shape and it failed to fulfil the conditions of s 3(1)(a).

6.20   A similar approach has been taken at the European level. A CTM application which reached the ECJ was for 'Companyline' for insurance services (*Deutsche Krankenversicherung v OHIM* (2000)). The ECJ upheld the OHIM's decision to refuse registration on the grounds the mark was devoid of distinctive character. It held that the two words 'company' and 'line' were generic words, denoting a line of goods or services, and their coupling without any modification giving them a distinctive character meant they were incapable of distinguishing. It was irrelevant that the word 'Companyline' as such was made up.

6.21   The CA revisited s 3(1)(a) in *Bach Flower Remedies (BFRL) v Healing Herbs (HHL)* (2000). Dr Edward Bach developed a set of remedies made from flowers. He deliberately disseminated his work widely. After his death in 1936, The Bach Centre carried on his work and sold his remedies commercially. They also continued to make available literature which included recipes and methods of treatment. In 1993, BFRL took over the business. Meanwhile, eight marks which included either the word 'Bach' or the words 'Bach Flower Remedies' had been registered in 1979, 1989 and 1991. HHL had been selling remedies made up from Bach recipes since 1989. It sought to have the registrations declared invalid. In the HC, Neuberger J held that the marks 'Bach' and 'Bach Flower Remedies' were invalidly registered because they were descriptive at the time of registration and had not, since then, acquired distinctiveness through use under s 3(1)(c) (see **6.25** below). BFRL appealed. The CA also found the marks to have been invalidly registered but on different grounds. Aldous LJ held first that a sign must fulfil the requirement of s 3(1)(a), before it can meet any of the grounds for registration set out in s 3(1)(b)-(d). This the marks had failed to do. In particular, the CA agreed with the finding of the HC that from before their registration until the present, the words 'Bach' and 'Bach Flower Remedies' were the common, generic name for the remedies. Although 'Bach' had begun life as a proper name, like 'wellington boot' it had through use acquired a descriptive meaning and could not, without further capricious addition, be capable of distinguishing. The CA then went on to consider how the meaning of the words as used was to be judged. The usage in question was by those engaged in the relevant trade or activity and normally this would be the 'average consumer' of the goods in question. The description of the average consumer was taken by the CA from a case decided by the ECJ, *Lloyd Schuhfabrik Meyer v Klijsen Handel* (2000). In *Lloyd*, the average consumer was deemed to be reasonably well informed, reasonably observant and circumspect. According to the CA, the task of the court was to inform itself, through evidence, of what the average consumer would know and then to ask the question as to whether he would say the words in question were a badge of origin. In this case, the CA held that he would not.

Marks which must satisfy the proviso

6.22 Signs which cannot satisfy the provisions of s 1(1) cannot be registered under s 3(1)(a). Some marks may satisfy s 3(1)(a) but still cannot be registered unless they have satisfied the proviso. There are three categories of marks which must satisfy the proviso to be registered. These are:

- marks devoid of distinctive character (s 3(1)(b))

- descriptive marks (s 3(1)(c))

- generic or customary marks (s 3(1)(d)).

The CA in *Bach* held that a mark which falls into any of these categories will only be considered for registration once it has satisfied s 3(1)(a) (see **6.18** above). Each category of mark will now be considered in turn.

Marks devoid of distinctive character (s 3(1)(b))

6.23 There are some marks which are not prima facie distinctive, for instance a common surname such as Smith. These marks may nonetheless become associated by the public with a particular product, because of the way they are used in the market place. If they have become distinctive of a particular trader through use, they will have satisfied the proviso and can be registered. In an early case following the passage of the TMA 1994, *British Sugar v Robertson* (1996), Jacob J set out two criteria for distinctiveness. The mark must be incapable of application to any anyone else and it must possess enough character that people would generally regard it as indicating the provenance of goods or services. 'North Pole' for bananas would be inherently distinctive on both counts. Conversely, some marks can meet neither of these criteria without first educating the public that they are trade marks. An example would be a common laudatory term for a product such as 'Treat', which was the mark at issue in *British Sugar*. If however, these latter marks do go on to become distinctive of a particular trader by educating the public through use, they well have satisfied the proviso and can be registered. Such words become trade marks, in the oft-quoted words of Geoffrey Hobbs QC in *AD200 TM* (1997), through 'nurture' not 'nature'.

6.24   The meaning of 'devoid of distinctive character' was considered by the CA in *Proctor & Gamble*. This concerned an application in respect of cleaning preparations, for the registration of a combination of the three-dimensional shape of a bottle, a label (without any wording) and colour. It is clear the applicant's purpose was to register the 'get-up' of its packaging (in this case the bottles which held its cleaning products) without its brand name, in order to discourage supermarket 'look alikes' packaged in the same way (see **5.52**). The registry had rejected the application, and, on appeal, so did the HC. In the CA, Robert Walker LJ held that the context in which distinctiveness fell to be assessed was that of other traders in competition with each other in the market place and 'to whom Parliament wished to accord proper protection but not exorbitant monopoly'. It was necessary to look at a visible sign or combination of signs which could by itself readily distinguish one trader's product from that of another competing trader. If differences became apparent only on close examination and comparison, neither could be said to be distinctive. By these criteria, the applicant's mark was not inherently distinctive but typical of the get-up of household cleaning products. Since no evidence of acquired distinctiveness through use was offered, the appeal failed.

Descriptive marks (s 3(1)(c))

6.25   There are some marks which consist exclusively of signs or indications serving to designate the kind, quality, quantity, intended purpose, value, geographical origin, the time of production of the goods or rendering of services, or 'other characteristics of goods or services'. Examples might be 'Jumbo', 'Mini', 'Personal' or 'Best', '24 Hour Service', 'Slim 'n Fit' for a slimming preparation (designating the intended purpose). Such wholly descriptive marks will only be registered if they have satisfied the proviso, by acquiring distinctiveness through use. Examples of marks which have been refused registration under s 3(1)(c) include 'Froot Loops' for fruit flavoured cereal (*Froot Loops Trade Mark* (1998)), 'Coffeemix' for coffee preparations suitable for mixing (*Coffeemix Trade Mark* (1998)) and 'Treat' for ice cream toppings (*British Sugar*). An application for a CTM for 'Baby-Dry' for diapers was refused by OHIM (a decision upheld by the ECJ). In *Philips*, the CA found that even after use the three-headed shaver mark consisted exclusively of an indication of the kind of goods for which it was registered and of the intended purpose of those goods. Some geographical names are prima facie registrable because they attach to very small areas or areas having no reputation for particular goods. Others are registrable only if they satisfy the proviso. 'Eurolamb' was not registrable because, inter alia, it designated the geographical origin of the goods and had not satisfied the proviso by acquiring distinctiveness through use *(Eurolamb Trade Mark* (1997)). Other characteristics of goods or services may amount to descriptions common in the trade (such as a red cap or gold cap for whisky). Again the proviso would apply to these examples.

Assessing distinctiveness

6.26 How is acquired distinctiveness to be assessed? In *Bach*, the CA found that the marks 'Bach' and 'Bach Flower Remedies' could not satisfy s 1(1) and so were not capable of registration under s 3(1)(a). There was no saving proviso. However, it also looked, purely hypothetically, at a different question. Suppose s 3(1)(a) had been satisfied, could it be said that these marks, which all the parties agreed were descriptive at the time of registration had subsequently acquired sufficient distinctiveness through use to satisfy the proviso. Morritt LJ referred to the ECJ decision in *Windsurfing v Boots* (1999), which had considered the question of acquired distinctiveness. In *Windsurfing*, the ECJ had considered whether the name of a well-known Bavarian lake, 'Chiemsee', could be registered for sportswear. It decided it could if its geographical designation had gained a new significance so it was no longer descriptive but identified the trade origins of the product. It then set out the criteria for assessing acquired distinctiveness, including how widespread and long-standing the use of the mark had been, how it had been promoted and so on. Furthermore, it was necessary for a significant proportion of the 'average customers' to see the marks as distinctive. In *Bach*, following *Windsurfing*, Morritt LJ held that the mark did not have to be universally recognised as distinctive. However, if the meaning of the mark remained ambiguous to the average consumer in the sense that it could be either distinctive or descriptive, it did not satisfy s 3(1)(c). On the basis of these criteria, the CA found that, even hypothetically, the Bach marks had not acquired the necessary distinctiveness for registration.

Distinctiveness and use

6.27   It is clear that use of a mark does not equal distinctiveness. The relationship between distinctiveness and use had been looked at in *British Sugar*. In 1992, the plaintiff, British Sugar, had registered the word 'Treat' for a range of dessert sauces and syrups, although it had been using the name 'Treat' since 1986. In 1995, the validity of its registration was challenged during infringement proceedings. The HC held that although this was a popular product which had been sold for many years prior to and since registration, the mark 'Treat' was not recognised by the public in a trade mark sense 'as a badge of origin'.

Generic or customary marks (s 3(1)(d))

6.28   Marks which are customary in current language or in bona fide and established practices of trade cannot be registered unless they satisfy the proviso and have acquired distinctiveness through use. This section covers 'generic' names which may have begun as the mark of a particular proprietor but are now used by the public to describe a general category of goods. In *Bach*, in the HC, Neuberger J found that the marks 'offended' against s 3(1)(d). However, it is submitted that following the decision in the CA, it will be unusual for a mark which cannot comply with s 3(1)(d) to have passed the test for s 3(1)(a) (see also, *Jeryl Lynn TM* (1999)).

Marks against the public interest (s 3(2)-(6))

6.29   Marks against the public interest may not be registered under any circumstances. There are no provisos. The three main categories are:

218

- prohibited shapes

- marks contrary to public policy

- other prohibited marks.

Each of these will be examined in turn.

Prohibited shapes (s 3(2)(a)-(c))

6.30   Signs which consist exclusively of shapes which result from the nature of the goods, shapes intended to obtain a technical result and signs which consist exclusively of the shape which gives substantial value to the goods cannot be registered. These prohibitions address concerns that the extension of the trade mark monopoly to shapes might conflict with other rights, such as design rights, registered designs and patents, which offer more limited protection (*Philips* (1998) per Jacob J). Each of these exclusions was looked at by the CA in *Philips* (see **6.17** above). First the CA considered s 3(2)(a) and asked whether the registered mark (taken as a three-dimensional shape) consisted exclusively of the shape which results from the nature of the goods themselves. According to the CA, what constitutes the 'goods themselves' depends upon how they are viewed as articles of commerce. Here they would be viewed in the trade simply as a type of electric shaver (not necessarily a three-headed one), so the mark did not result from the nature of the goods since electric shavers come in diverse shapes. Second, the CA considered s 2(3)(b) and asked whether the shape was necessary to achieve a technical result. It took the view that the proper question to ask is does the shape solely achieve a technical result, whether or not other shapes may obtain the same result. It decided that it did, and therefore the registration fell foul of this section. (Interestingly, other European courts have come to an opposite conclusion, eg the Swedish case, *Ida Line AG v Philips* (1997) based on the same facts, and the ECJ has now been asked to adjudicate on the correct approach to the registration of functional shapes.) Third, the CA considered s 2(3)(c) and asked whether the shape gave substantial value to the goods. This was understood to mean did the shape add substantial value to the goods because it had eye appeal. Here the shape was no more appealing (in other words, had no more value) than other shapes of electric razors. The mark did not fall foul of s 3(2)(c).

Contrary to public policy (s 3(3)(a))

6.31 Marks which are contrary to public policy or to accepted principles of morality, such as marks likely to be deemed religiously offensive, racist, sexist or obscene are prohibited. The TMA 1938 had a similar prohibition, under which 'Hallelujah' was denied registration in 1976 (*Hallelujah Trade Mark* (1976)). In more recent times, French Connection Ltd has successfully registered 'FCUK' as a trade mark, although the mark has not necessarily found favour with members of the judiciary (*French Connection v Sutton* (2000)).

Other prohibited marks (s 3(3)(b)-3(6))

6.32 Deceptive marks are prohibited. In *Jeryl Lynn*, the respondents had registered 'Jeryl Lynn' as a trade mark for medicines generally. 'Jeryl Lynn' was actually the name of a specific mumps virus which had been isolated by the respondent, and used in a mumps vaccine. The applicants sought to have the mark declared invalid, inter alia, because it was the generic name for the virus. Laddie J held that the mark was invalid because it failed to satisfy s 3(1)(a). He also held that the mark was deceptive, because as it was generic and descriptive only of one particular virus. It could not be used on other products without misdescription. Marks which are contrary to UK or Community law are also prohibited (s 3(4)) and the royal coat of arms may not be registered (s 4). Finally, s 3(6) prohibits registration of a trade mark if or to the extent that the application is made in bad faith. Most commonly, the applicant is not the owner of the mark, perhaps he is a franchisee, or else he has no intention of using the mark or, at least, not in relation to all the goods he specifies (*Mickey Dees (Nightclub) Trade Mark* (1998)). There is no general test set for what constitutes bad faith, but in *Gromax v Don & Low* (1999) Lindsay J said that dealings made in bad faith included not only 'dishonest dealings', but also 'those which fell short of the standards of acceptable commercial behaviour observed by reasonable and experienced men in the area being examined' (also *Road Tech v Unison* (1996)).

Relative grounds for refusal of registration

6.33 The relative grounds for refusal of registration are set out in s 5. They are termed 'relative' since the mark will be refused registration, not because of any quality intrinsic to itself, but because it conflicts with an earlier trade mark or right. Earlier marks, identified in s 6, may be

UK marks, CTMs, marks registered under the Madrid Protocol and 'well-known' trade marks entitled to protection under Article 6bis of the Paris Convention (see **6.68** below). The relative grounds for refusal of registration are the same grounds which form the basis for infringement proceedings under s 10 where of course the issue is also whether a later sign conflicts with an earlier trade mark (**6.55** et seq).

Grounds for conflict

6.34 The four general situations in which marks may conflict for the purposes of opposing a trade mark registration (or founding an infringement action) are looked at below. They are:

- identical marks on identical goods and services (s 5(1))

- identical marks on similar goods and services, with the proviso that there exists a likelihood of confusion on the part of the public which includes the likelihood of association with the earlier mark (s 5(2)(a))

- similar marks on similar or identical goods and services and the above proviso applies (s 5(2)(b))

- identical or similar marks on goods and services which are not similar, with the proviso that the use of the later mark without due cause would take unfair advantage of, or be detrimental to, the distinctive character of the earlier mark (s 5(3)).

Identical marks on identical goods and services (s 5(1))

6.35 A mark which is identical to an earlier registered mark and used in relation to the same goods and services will not be registered. The level of identity between the marks must be very high. The marks 'Origin' and 'Origins', both used in relation to clothing, were held to be similar but not identical (*Origins Natural Resources v Origin Clothing* (1995)).

Identical marks on similar goods and services and similar marks on similar or identical goods and services (s 5(2)(a)-(b))

6.36 In these circumstances, conflict between a later mark and an earlier mark is not inevitable. It will arise only if the proviso applies and there exists a likelihood of confusion on the part of the public which includes the likelihood of association with an earlier mark. The meaning of this section, and in particular the proviso, has provoked a great deal of controversy, since how it is interpreted will determine, in large measure, the extent to which the EU trade mark regime recognises the concept of 'dilution'. In *British Sugar*, Jacob J suggested that a discrete three-stage approach should be taken to applying this section. First, ask whether the marks are the same or similar. Next ask whether the goods are the same or similar. Finally ask whether the proviso applies and there is a likelihood of confusion including a likelihood of association between the two marks. If the answer to all three questions is positive, then there will be conflict. However, subsequent decisions by the ECJ have made it clear that rather than applying a staged test, it is necessary to take a 'global approach' to interpreting this section. In other words, the answer to any of the three questions posed by Jacob J may depend upon how the other two have themselves been answered. What this means and the consequences for protecting marks from dilution is examined in the following paragraphs, beginning with the meaning of the proviso.

The proviso: (i) the early years

6.37 The wording of s 5(2)(a)-(b) was new to the TMA 1994 and comes directly from Art 4(1)(b) of the TM Directive. It is generally accepted that 'likelihood of confusion' in the proviso means the likelihood that the public will be confused as to the origin of the marks. However, some EC member states, especially the Benelux countries, have gone on to argue that the addition of the key words, 'including a likelihood of association' to the proviso extends the protection given to trade marks beyond their function as indicators of origin to include protection for their commercial value, or reputation, which might be diluted by a simple association with another mark even when the public is not confused as to origin. The first UK case to consider the meaning of the proviso was *Wagamama*. The plaintiff was the proprietor of the mark 'Wagamama' for restaurant services and operated a London restaurant under that name. The defendant operated an Indian restaurant under the name 'Raja Mama'. The plaintiff sued for infringement, arguing both classic infringement as to trade origin as well as the likelihood of association. Laddie J accepted that there was a likelihood of confusion but rejected the argument that the likelihood of association imported the non-origin concept of dilution into UK law. Instead, he took the view that 'likelihood of association' derived from previous domestic case law by which marks are 'associated in the sense that one is an extension of the other or that they are derived from the same source.' Likelihood of association was contained within the 'classic' English concept of 'likelihood of confusion'. The *Wagamama* decision was widely criticised by those who preferred an anti-dilution approach such as the one recognised in Benelux law, and reflected in the Benelux case, *Claeryn/Klarein* (1975). Claeryn was a well-known alcoholic drink and Klarein a toilet cleaner. There was no argument that the public would believe the products originated from the same source. They would not. What the drinks marker argued was that if the 'Klarein' mark continued to be used, the public would associate the two products and that the reputation of the 'Claeryn' mark and therefore its value would suffer. The Benelux court accepted that there was a likelihood of association, although not confusion as to source, and the drinks maker won its case. It fell to the ECJ to decide whether the broad Benelux or the narrow UK interpretation of 'likelihood of association' would prevail under the TM Directive.

The proviso: (ii) Sabel and beyond

6.38   The issue was decided by the ECJ, in the case *Sabel v Puma* (1998). Puma was the registered proprietor of two German trade marks comprising bounding puma and leaping puma devices, registered in respect of jewellery and leather goods. Puma opposed the registration of Sabel's sign of a bounding cheetah device with the name 'Sabel' also for jewellery. The German Supreme Court decided that the marks were not sufficiently similar to give rise to a likelihood of confusion as to origin, but that the similarity of the 'semantic' content of the marks, that is the bounding felines, might give rise to a likelihood of association. Would this be sufficient grounds for Puma to oppose registration of the Sabel mark? The ECJ held that it would not. It ruled that a likelihood of association was merely one element of a likelihood of confusion as to origin not a separate ground for opposition. The ECJ then went on to consider how the likelihood of confusion should be assessed. It said that it must be appreciated 'globally', taking into account various factors, including:

* the recognition of the trade mark on the market

* the association which can be made between the registered mark and the sign

- the degree of similarity between the mark and the sign and the goods and the services.

As to assessing the similarity of the marks themselves, the ECJ's remarks are worth quoting in full:

> The global appreciation of the visual, aural or conceptual similarity of the marks in question, must be based on the overall impression given by the marks, bearing in mind, in particular, their distinctive and dominant component. The wording of Art 4(1)(b) of the Directive—'...there exists a likelihood of confusion on the part of the public...'—shows that the perception of marks in the mind of the average consumer of the type of goods or services in question plays a decisive role in the likelihood of confusion. The average consumer normally perceives a mark as a whole and does not proceed to analyse its various details.
>
> In that perspective, the more distinctive the earlier mark, the greater will be the likelihood of confusion. It is therefore not impossible that the conceptual similarity resulting from the fact that two marks use images with analogous semantic content may give rise to a likelihood of confusion where the earlier mark has a particularly distinctive character, either per se or because of the reputation it enjoys with the public.

The definition of who constitutes the 'average consumer' was given in the later case of *Lloyd Schuhfabrik* (see **6.21**)). In *Lloyd Schuhfabrik*, it was also noted that in assessing the likelihood of confusion, account should be taken of the fact that the average consumer will rarely have a chance to make a direct comparison between the two marks and that his level of attention is likely to vary according to the category of the goods or services in question. Returning to *Sabel*, the ECJ held that neither of the marks was particularly distinctive, and their use did not give rise to a likelihood of confusion.

The proviso: (iii) Wagamama endorsed?

6.39 Does *Sabel* endorse the UK approach to the proviso? It appears to do so since it says that the likelihood of association helps to define the scope of the likelihood of confusion, it is not a separate factor in finding conflict. However, those favouring anti-dilution measures might also take some comfort from *Sabel*. The ECJ also appears to be saying that in deciding whether marks or goods are similar enough to cause confusion, the distinctive character of the earlier mark, its reputation, and the likelihood that the public might associate the two marks may all be taken into account as well. In other words, the more distinctive the earlier mark, the greater will be the likelihood of confusion, and therefore marks with a highly distinctive character, either per se or because of their recognition on the market, enjoy broader protection than marks with a less distinctive character (*Lloyd Schuhfabrik*). Some might argue that the ECJ has simply side-stepped the confusion/association debate by widening the circumstances in which 'origin' confusion will be found.

6.40 *Sabel* was followed in the first UK trade mark case under the TMA 1994 to reach the CA, *The European v The Economist* (1998). The plaintiff had registered a device mark incorporating the words 'The European' as the masthead of its newspaper. The device also included a decorative element, a dove holding a globe. The defendant published a weekly newspaper, whose masthead included the words, 'European Voice'. The plaintiff claimed infringement, on the basis of similar marks on identical goods plus the proviso. It lost in the HC and appealed. The CA considered whether there was a likelihood of confusion on the part of the public due to the similarity between the defendant's sign and the plaintiff's mark. It held that the question was one of degree. Marks could be similar and not conflict as long as they did not give rise to confusion. In deciding if these marks were confusingly similar, the CA adopted the *Sabel* guidelines, including the fact that the more distinctive the earlier mark the greater will be the likelihood of confusion. In this case, the CA held the converse was also true, that is the more descriptive and less distinctive the earlier mark, the less likelihood of confusion. It held that the word 'European' in the plaintiff's device, which was its most distinctive element and the only word it had in common with the defendant, was seen by the public as an ordinary descriptive word and not a badge of origin. As a result, the marks were not confusingly similar and the appeal failed.

Defining distinctiveness

6.41 The ECJ considered the question of distinctiveness in *Lloyds Schuhfabrik*. It held that in determining the distinctive character of a mark and, accordingly, in assessing whether it is highly distinctive, it is necessary to make 'a global assessment of its capacity to identify the goods or services for which it has been registered as coming from a particular undertaking (and hence its capacity to distinguish). It went on to say that it is appropriate to use a quantitative assessment of the degree of public recognition attained by a mark to determine whether it has a strong distinctive character.

Are the marks similar?

6.42 *Sabel* set out the broad test for determining whether marks are confusingly similar. In *Origins*, the context in which the test should be applied was summarised by Jacob J:

> It requires the court to assume that the mark of the plaintiff is used in a normal and fair manner in relation to the goods for which it is registered and then to assess a likelihood of confusion in relation to the way the defendant uses the mark, discounting external matter or circumstances. The comparison is mark for mark.

(For the earlier case on which the *Origins* test was based, see *Pianotist Co's Application* (1906)). It is submitted that *Origins* is now overruled to the extent that, in judging similarity between marks, courts can take into account the 'external matter' of the earlier mark's reputation or its distinctiveness (*Sabel*). But the rule that the comparison is physically mark for mark still holds. In the 'Penguin/Puffin' passing off case (see **5.9** above), the similarities between the biscuits' packaging as a whole was sufficient to found a passing off action but, stripped of extraneous matter, the sign 'Puffin' on the defendant's biscuit did not infringe the plaintiff's mark 'Penguin' (*United Biscuits*). The test for similar marks was also looked at in *Lloyds Schuhfabrik*. A German company distributed shoes under the mark 'Lloyd'. A Dutch company marketed shoes under the mark 'Loints' and sold them in Germany. Among the questions for the ECJ was whether the aural similarity between the marks was sufficient to find a likelihood of confusion. The ECJ ruled that a mere aural similarity was sufficient to create a likelihood of confusion. In reaching its judgment, the ECJ said that in order to assess the degree of similarity between the marks concerned it was up to the national courts to determine the degree of visual, aural or conceptual similarity between them and, where appropriate, to evaluate the importance to be attached to these elements, taking into account the category of goods or services in question and the circumstances in which they are marketed.

6.43 It is submitted that, in light of *Lloyds Schuhfabrik*, case law developed before the TMA 1994 for judging whether marks are similar, may still have some relevance. This was the approach taken by the registry in

226

Ener-cap TM (1999). There follows some of the most basic cases, decided before the TMA 1994 which may provide a useful guide to assessing the extent of the similarity between marks. If the mark is highly distinctive, for instance an invented word such as Kodak, then the threshold for what is assumed may be confusing similarity is lower (*Wm Bailey (Birmingham) 'Erectiko'* (1935)). In any comparison of two marks, less weight may be given to elements which are common to the trade, so Coca Cola was unable to prevent registration of Pepsi Cola (*Coca Cola v Pepsi Cola* (1942)). First syllables of words may be given more weight than later syllables because they achieve more public recognition, so Seda Seltzer was allowed despite the mark Alka Seltzer (*R Demuth* (1948)), but if the words are invented they have been considered as a whole, so Accutron was not allowed because of Accurist (*Accutron* (1966)). Where the goods are expensive or for a specialist market, purchasers will take more care and are therefore less likely to find two similar marks confusing. 'Lancer' was allowed for mass market cars despite opposition from the manufacturers of the up-market 'Lancia', since the risk of confusion 'was unlikely to survive the mechanism of purchase.' The marks sounded similar when spoken but the goods were not likely to be ordered by telephone (*Lancer TM* (1987)). Even with the new guidelines from the ECJ, it is still the case that the law relating to similar marks is voluminous and not always consistent. The courts have described the exercise of whether two marks are confusingly similar as an art rather than a science, to which according to Laddie J in *Wagamama*, 'the judge brings his own, perhaps idiosyncratic pronunciation and view or understanding of them.'

Are the goods (or services) similar?

6.44 Thus far this chapter has considered the criteria for deciding whether marks are confusingly similar. The next question to ask is whether the goods (or services) are sufficiently similar for the purposes of s 5(2)(a)-(b). *British Sugar* was the first UK case to address the issue of similar goods under the TMA 1994. Later the ECJ looked at similar goods in *Canon v MGM* (1998). Following *Canon*, Jacob J's approach in *British Sugar* continues to have relevance. *Canon* is looked at below (see **6.46**), but first the *British Sugar* approach will be considered. Because the TM Directive does not set out a test for similar goods, it was held in *British Sugar* that the test for 'similar goods' was similar to that for 'goods of the same description' under the TMA 1938, and therefore previous case law was relevant. The original test for goods of the same description was set out in *Jellinek* (1946), which identified three questions to be asked. First, what are the nature and composition of the goods. Second, what is the respective use of the articles. Last, what are the trade channels through which the commodities are bought and sold.

Applying Jellinek

6.45 The *Jellinek* test was applied in *British Sugar*. British Sugar marketed a dessert sauce and syrup under the registered mark 'Treat'. The defendants marketed a spread called Robertson's Toffee Treat. British Sugar claimed trade mark infringement. In his judgment, Jacob J examined, inter alia, whether the goods were of the same description. In holding that they were not, Jacob J applied the three *Jellinek* criteria, but asked further questions. In the case of self-service consumer items such as these, where in practice are they found or likely to be found in supermarkets and in particular, are they likely to be found on the same or different shelves? What is the extent to which the respective goods and services are competitive, taking into account how the trade classifies the goods? In this case, the two products were not in direct competition and they would be found in different places in supermarkets. Their physical natures were 'somewhat' different as one was pourable and one needed spooning. They were not similar goods. This case demonstrates how the *Jellinek* test may be adapted to reflect modern marketing conditions. When most goods were sold in small or specialist shops, rather than in supermarkets, the question of their proximity on the shelves did not arise. New channels of trade are constantly emerging—television shopping channels or e-commerce. It is likely these questions will change again.

The test for similar goods post-Canon

6.46 Inevitably, the ECJ was called upon to address the issue of what criteria should be employed in deciding whether or not goods are similar for the purposes of finding conflict. In *Canon v MGM* (1998), MGM applied to register 'Cannon' for video cassettes, production, distribution and projection of films for cinema and television. Their application was opposed by Canon who had registered the mark 'Canon' for cameras, projectors, television and recording equipment. The question put to the ECJ was whether, when determining whether the similarity of the goods and services covered by the two marks at issue is sufficient to give rise to a likelihood of confusion, the distinctive character of the earlier mark, in particular its reputation, must also be taken into account. These latter factors had not been considered relevant in *British Sugar*. The ECJ held that they should. It said that in addition to looking at the sort of evidence of similarity between the goods and services which had been considered in *British Sugar*, the distinctive character and in particular the reputation of the earlier trade mark was also relevant for determining whether the similarity between the goods and services covered by the two trade marks was sufficient to give rise to a likelihood of confusion.

The global approach summarised

6.47   It was suggested above (**6.36**) that the discrete three-stage test put forward by Jacob J in *British Sugar* for assessing whether conflict has arisen under s 5(2)(a)-(b) has been superseded by the 'global approach' formulated by the ECJ. Under this approach the three elements in finding conflict, similarity of marks, similarity of goods (or services) and the likelihood of confusion are all, in a sense, mutually dependent. In *Canon*, the ECJ summarised this approach. It said:

> A global assessment of the likelihood of confusion implies some interdependence between the relevant factors, and in particular a similarity between the trade marks and between these goods and services. Accordingly, a lesser degree of similarity between these goods and services may be offset by a greater degree of similarity between the marks and vice versa. It follows that ... registration of a trade mark may have to be refused, despite a lesser degree of similarity between the goods or services covered, where the marks are very similar and the earlier mark, in particular its reputation, is highly distinctive.

Marks with a reputation on dissimilar goods (s 5(3))

6.48   A conflict arises when identical or similar marks are used on dissimilar goods (or services) where the earlier mark has a reputation in the UK (or a CTM in the EC) and the proviso applies, that is that the use of the later mark without due cause would take unfair advantage of, or be detrimental to, the distinctive character of the earlier mark. The wording of s 5(3) was taken from Art 5(2) of the TM Directive. In the early case of *British Sugar*, Jacob J suggested that *Claeryn* might well provide a model for the sort of situation to which this section would apply.

What is a reputation?

6.49   The ECJ considered the criteria for assessing whether a mark has a reputation for the purposes of Art 5(2) in *General Motors (GM) v Yplon* (2000). Yplon had registered 'Chevy' for cleaning products in Benelux and GM wanted to restrain use of the mark on the grounds that it diluted the reputation of its own trade mark 'Chevy' for cars, and damaged its advertising function. Yplon responded that GM had not shown that its mark had a reputation in the Benelux countries. The ECJ was asked by the national court for the proper construction of 'repute of the trade mark'. The ECJ made clear that Art 5(2) was intended to apply only when the public had sufficient knowledge of the earlier registered mark so that when confronted with the later mark, it might make an association between the two even if they were used for different products or services, and, as a result of this association, the earlier mark might be damaged. It then went on to list a number of factors relevant to assessing whether the earlier mark has a reputation. First, the relevant public with whom the mark must have acquired a reputation is the public 'concerned with the trade mark'. The relevant public might, depending upon the product, be either the general public or a more specialised public, for instance traders in a specific sector. The necessary degree of knowledge is then reached when the earlier mark is known by a significant part of the relevant public. It is up to the national court to decide if it has been reached by taking into account all the relevant facts, including the trade mark's market share, the intensity, geographical extent and duration of its use, and the size of the investment made in promoting it. To have a reputation, a mark does not have to be known throughout a member state, as long as it is known in a 'substantial' part of it.

Applying the proviso

6.50   It is not enough that the earlier trade mark has a reputation and that a later identical (or similar) trade mark is used on dissimilar goods or services, the proviso must also apply so that the use of the later mark without due cause would take unfair advantage of, or be detrimental to, the distinctive character of the earlier mark. In *General Motors*, the ECJ held that if, based on the above criteria, the national court decides a mark has a reputation, it should then go on to examine whether it has been detrimentally affected without due cause. Crucially, it observed that the stronger the earlier mark's distinctive character and reputation, the easier it will be to find that detriment has been caused to it. In addition, under s 5(3) there is no need for there to be a likelihood of confusion between the two marks. This was made clear in *Sabel* (although for a dissenting view, see Michaels 'Confusion in and about Sections 5(3) and 10(3) of the Trade Marks Act 1994' (2000) EIPR 335).

6.51 The reach of s 5(3) was tested in two UK cases with remarkably similar facts. In *Oasis Stores TM Application* (1998), the applicant sought to register 'Eveready' for condoms. The application was opposed by Ever Ready plc which had a number of registered trade marks for inter alia torches and batteries. On the basis of s 5(3), Ever Ready argued that the registration would take unfair advantage of the reputation of its mark and would be detrimental because undesirable associations would be made by the public. The argument was unsuccessful. The Registrar took the view, inter alia, that because the products were so different, there was no likelihood that the public would make any association between them despite the similarity of the marks. However an opposite result was reached in *Sheimer's TM Application* (2000). The application was for the mark 'Visa' for condoms. It was opposed by Visa International who had registered 'Visa' for financial services (including credit cards). Registration was refused and the applicant appealed. The appeal was unsuccessful. It was held that the opponent's mark was well known with a strong and distinctive character and reputation in the UK and the use of the word 'Visa' for the applicant's products would, without due cause, damage the distinctive character of the earlier mark. There would be 'cross pollination' between the applicant's use of 'Visa' and the opponent's use. As the condom mark became known it would affect how the opponent's mark was also known, and so would be detrimental to its distinctive character. What distinguishes the Eveready from the Visa application? It has been suggested that in the case of *Oasis,* the public might make a natural connection between the word 'Eveready' and the goods to which it attaches, ie condoms, but not necessarily to batteries or other Ever Ready goods. However, as the word 'Visa' had no natural connection with condoms, the public would be more likely to associate it with the credit card, despite the applicant's argument that 'Visa' was a 'humorous' allusion to the concept of 'permission to enter' (Rawkins 'Entry Denied: Visa for Condoms Rejected in the UK' (2000) TMW 22).

Conflicts with earlier rights

6.52 A mark will not be registered which conflicts with an unregistered mark, which would be protected under the law of passing off (s 5(4)(a)).

Proprietors of other earlier rights, particularly those given by virtue of the law of copyright, design right or registered designs, are also protected from the registration of a later mark, which would infringe those rights (s 5(4)(b)). An example might be an application for a shape trade mark, say a bottle, which infringes a registered design, or a jingle, which would infringe a copyright. These will not be registered. In *Ann Frank Trade Mark* (1998), the foundation which owned Anne Frank's literary estate tried unsuccessfully to have the trade mark 'Anne Frank' held by the Anne Frank House, revoked because it claimed to have the copyright in her signature. It was defeated because it was held, inter alia, that there is no copyright in a signature.

Consent/honest concurrent use

6.53 All the grounds for refusal in s 5 may be overcome if the proprietor of the earlier mark or right gives his consent to registration of the later mark (s 5(5)). If consent is given, the Registrar has no discretion (as under the TMA 1938) to refuse registration of the later mark even if there will be confusion between the two marks. This is another indication of the deregulatory nature of the TMA 1994. The Registrar shall also accept an application for registration even though it conflicts with an earlier trade mark or an earlier right, if the applicant can show that he has made honest concurrent use of the trade mark for which registration is sought (s 7) and there is no opposition from the proprietor of the earlier right (*Road Tech v Unison Software* (1996)). The definition of what constitutes honest concurrent use lies in previous case law, as there is no similar provision in the TM Directive (s 7(3)). Factors to be taken into account are: the extent of use, the degree of confusion likely to ensue, the honesty of the concurrent use, whether any instances of confusion are proved and the relative inconvenience caused to the public if both marks are registered (*Club Europe Trade Mark* (2000)).

Infringement

6.54 The proprietor of a registered trade mark has exclusive rights in the trade mark which are infringed by its use in the UK without his consent (s 9). The acts amounting to infringement are set out in s 10. The right to commence infringement proceedings arises once the trade mark has been registered. But infringement itself (and so the starting date

232

for calculating damages) dates from the date of registration which under s 40(3) is defined as the date of the filing of the application for registration. Although s 9 mentions only the rights of the proprietor, under certain conditions assignees and licensees can also bring infringement proceedings.

The grounds for infringement

6.55 The four main grounds for infringement are set out in s 10(1)-(3). They are the same as the relative grounds for refusal of registration (s 5(1)-(3))(see **6.33** et seq). They are:

- use of an identical sign in relation to the identical goods and services for which the trade mark is registered (s 10(1))

- use of an identical sign in relation to goods and services similar to those for which the trade mark is registered with the proviso that there is a likelihood of confusion on the part of the public including the likelihood of association (s 10(2)(a))

- use of a similar sign in relation to goods and services identical or similar to those for which the mark is registered and the proviso applies (s 10(2)(b))

- use of an identical sign in relation to dissimilar goods and services where the mark has a reputation in the UK with the proviso that the use of the sign, being without due cause, takes unfair advantage of, or is detrimental to, the distinctive character or repute of the mark (s 10(3)).

The key difference between s 5 conflict and s 10 infringement is that under the former the comparison is mark for mark while, under the latter, the comparison is mark for sign. The significance of this difference is looked at below (**6.57**).

What constitutes infringing use?

6.56 To infringe, the sign must be used in the course of trade which includes any business or profession (s 103). Infringing use is generally defined as use of a trade mark, or of a sign, identical with, similar to, or likely to be mistaken for a trade mark (s 103(2)). Actual uses of a sign for the purposes of infringement are set out in (s 10(4)-(5)) and include use in advertising (including, of course, radio advertising where there might be aural confusion (*Lloyds*)), exposing goods for sale under the sign or affixing the infringing sign to goods and packaging. In *Trebor Bassett v Football Association* (1997) it was not infringing use, in this case of the English football team's three lions crest (a registered trade mark), to distribute cards bearing photographs of the players where the crest was visible on their shirts. In *Beaumatic v Mitchell* (2000), infringing use was held to include the application of the trade mark on packaging in the UK for goods which were to be shipped abroad.

Non-trade mark use

6.57   In *British Sugar*, it was said that in order to constitute infringing use, use of a sign need not be in a 'trade mark sense'—that is as an indicator of origin of the goods or services of either the plaintiff or the defendant. According to Jacob J, to find infringement, the court is merely required to determine whether the sign is used by the defendant in the course of trade and then to consider whether this use falls within one of four categories of infringement listed above (see **6.55**). The correct comparison is 'mark for sign', excluding added matter (*British Sugar*). In *British Sugar* the defendant marketed a product 'Robertson's Toffee Treat'. The plaintiff's registered mark was 'Treat'. The relevant comparison was mark for sign disregarding added matter (ie 'Robertson's Toffee') and the identity of the plaintiff's mark 'Treat' and the defendant's sign 'Treat' was clear. It was irrelevant to a finding of infringement that Robertson's used 'Treat' purely in a descriptive sense, although it would subsequently provide Robertson's with a defence under s 11(2)(b) (see **6.72** et seq). Nonetheless, there was no infringement, in this case because the goods to which the mark and sign applied were not similar (see **6.55**). Since *British Sugar*, the question of non-trade mark use in relation to infringement has been a matter of some controversy. In *British Sugar*, Jacob J pointed to the wording of s 10, which was taken from the TM Directive, and in particular the use of the word 'sign' rather than 'mark' in setting out the relevant comparison for finding infringement (**6.55** above). According to Jacob J it followed from this that the later sign did not need to be used in a trade mark sense to infringe. In *Philips*, the CA followed Jacob J's approach and agreed that the infringement provisions did not call for the later sign to be used in a trade mark sense. The CA pointed out instead that s 11 of the TMA 1994 listed a number of exclusions which would almost certainly provide a defence against infringement for a sign used in this way.

Finding infringement

6.58 The three main circumstances (treating s 10(2)(a) and (b) together) in which infringement arises are looked at below. A more detailed discussion of these circumstances is to be found above in the discussion of the relative grounds for refusal of registration under s 5, where the same grounds for conflict apply (see **6.34** et seq).

Identical marks on identical goods (s 10(1))

6.59 The correct comparison for the purpose of finding infringement is mark for sign excluding added matter (*Origins*). The criteria for such a comparison have been set out in above (see **6.42**).

Identical or similar marks on identical or similar goods (s 10(2))

6.60 The infringement provisions of the TMA 1938 did not extend to identical or similar signs on similar goods (or in the words of the TMA 1938 to 'goods of the same description'). Now all trade marks, including those registered before the TMA 1994, are covered by s 10(2). The criteria for the comparison of marks and of goods and services in order to establish similarity are set out in the discussion above of s 5(2)(a)-(b) under the relative grounds for refusal of registration (see **6.33**). It is, of course, necessary for the proviso to apply so that there must be a likelihood of confusion on the part of the public including the likelihood of association for there to be infringement.

Marks with a reputation on dissimilar goods s 10(3)

6.61 The basic criteria for finding infringement under s 10(3) are set out above in the discussion of conflicting marks under s 5(3) (see **6.48** et seq). It is necessary to show that the proviso applies and the use of the sign, being without due cause takes unfair advantage of, or is detrimental to, the distinctive character of the earlier mark.

6.62 In *British Telecommunications v One in a Million* (1999), the plaintiffs succeeded in a s 10(3) infringement action as well as in an action for passing off (see **5.28** on passing off). The defendants had registered a number of domain names without the owners' consent including bt.org, marksandspencer.co.uk, etc. There were no web sites attached to them. The defendants admitted that they had no intention of using the marks and intended to sell them. The CA held that since the domain names were registered to take advantage of the distinctive character and reputation of the marks, this was unfair and detrimental and s 10(3) infringement was made out. Despite cases such as this, it is increasingly the case that internet domain name disputes will be settled at the international level, and appropriately so. Both WIPO through its Arbitration and Mediation Centre and ICANN (the Internet Corporation for Assigned Names and Numbers), a non-profit organisation responsible for internet allocation, have established 'uniform-domain-name-dispute-resolution' policies. Their aim is to arbitrate domain name disputes. ICANN has an expedited procedure where there has been a complaint of abusive registrations, such as by 'cybersquatting', of which the above case would presumably be an example.

Comparative advertising (s 10(6))

6.63 Until the TMA 1994, it was not possible for an advertiser to compare his product to that of a competitor, by reference to the competitor's registered trade mark. The TMA 1994 allows comparative advertising. This was a UK government decision, so the wording of s 10(6) is not taken from the TM Directive. Recently, the EU has enacted the Directive on Comparative Advertising 97/55/EC which amends the Directive 84/450/EEC on Misleading Advertising to include comparative advertising and was implemented in the UK by the Control of Misleading Advertising (Amendment) Regulations 2000. Section 10(6) of the TMA reads:

> Nothing in the preceding section [sections 10(1)-(3) on infringement] shall be construed as preventing the use of a registered trade mark by any person for the purpose of identifying the goods or services as the those of the proprietor or licensee, provided that any such use otherwise than in accordance with honest business practices in industrial and commercial matters shall be treated as infringing the registered trade mark if the use without due cause takes unfair advantage of, or is detrimental to, the distinctive character of the mark.

Interpreting s 10(6)

6.64 In *Barclays' Bank v RBS Advanta* (1996), the plaintiff was the proprietor of the registered trade mark, 'Barclaycard', and the defendant intended to launch a competing credit card, the 'RBS Advanta Visa'. The defendant's advertising material compared the two cards, in particular listing 15 reasons why its card was a 'better' card, and setting out a table naming 'Barclaycard'. The defendant did not point out that six or seven of these reasons were common to 'Barclaycard' or that 'Barclaycard' provided services the defendant did not. The plaintiff wanted an injunction to prevent publication of the advertisement on the grounds that it infringed the proviso to s 10(6). Laddie J found that in deciding whether the proviso applies it must be broken down into its three constituent parts.

Part I: use must be honest

6.65   This is an objective test. Does the advertisement fall within what reasonable people would regard as honest. It can be assumed that a reasonable person will be aware that in the field of advertising, there is much puffery and hyperbole. However, if that same reader on being given the full facts is likely to say that the advertisement is not honest, because it is significantly misleading, then it is infringing.

Part II: honest practices in industrial and commercial matters

6.66   Many traders and professions have agreed codes of conduct in relation to advertising. However, Laddie J said that these had little direct relevance. 'Honesty has to be gauged against what is reasonably to be expected by the relevant public of advertisements for the goods and services in issue.' Thus, it appears, for instance, that the honesty of an advertisement which compares two luxury sports cars might be differently judged to one comparing second hand cars. In a later case it was held that use was dishonest practice if the confusion was significantly misleading to a substantial proportion of the reasonable audience (*Vodafone v Orange* (1997)). In *Cable & Wireless v British Telecommunications (BT)* (1998), the HC looked again at what was meant by 'honest business practices'. In this case, BT produced a pamphlet comparing the costs of their services against those of the plaintiff by making reasonable estimates of the plaintiff's pricing. It was held that the test of honesty was an objective one in that the question was whether a reasonable trader could honestly have made the statements based on the information he had. A person who knowingly put forward a false claim could not be said to be acting in accordance with honest practices. In this case, BT's statements were more likely to be true than false, and it had not been shown that they were ones which an honest trader having the information which BT had would not have been prepared to make. There was no infringement.

Part III: '...if the use without due cause...repute of the mark'

6.67   In *Barclaycard*, it was held that to be infringing, use of the claimant's mark must give some advantage to the defendant or inflict some harm on the character or repute of the mark which is above the level of *de minimis*. In *Barclaycard*, it was not dishonest to omit to mention that 'Barclaycard' also offered similar services because it was assumed that the public would understand that the advertisement taken as a whole was meant to convey the meaning that the 'Advanta' card was believed to offer the customer a better deal. In the recent case of *Emaco v Dyson* (1999) (where the two vacuum cleaner manufacturers each published comparisons of the other's suction powers), the court found that both sides had made false representations and that the use of each other's trade marks having fallen short of 'honest practices', was without due cause and detrimental (Wilkinson 'Suction Wars: Comparative Advertising in the UK after Electrolux v Dyson' (1999) TMW 18).

Well-known marks (s 56)

6.68   This section which implements Art 6bis of the Paris Convention gives limited protection to well-known marks which are not registered in the UK. It allows the proprietor to obtain an injunction against the use in the UK of an identical or similar trade mark in relation to identical or similar goods or services where use is likely to cause confusion. He may also prevent registration of a later conflicting mark or seek to have it declared invalid. But he does not have the right to claim damages nor can he act against the use of his mark on dissimilar goods. Under s 56, there is no need for the proprietor to carry on business or have any goodwill in the UK to obtain injunctive relief, as would be the case if an action was brought under passing off (*Anheuser-Busch v Budejovicky Budvar* (1984)) (**5.12** above). It is also worth noting that TRIPS goes further and extends the protection given under Art 6bis to goods or services which are not similar to those in respect of which the mark is registered, provided that use of the mark would 'indicate a connection between these goods or services and the owner of the registered trade mark and provided that the interests of the owner of the registered trade mark are likely to be damaged by such use'. A well-known mark is not defined in the TMA 1994, but presumably will have to command a very high degree of consumer recognition, greater than that for marks with a reputation, a view confirmed by the AG in *General Motors* . In *Philips*, the plaintiff claimed to have protection under s 56 as an alternative to trade mark protection. Jacob J observed that since s 56 is intended to give the trade mark owner equivalent protection to that which he would have under passing off, if he had the requisite goodwill in the UK, then to succeed under s 56 he must be able to show confusion or deception in 'a passing-off sense'.

Limits on the protection afforded by registration

6.69   As presently interpreted by the UK courts, s 10 allows for the possibility that a 'sign' may infringe an earlier registered mark even if it is not used in a 'trade mark sense' **(6.57)**. Section 11 provides five defences which may be raised to avoid a finding of trade mark infringement. It is important to remember that the exceptions to trade mark infringement set out in s 11 are only invoked after a finding of infringement has been made.

Defence 1: overlapping registrations

6.70   A trade mark is not infringed where another registered trade mark is used in relation to the goods or services for which the latter is registered (s 11(1)). Both marks are validly on the register and both are entitled to protection. However, it is open to either proprietor to seek to have his opponents registration declared invalid **(6.85** et seq).

Defence 2: use of own name

6.71   A trade mark is not infringed by the use by a person of his own name and address provided the use is in accordance with honest practices in industrial or commercial matters (s 11(2)(a)). This defence, which is available to businesses and companies as well as individuals, will only apply if the whole business name is used (*Origins*). In *Nad Electronics v NAD Computer Systems* (1997), Ferris J held that the use of an own name is protected only if it is bone fide, that is to say innocently applied to goods or used in relation to goods, without the intention to mislead or confuse others or to attract another trader's goodwill.

Defence 3: descriptive use

6.72   A trade mark is not infringed by the use of indications concerning the kind, quality, quantity, intended purpose, value, geographical origin, the time of the production of goods or of rendering of services or other characteristics of goods or services provided the use is in accordance with honest practices in industrial or commercial matters (s 11(2)(b)). As the law now stands, a sign, even if it is not used in a trade mark sense but purely descriptively, may infringe (see **6.57** above). But provided the use is honest, s 11(2)(b) will provide a defence. The protection offered by s 11(2)(b) is particularly important since, in theory, it is possible under the TMA 1994 to register any descriptive sign provided it has acquired sufficient distinctiveness through use. As a result, but for the protection afforded by this section, increasing numbers of common descriptive words would be effectively off limits to other traders.

6.73   This defence was successful in *British Sugar*. The defendant referred to its product as 'Robertson's Toffee Treat'. This was held to be infringement because the comparison was simply mark for sign excluding added matter, that is 'Treat' for 'Treat' whether or not the defendant had used the word 'Treat' in a trade mark sense. In fact, the defendant had not used the words 'Toffee Treat' as an indication of origin, but as a description of its product. So although the defendant had infringed the 'Treat' mark by using an identical sign, it was protected by s 11(2)(b) because it had used it purely in a descriptive sense and not as a badge of origin. It follows that whereas the test for infringement under s 10(1)-(3) is to compare mark to sign, the test for descriptive use under s 11(2)(b) is to consider the whole context in which the contested sign is employed. According to Jacob J in *British Sugar*, whether the descriptive word is used, by the defendant, as a trade mark is a question of fact. Would a member of the public take it as a badge of origin? In *British Sugar*, it was held that where use is descriptive to some but has a trade mark significance to others it will not be protected. This approach was endorsed by the CA in *The European* where it was observed that the purpose of s 11(2)(b) was to permit the fair use of the plaintiff's registered mark to indicate the characteristics of the defendant's goods or services, but not to perform the dual function of indicating both their characteristics and their trade origin. In *Philips*, the CA found that Remington's use of a three-headed shaver was protected under s 11(2)(b)

240

in that it was an indication of the kind of shaver and its intended purpose. It also endorsed Jacob J's view in the HC that even though Remington had copied the plaintiff's shaver, its use was honest (since without such copying 'the development of competition would be eroded'). The same may not have been true, however, if it had copied a valid intellectual property right.

6.74   Another interesting case where the use of a trade mark was held to be descriptive was *Bravado v Mainstream Publishing* (1996). It concerned a book entitled *A Sweet Little Mystery—Wet Wet Wet—the Inside Story* about the pop group Wet Wet Wet. The group alleged that the book's title infringed its registered trade mark 'Wet Wet Wet' in relation to printed matter. In this early case the court held that infringing use must be use in a trade mark sense. Lord McCluskey found that the mark was being used in a trade mark sense since the defendants had used the words 'Wet Wet Wet' on printed matter and on the face of it there was infringement. But he also held that there was a defence available under s 11(2)(b) because the defendant was using the trade mark purely descriptively, as an indication of what the book was about. Lord McCluskey said it would be wrong if trade mark registration prevented a publisher from using a protected name in the title of a book about a company or a product, or indeed prevented the media as a whole from referring to a product by it registered name. For the courts to decide otherwise would seriously inhibit freedom of the press, for instance in reporting corporate misdeeds.

Defence 4: intended purpose

6.75   It is not an infringement to use the trade mark where it is necessary to indicate the intended purpose of the product or service (in particular, as accessories or spare parts) provided the use is in accordance with honest practices in industrial or commercial matters (s 11(2)(c)). A trader who supplies spare parts for or makes repairs to a particular branded product may make this clear to the public. But he must be careful. He may say, for example, 'This film is suitable for a Kodak Camera' (to cite an example given by the CA in *Philips*) but not 'We supply Kodak film' if the film he supplies is not produced by Kodak. The ECJ examined this defence in *BMW v Deenik* (1999). Mr Deenik sold, repaired and maintained second-hand BMW cars and advertised using phrases such as 'Repairs and maintenance of BMW' and 'BMW specialist'. The ECJ was asked whether the proprietor of a trade mark can prevent another person from using the mark to inform the public that he carries out the repair and maintenance of goods carrying the mark and put on the market by the proprietor. In particular, can the proprietor prevent the advertiser from creating the impression that his business is affiliated to the trade mark owner if the manner in which he advertises means there is a good chance the public might be given that impression? The ECJ held inter alia that a proprietor is not entitled to prevent a third party from using the mark for the purpose of informing the public that he carries out the repair and maintenance of goods covered by the trade mark and put on the market with the proprietor's consent. Nor can he be prohibited from informing the public that he is a specialist in the sale, repair or maintenance of such goods. But this protection is lost if in either case the mark is used in such a way as to create an impression that there is a commercial connection between the two undertakings and in particular that the reseller's business is affiliated to the trade mark proprietor's distribution network or that there is a special relationship between the two.

6.76 In the later UK case, *Volvo v Heritage* (2000), the HC considered the meaning of the proviso to s 11(2)(c). The claimants owned the registered mark 'Volvo' for inter alia the maintenance and repair of cars. The defendant had been an authorised Volvo dealer. When its dealership was revoked, it continued to use the word 'Volvo' accompanied by the words 'specialist' and 'independent', albeit in smaller lettering, on signs and on their letterhead. The claimant alleged infringement and the defendants claimed protection under s 11(2)(c). Rattee J held that the defendants had infringed. He then looked at the s 11(2)(c) defence and, in particular, the proviso. He said that honest use was judged by an objective standard, citing *Cable & Wireless* (see **6.66** above). In this case, the defendant's use of the mark in the context of its having previously been an authorised Volvo dealer was calculated to cause at least confusion and possibly some belief in the minds of customers that there was still a trading connection with the claimant. No reasonable motor trader would say that this constituted honest use in the course of trade. The defence failed.

Defence 5: local signs

6.77 A registered trade mark is not infringed by the use in the course of trade in a particular locality of an earlier right which applies only in that locality (s 11(3)). Examples of what might be protected are a pub sign or a local service.

Losing the mark

6.78   Trade mark registration endows on a proprietor an indeterminate monopoly in the sign which is the subject matter of the mark. But there are various ways in which a trade mark monopoly may be lost either voluntarily or involuntarily. In the former case, a proprietor of a trade mark may surrender his mark voluntarily (s 45). A proprietor may also lose his mark involuntarily either by having it revoked or through a finding of invalidity. Each of these is examined below.

Revocation

6.79   A trade mark which has been validly registered may for a number of reasons, be taken off the register (s 46). An application for revocation may be made by any person (to the Registrar or the court) (s 46(4)). In practice, this will almost certainly be someone who has competing trade interests with the registered proprietor, perhaps a trade rival who has been accused of infringing the registered mark. There are three general grounds for revocation looked at below:

- non-use

- the mark has become generic

- the mark has become deceptive.

Non-use

6.80   Non-use of the trade mark for a period of five years since registration or use which has been suspended for an uninterrupted period of five years may lead to the trade mark being revoked (s 46(1)(a)-(b)). Use must be by the proprietor or with his consent, so that use can be by a licensee or perhaps by a subsidiary company. There must be genuine use in the UK in relation to the goods or services for which the mark is registered, when there are no proper reasons for non-use. If a registered proprietor claims that there has been use made of his mark, the onus of showing use rests with him (s 100). The proprietor is afforded a defence from non-use of his registered mark if he can show that he has used a different mark which incorporates the essential elements of the registered mark (s 46(2)). In *Elle TM* (1997), the use of 'ELLE' in upper case letters was held not to be the same as use of a lower case 'elle' inside a circle with an arrow attached.

6.81 A challenge for non-use can be overcome if there are 'proper' reasons. In *Invermont TM* (1997), 'proper' was defined as 'apt, acceptable, reasonable, justifiable in all the circumstances'. It is meant to cover not normal situations or routine difficulties in the trade, but abnormal situations, 'or perhaps some temporary but serious disruption affecting the proprietor's business.' In *Invermont*, the proprietor had registered 'Invermont' for alcoholic beverages, and argued that non-use was due to the lengthy and complicated process of introducing a new brand onto the market. The Registrar held this was not a proper reason since such delays and difficulties were normal to the trade as a whole. Similarly, in *Cabanas Habana TM* (2000), the proprietor of this mark for cigars failed to convince the TMR that the US embargo on Cuban products constituted a proper reason for non-use of its mark. The embargo had been in force for 33 years and had become a normal condition of trade.

Generic marks

6.82 A mark may be revoked on the grounds that, in consequence of the activity or *inactivity* of the proprietor, it has become the common name in the trade for a product or service for which it is registered (s 46(1)(c)). Obviously, it is crucial for proprietors actively to police the use of their marks, for instance, ensuring that licensees use them correctly, pursuing infringers and ensuring that if a word mark is applied to their goods it is perceived as a trade mark. This may be done by presenting the mark in a fanciful way so that it is not taken to be the name of the product itself.

Misleading marks

6.83 A trade mark may be revoked because as a consequence of the use made by the proprietor, or with his consent, in relation to the goods or services for which it is registered, it is liable to mislead the public, particularly (but not exclusively) as to the nature, quality or geographical origin of the goods and services (s 46(1)(d)). In *Avnet v Isoact* (1998), Jacob J suggested that the most common ground for revocation under s 46(1)(d) was likely to be if the proprietor did not use the mark on the goods or services for which it was registered. In *Gromax*, other grounds for deception were suggested. The plaintiffs were challenging the registration of the defendants mark 'Gro-Shield'. They claimed it was deceptive because not all the goods sold under the mark had been manufactured by the defendant. The HC rejected this argument for revocation because the defendants had a substantial connection with the manufacture of the goods, although they did not make all of them. The plaintiffs also claimed that the goods sold under the mark 'Gro-Shield' and manufactured by the defendants signified only goods sold by the plaintiffs and, if sold by anyone else, the mark would be misleading. This argument too was rejected, the HC finding that there was a close connection in the course of trade between the defendants as owners of the mark and goods in relation to which it was used even if the goods were sold by someone else.

Consequences of revocation

6.84 If a trade mark is revoked, it is taken off the register and the mark ceases to have protection from that date, unless the Registrar believes the grounds for revocation existed at an earlier date. Its erstwhile proprietor will not be liable for infringement of an identical or similar mark during the period his mark was registered. The grounds for revocation go to the heart of the trade mark as a monopoly right. They recognise that a proprietor must justify his monopoly through his activities in the market place. If the proprietor misuses the mark either through action or inaction, he loses his right to a monopoly in it. In effect, the proprietor's property, his right to exclusive use of the mark, will be confiscated.

Invalidity

6.85 There are three grounds for a finding that a trade mark has been invalidly registered (s 47). They are:

- breach of absolute grounds for refusal of registration

- an earlier registered mark

- bad faith.

Each of these is examined below.

Breach of absolute grounds for refusal of registration

6.86 A mark will be declared invalid if it was registered in breach of the absolute grounds for refusal of registration (see above **6.18** et seq), unless in the case of the grounds set out in s 3(1)(b)-(d) it has, after registration, acquired a distinctive character in relation to the goods and services for which it is registered (s 47(1)). It is worthwhile looking at a hypothetical example of the application of s 47(1). 'Fizzy' is registered as a mark for a new brand of carbonated water by X. Y, who has been accused of infringing the 'Fizzy' trade mark by marketing a mineral water under the unregistered mark 'Phizzy', seeks to have 'Fizzy' declared invalid on the grounds that the mark is devoid of distinctive character (s 3(1)(b)), is too descriptive (s 3(1)(c)) and is a sign which has become customary in current language (s 3(1)(d)). On the face of it, Y will probably succeed. But X, after registering 'Fizzy' had mounted a nationwide advertising campaign, involving the entire Manchester United football team and the group Oasis. Over the year following registration 'Fizzy' had become *the* water to drink, and the public will only be satisfied if they are sold 'Fizzy' fizzy water. 'Fizzy' may have succeeded in acquiring, subsequent to registration, a distinctive character in relation to the goods which will save it from a finding of invalidity.

6.87 In *Bach*, the CA held that it was impossible to reach a conclusion under s 47(1) as to whether a mark had acquired distinctive character through use without first identifying whether the mark was actually capable of having a distinctive character or of acquiring a distinctive character by further use before or after the date it was registered. In other wards, it is no use applying the proviso to s 47(1) if the sign cannot fulfil the requirements of s 1(1) or s 3(1)(a) (see above **6.21**). In *British Sugar*, the defendant, Robertson attacked the validity of the mark 'Treat' on all four grounds of s 3(1), including s 3(1)(a) that it was not a sign capable of distinguishing as defined in s 1(1). The court first looked at whether 'Treat' was devoid of distinctive character under s 3(1)(b) following the logic that if it was not devoid of distinctive character it must satisfy s 3(1)(a). In light of the *Bach* decision, it is submitted that s 3(1)(a) should have been considered first. Nonetheless, *British Sugar* remains relevant to understanding how s 3(1)(b)-(d) will apply to a finding of invalidity. Jacob J found that at the time of registration, 'Treat' was not sufficiently distinctive to merit registration, despite the fact that it had been used for five years prior to registration. (As has been suggested above, in **6.27**, evidence of use is not necessarily the same as evidence of distinctiveness.) Furthermore, the word 'treat' was a laudatory word and common in the trade. The onus then shifted onto British Sugar to show that 'Treat' had acquired the requisite distinctive character subsequent to registration to stay on the register and this British Sugar was unable to do. British Sugar did show considerable use, for instance Treat had 50% of the ice-cream topping sector. Polls indicated public recognition of the product, but it was held this was not the same as a public perception of 'Treat' as a trade mark. What then is the level of recognition needed for distinctiveness? Jacob J said because there is no guidance in TMA 1994 the question was left to the common sense of the judge and was one of degree. If the word is a common word, that is almost a household word (as was 'treat'), then compelling evidence is needed, such as universal or near universal acceptance of the sign as a trade mark, among the relevant public. Here, a figure of 90% was suggested. However, if the mark is used on specialist goods, a different, smaller public might of course be considered. 'Treat' had not achieved this level of recognition and was invalidly registered. Following the decisions in *Bach and Windsurfing*, however, the criteria for assessing distinctiveness are more clear cut (see **6.26** above).

An earlier registered mark

6.88 A registration will be declared invalid if there is an earlier registered mark to which the conditions apply as set out in s 5(1), (2) or (3), which describe the relative grounds for refusal of registration (see **6.33** et seq) or there is an earlier right in relation to which the conditions set out in s 5(4) are satisfied so that there is a conflict with the later registered mark (s 47(2)). The conditions for such conflict have been described above in the discussion of s 5 and also of infringement (s 10) (**6.54** et seq). In *Anne Frank* (**6.52** above), the applicant sought unsuccessfully to have the respondent's trade mark 'Anne Frank' declared invalid under s 47(2) because it claimed to have a prior right, that is the copyright in her signature.

Bad faith

6.89 If there was bad faith in the registration of the mark, a mark will be declared invalid (s 47(4)). What constitutes bad faith was identified in the discussion of the absolute grounds for refusal of registration, in particular s 3(6) (see **6.32** above). In *Avnet*, Jacob J identified the most likely ground for a finding of bad faith to be whether the proprietor uses his mark for the goods and services covered by registration (also the most likely ground for revocation of a deceptive mark (**6.76**). In *Mickey Dees TM* (1998), the Registrar found that applicant had acted in bad faith as he was not in a position to provide the full range of services listed on the registration and the mark was declared invalid.

Consequences of a finding of invalidity

6.90 If a registration is found to be invalid the effect is as if the mark had never been registered and therefore infringement proceedings can cover the period during which it was invalidly registered. But any past or closed transactions relating to the expunged mark are not affected.

Consent and acquiescence

6.91 A conflict with an earlier mark or right can be overcome if the proprietor of the earlier mark or right consents to the registration (s 47(2)) (see **6.53** above).

Licensing and assignments

6.92 A registered trade mark is a personal property right (s 2(1) and s 22). It is transmissible by assignment, testamentary disposition or by operation of the law in the same way as other personal or moveable property (s 24). It can also be charged. The two most common circumstances in which a trade mark will be used by someone other than its original proprietor are if it has been assigned or licensed.

Assignments

6.93 Assignments must be in writing signed by or on behalf of the assignor and, in contrast to the position with unregistered marks, need not include the goodwill attached to the mark (see **5.13** on passing off).

248

Assignments may be limited to apply to some, but not all, of the goods or services in relation to which the mark is registered or limited so that the assigned trade mark can be used only in a particular locality or in a particular manner (s 24(2)(a)-(b)). As a result, it is entirely possible to have a single trade mark owned by two different proprietors being used for similar goods throughout the UK, or on the same goods in different parts of the UK. The TMA 1938 contained provisions which enabled the TMR to reject assignments which rendered the mark deceptive. By contrast, under the deregulatory TMA 1994, such assignments are freely allowed, although marks which become deceptive by virtue of an assignment may be revoked (s 46(1)(d)). Although there is no requirement that an assignment must be registered, as was true under the TMA 1938, assignments are defined as 'registrable transactions' (s 25) and there are clear advantages to registration in the case of infringement.

Licensing

6.94   Licences like assignments may be limited, for instance, to some but not all of the goods or services for which the trade mark is registered or in relation to use in a particular manner or in a particular locality (s 28(1)(a)-(b)). As a result, there is the same potential for a licensed mark to become deceptive, as there is with limited assignments. The TMA 1938 was the first to allow licensing of trade marks, but the registered users regime was hedged with restrictions intended to protect the public from deceptive marks. Now the licensing regime is effectively deregulated, and it is left to the self-interest of the licensor to ensure that his mark does not become deceptive.

Rights of licensees

6.95   There are two kinds of licence, an exclusive licence, where the licensee uses the mark to the exclusion of all other persons, including the licensor (s 29) and non-exclusive licences (including sub-licenses) (s 28). The rights of exclusive licensees are different from those of non-exclusive licensees (see ss 30 and 31). Like assignments, both exclusive and non-exclusive licences are registrable transactions (s 25) and there are advantages to registration in relation to infringement actions. If a licensee steps outside the terms of his licence, he will certainly be in breach of contract but will he also be infringing the trade mark? Article 8(2) of the TM Directive says he will be, if he contravenes any provisions

249

relating to the duration of the licence, the form of the mark, the scope of the goods and services, the territory or the quality of the goods and services he provides. There is no similar provision in the TMA 1994. However, if the licensee acts beyond the scope of his licence, it is submitted that he is using the mark without the consent of the proprietor and could therefore be subject to infringement proceedings. Use of a mark by a licensee, rather than the proprietor, is sufficient to prevent a mark being revoked for non-use (s 46).

Character merchandising

6.96 It has been suggested that an action for passing off has traditionally offered the most effective means to protect character merchandising (see **5.62** on passing off). Certainly, until the TMA 1994, the registered trade mark regime offered little comfort in this area. The TMA 1938 explicitly forbade 'trafficking' in a mark, which meant dealing in the mark as a commodity in its own right, in situations where there would be no trade connection between the proprietor of the mark and the goods or services for which it was registered (a common situation in character merchandising). The fear was that the buying public could not depend upon the mark to be any guarantor either of origin, or indeed of quality. In recent years, the restrictions on trafficking were widely criticised, particularly by those involved in character merchandising, who were generally denied the protection of trade mark registration for their characters (*Re American Greeting Corporation's Application 'Holly Hobbie'* (1984)). When the government swept away the registered users category in the TMA 1994 Act, thereby allowing trafficking in marks, it justified its action by citing the greater sophistication of the buying public. In other words, today's canny consumers will not necessarily expect that the rights holder in the character had actually produced the goods on which it appears, but they will assume the merchandiser has a legitimate licence to use the character. This view was endorsed by the courts in the 'Ninja Turtle' passing off case (*Mirage Studios v Counter Feat Clothing* (see **5.65** above)).

Elvis Presley and character merchandise

6.97 Nonetheless, the recent decision in *Elvis Presley TM* (**5.67**) indicates that the registered trade mark regime still offers only limited comfort to character merchandisers. The applicants (Enterprises), the successors to Elvis Presley's merchandising business, sought to register the marks 'Elvis' and 'Elvis Presley' for toiletries. Opposition came from a Mr Shaw who had registered the mark 'Elvisly Yours', on the grounds that the applicant's marks would be confusingly similar and that they lacked sufficient distinctiveness for registration. The application was under the TMA 1938, but the HC and the CA made clear their judgments would be relevant to the TMA 1994. In his leading judgment in the CA, Walker LJ held that the marks lacked the requisite distinctiveness for registration because by the date of the application the marks, rather than acting as a badge of origin, had come to be descriptive of the goods to which they attached. The public bought Elvis memorabilia because it carried his name or image—they wanted 'Elvis soap' or 'Elvis perfume' and were indifferent as to its trade source. Or, according to Walker LJ, paraphrasing Laddie J's judgment in the HC: 'The commemoration of the late Elvis Presley is the product, and the article on which his name or image appears...is little more than a vehicle.' In effect, the marks had become so much a part of the language as to be descriptive of the goods rather than distinctive of their source and it would be wrong to deny other traders an opportunity to use them by allowing them to be registered (see also *Tarzan Trade Mark* (1970)).

6.98 More generally, in *Elvis Presley*, the CA rejected the idea that the public will automatically assume that character merchandise comes from a particular source (thus giving a narrow interpretation to the Ninja Turtle case (for the position in passing off, see **5.65** et seq)). Following *Elvis*, it will now be up to the applicant to prove a trade connection in the minds of the public between the mark and the merchandise in order to secure registration, something that will become increasingly difficult as the character or personality achieves greater public recognition. Indeed, it may be virtually impossible if the character is already a household name at the time of the proposed registration, as was the case with Elvis Presley. The CA was only willing to concede that the public may well make the trade connection more readily if there is also a connection between the character and the product against which the application is made. It gave what, for some no doubt, was the obscure example of Geoffrey Boycott and cricket bats. Following *Elvis*, TMR practice is to accept applications for the names of famous people where the goods or services are connected with their fame, such as pop groups for CDs. Clearly, a character merchandiser would be well advised to register his character or name before it achieves widespread fame. Other advice may be to seek to register a stylised name for a real person, such as 'Gazza' for the footballer, Paul Gascoigne.

Remedies

6.99 Infringement proceedings cannot begin until the date upon which the trade mark is first registered, although damages for infringement will be recoverable from the mark's priority date. In all legal proceedings relating to a registered trade mark, the registration of a person as proprietor of a trade mark shall be prima facie evidence of the validity of the original registration (s 72). Trade mark actions are brought exclusively in the HC, but it is unusual for a trade mark action to come to full trial. The proprietor's primary concern is generally to prevent further use of an infringing mark as quickly as possible. Interim injunctions are a crucial tool and if an injunction is obtained, it is frequently the case that the matter is settled with the payment of costs and a token sum for damages by the defendant (who is probably uninterested in continuing to invest in a mark he may be prevented from using in the future). The defendant may, of course, counter attack by seeking to have the claimant's mark declared invalid or revoked. The injured proprietor should therefore always combine an action for infringement with one for passing off. If he loses his registration in the course of the proceedings, he may yet be able to argue that the defendant's use amounts to passing off (*United Biscuits* is an example, see **5.9** above). The claimant is entitled to all such relief by way of damages, injunctions and accounts of profits or otherwise as is available in respect of any other property rights (s 14(2)). Specific remedies include an order for the erasure of an infringing sign (s 15) or for the delivery up of goods, materials or articles which bear it (s 16).

Groundless threats

6.100 Groundless threats to bring infringement proceedings are actionable if they are directed against anyone other than the individual who applies the mark to the goods or packaging, imports the goods, or supplies services under the mark (s 21(1)). This provision is typically intended to prevent the intimidation of third parties, such as shops which sell goods bearing infringing marks, as a means of bringing indirect pressure to bear on the primary infringer. In *Prince v Prince Sports Group*

(1998), the plaintiff had the registered mark 'Prince' for computers and the registered domain name 'prince.com' with Network Solutions (the US domain name register). The defendants who sold sporting goods and had only a US registered mark 'Prince' wrote to the plaintiffs threatening to sue for UK trade mark infringement, sending a copy of the letter to Network Solutions. The HC found both these letters amounted to groundless threats and were actionable. The test was an objective one. Would the ordinary reader see them as a threat. There is however nothing to prevent a proprietor threatening passing off proceedings against whomever he pleases. There are similar provisions against groundless threats in relation to patents and to registered designs.

Criminal sanctions

6.101 The criminal provisions are primarily designed to catch those involved in counterfeiting operations, where civil remedies are both inadequate and often difficult to enforce. The prerequisite to finding an offence has been committed is that the defendant must have acted with a view to gain to himself or another or with intent to cause loss to another and without the consent of another (s 92). Criminal sanctions apply only to use of the mark in relation to goods not services, and only to the use of trade marks, identical to or likely to be mistaken for the registered trade mark (a higher standard of similarity than similar trade marks protected by civil remedies). The goods concerned must be the goods in respect of which the trade mark is registered or, if not, the trade mark has a reputation in the UK and the use of the sign would take unfair advantage of, or be detrimental to, the distinctive character or repute of the mark (s 92(4)). It is a defence for the person accused to show that he believed or that he had reasonable grounds to believe that the use of the sign in the manner in which it was used or was to be used was not an infringement of the registered trade mark (s 92(5)). It follows that one defence against criminal sanctions would be a recourse to the infringement provisions of the TMA 1994, in order to prove the sign was not infringing.

Trade marks and the EC

6.102 Like patents and other intellectual property rights, trade mark protection may conflict with the prohibitions set out in Art 28 of the Treaty of Rome. National trade mark law (and now the CTM) endows a proprietor with a monopoly right to use his mark in the relevant territory, and, again like patent rights, may allow him to keep out the goods of others. Trade mark protection has nonetheless been justified by its role as an indicator of origin and quality (see the essential function of the mark and its specific subject matter given in *Bristol-Meyers Squibb*, **6.3** above). Thus, Art 30 (previously Art 36) of the Treaty of Rome recognises that there can be a public interest in the monopoly rights afforded by trade mark protection. However, again like patents, the existence of such a monopoly right must not constitute a means of arbitrary discrimination or disguised restriction on trade between member states.

6.103   In practice, the territorial monopoly endowed by trade mark protection can be, and indeed has been, effectively used to partition the market and impede the free movement of goods. The ECJ has built up a body of case law which has sought to balance the sometimes conflicting imperatives of promoting free competition and protecting the rights of trade mark proprietors. In doing so, it has relied on two closely related principles, 'exhaustion of rights' (which has already been considered in relation to copyright and patents) and 'common origin'.

Exhaustion of rights in the EEA

6.104   Section 12(1) of the TMA (implementing Art 7(1) of the TM Directive) states that a registered trade mark is not infringed by the use of the mark in relation to goods which have been put on the market in the EEA under the trade mark by the proprietor or with his consent. To what extent can a proprietor nonetheless use trade mark rights to prevent competition from parallel imports? In *Centrafarm v Winthrop* (1975) (see also *Centrafarm v Sterling* in relation to patents, **2.98**), the American company Sterling Drug had subsidiaries in the UK and the Netherlands [Winthrop BV]. Sterling granted both companies a patent licence to produce its drug 'Negram'. Each was also the registered proprietor of the mark 'Negram' in its respective country. Centrafarm bought Negram in the UK, where because of government price controls it was sold more cheaply, and marketed it in the Netherlands. Winthrop BV unsuccessfully sued for trade mark infringement. In reaching its decision, the ECJ was concerned to define the specific subject matter of the industrial property right protected by the first part of Art 36 (now Art 30). It was held to be the guarantee to the proprietor of a trade mark that he has the exclusive right to use the trade mark for the purpose of putting the product into circulation for the first time and therefore to protect him against competitors wishing to take advantage of the status and reputation of the mark by selling products illegally bearing the mark. In this case, the plaintiff had already exhausted his rights by putting the goods into circulation for the first time. Further circulation of these goods within the EC could not be prevented on the grounds of trade mark infringement.

Disguised restriction of trade

6.105 The extent to which Art 30 will safeguard the subject matter and essential purpose of trade marks must be considered together with the question of whether the granting of that protection will lead to a disguised restriction of trade. If it does, then protection may be withdrawn. Typically, this question will arise if a proprietor registers different marks for the same product in different member states. In *Centrafarm v American Home Products* (1978), American Home Products marketed the same drug as Serenid in the UK and as Seresta in the Netherlands. Because of domestic price controls, the UK product was cheaper. Centrafarm bought Serenid in the UK and sold it, remarked as Seresta, in the Netherlands. American Home Products sued for trade mark infringement in the Netherlands and the case went to the European Court. The ECJ found that a proprietor of a trade mark which is protected in one member state is justified pursuant to the first sentence of Art 36 (now Art 30) in preventing a product from being marketed by a third party in that member state even if previously the product had been lawfully marketed in another member state under a different mark by the same proprietor. Thus, in principle it may certainly be lawful for the manufacturer of a product to use different marks in different member states for the same product. However, if such a practice is followed by the proprietor of the marks as part of a system of marketing intended to partition the market artificially that would constitute a disguised restriction of trade for the purposes of Art 36. According to the ECJ in *Centrafarm*, the test for whether a proprietor was using trade mark protection as a disguised restriction of trade was a subjective one, that is what did the trade mark proprietor intend?

Changing the 'condition' of the goods

6.106 Section 12(2) of the TMA 1994 (implementing Art 7(2) of the TM Directive) states that exhaustion of rights within the EEA does not apply where there exist legitimate reasons for the proprietor to oppose further dealings in the goods (in particular, where the condition of the goods has been changed or impaired after they have been put on the market). Section 12(2) thus provides a possible alternative avenue for trade mark proprietors to control the further marketing of their goods. It is one they have been keen to use. It has raised the fundamental question of the extent to which a proprietor can object to the way in which a parallel importer changes the condition of his goods or uses or applies his mark. This question has given rise to considerable case law, both European and domestic. Much but not all of this case law has involved the repackaging or rebranding of pharmaceuticals, typically in order to conform to national regulations or standards (such as, for instance, that labels and instructions are in the appropriate language). *Centrafarm v American Home Products* concerned rebranding of the goods. It was held that rebranding by the parallel importer was allowed only if it could be shown that the intention of the proprietor in using the different marks was to partition the market, which was a subjective test. The slightly earlier case of *Hoffman La Roche v Centrafarm* (1978) related to repackaging. In *Hoffman La Roche*, the ECJ held that the repackaging of goods was not an infringement of the mark and could not be used by the proprietor to prevent parallel imports as long as repackaging did not effect the specific subject matter of the trade mark (for instance, by obscuring the origin of the goods or by altering their condition). In *Hoffman La Roche*, the test for whether repackaging was non-infringing was an objective one. Would the proprietor's objection to repackaging result in the artificial partitioning of the market?

The test of necessity

6.107 But when would it be legitimate for a parallel importer to repackage the goods? This was the question raised in the recent case of *Bristol-Myers Squibb v Paranova* (1996). In *Bristol-Myers*, the ECJ held that repackaging was acceptable but only if it was 'necessary' in order to market the product in the country of importation. The test of necessity was held to be an objective one. In this case the ECJ gave as an example of necessity repackaging by a parallel importer if different package sizes are used in different member states. In *Bristol-Meyers*, the ECJ also set out certain obligations that parallel importers have in relation to repackaging, most notably to give the trade mark owner notice of their intentions. Conversely, the ECJ noted that poor presentation by the repackager might damage the trade marks reputation and the trade mark owner may oppose the parallel importation of products in which the repacking is defective, untidy or of poor quality. (For similar principles applied to non-pharmaceutical products, see *Frits Loendersloot v George Ballantine* (1998).)

Rebranding the goods

6.108   Most recently, in *Pharmacia and Upjohn v Paranova* (2000), the ECJ in effect reversed itself in *Centrafarm v American Home Products* and held that the test for whether rebranding was non-infringing was also an objective one. It did not depend upon the intent of the trade mark owner when selecting different marks in different member states. Instead the ECJ applied the criterion of 'necessity' to rebranding. In other words, rebranding may be permitted if it was objectively necessary to obtain access to the market in the state of importation. Necessity would arise if the 'rules or practices' in the country of importation would prevent the product in question from being marketed, for instance if its consumer protection laws prohibited the use of the original trade mark on the grounds that it was 'liable to mislead' consumers. Following *Upjohn*, it is up to each member state to determine whether there is a sufficient degree of necessity to justify rebranding. However, necessity is not satisfied if the reason for rebranding is simply for the parallel importer's commercial advantage. It has been suggested that the test of necessity set out in *Upjohn* will also be the same for repackaging.

6.109   A recent UK case looked at the issue of necessity in relation to repackaging and rebranding. *Glaxo v Dowelhurst (No 2)* (2000) was concerned with the rebranding of pharmaceuticals which had been the subject of parallel importation from other EEA member states into the UK. The claimants sued for infringement of trade mark. They argued, following *Upjohn*, that if repackaging of products was permissible only if it was necessary, then repackaging that was not strictly necessary was infringing, even if it did no harm to the goods or the specific subject matter of the mark. Laddie J disagreed. He took the view that as long as the specific subject matter of the mark was not damaged by repackaging or by rebranding or by use of the mark to advertise the goods, the proprietor could not object just because such repackaging or rebranding was not necessary. According to Laddie J to recognise such an objection would place a general restriction on the free movement of goods and allow trade mark proprietors to use national trade mark rights to override the free market. Only if such repackaging or rebranding caused substantial damage to the specific subject matter or the essential function of the mark would the test of necessity came into play. In these circumstances, repackaging or rebranding would only be indulged to the extent that they were necessary. Other member states have taken a different view of necessity, reflecting the interpretation put by the claimants in *Glaxo v Dowelhurst*. Following this case, the question of the proper interpretation of necessity has been referred to the ECJ by the UK court.

Changing the 'mental' condition of the goods

6.110   It is submitted that the difference in approach between the UK courts and other member states over the question of necessity reflects the different emphasis placed upon the role of trade marks. In the UK, the courts typically emphasise the trade mark's function as an indicator of origin. Other member states are more likely to recognise the extrinsic qualities of trade marks and so look sympathetically on attempts to prevent dilution of a mark's reputation through repackaging and rebranding, even if the origin function is unaffected. It has already been noted that in *Bristol-Meyers*, the ECJ suggested that trade mark proprietors might object to repackaging if it led to poor presentation and hence to damage to the trade mark's reputation. This approach was confirmed in *Christian Dior v Evora* (1998). The ECJ was asked whether legitimate reasons for opposing further dealing in parallel imports extended to use of the brand which would impair or change the 'mental' condition of the goods rather than their physical condition, in this case the manner in which the reseller advertised the goods. The facts were that Dior France had sought to maintain the high prices paid for its goods and its luxurious image by distributing its perfumes only through exclusive outlets. Evora operated a chain of chemist shops in the Netherlands and sold Dior perfumes obtained through parallel imports. It advertised the perfumes in leaflets which reproduced Dior's marks and also advertised similar goods which were not all of the same quality. The ECJ was asked first whether a reseller can use the marks attached to the goods for advertising purposes. It held that they could. The second question was whether the proprietor could object because the way the reseller uses the mark damages its prestigious image so that the advertising function (or reputation of the mark) is endangered. Again the ECJ answered in the affirmative. Finally, it was asked whether such damage constitutes a legitimate reason which would allow the proprietor to oppose the marks use for further commercialisation. Once again the ECJ said that it did. The proprietor could oppose use of the mark where, given the specific facts of the case, use of the trade mark to advertise the goods damaged its reputation, for example in an advertising leaflet which puts the mark in a context which seriously detracts from its image. In *Zino Davidoff v A&G Imports* (1999) which involved the parallel import of luxury cosmetics from outside the EEA, the HC gave a narrow interpretation of the *Dior* guidelines. Laddie J accepted that legitimate reasons for a proprietor to object to further commercialisation of his goods encompassed impairment to both their 'physical' or 'mental' condition, but such damage must be substantial. Nor did it mean anything that might undermine the mark's luxury image (such as, for instance, selling the goods at a lower price). In this case, obliteration of the batch codes (marked on the goods) by the defendant was not sufficient. In the later case of *Glaxo v Dowelhurst*, Laddie J appeared to narrow the *Dior* guidelines further still by suggesting that sufficient damage to a mark's reputation must constitute damage to its specific subject matter (see above **6.3**) and not simply general damage to its image. Whether this interpretation is correct will inevitably fall to be decided by the ECJ.

Common origin

6.111   The principle of exhaustion of rights depends upon the fact that the proprietor has given his consent to the first marketing of the goods bearing his mark in a Member State. What is the situation where no such consent has been given? In *Van Zuylen v Hag* (1974), known as 'Hag I', the Hag trade mark for decaffeinated coffee had originally been owned by a German company, which had sold the product in Belgium and Luxembourg. After World War I, the right to the Hag trade mark was sequestered as enemy property and passed through assignment to the Van Zuylen company. The German company Hag, planned to export coffee into Belgium bearing the 'Hag' mark and Van Zuylen alleged trade mark infringement. In this case, Van Zuylen had certainly not consented to the first marketing of these particular goods. However, the ECJ found that where the trade marks have a common origin the rights of one trade mark owner could not be used to prevent the parallel import of goods bearing the same mark into its territory. *Hag I* was widely criticised as pushing the exhaustion of rights principle beyond sensible boundaries.

The decision in *Hag II* (*SA CNL-SUCAL v Hag* (1991)) seemed to justify this criticism. Now the German company sought to prevent the importation of coffee under the mark 'Kaffee Hag' into Germany by Van Zuylen. In what amounted in effect to a reversal of its earlier decision, the ECJ found that trade mark protection could be used to prevent such imports. The ECJ based its decision on the principle that for a trade mark to fulfil its role it must offer a guarantee that all goods bearing it have been produced under the control of a single undertaking which is accountable for its quality. Here, because of the forcible expropriation of the 'Hag' mark, the goods were being marketed without the German company's consent and it effectively had no control over the quality of the goods marketed under the 'Hag' mark.

Ideal standard

6.112 The finding in *Hag II* was generally understood to mean that the exhaustion of rights principle did not apply where there had been no consent to the division of trade mark ownership in different member states. This view was radically altered by the decision of the ECJ in *IHT v Ideal Standard* (1995). American Standard Group held through its German and French subsidiaries the trade mark 'Ideal Standard' for sanitary fittings and heating equipment in Germany and France. In 1984, the French company assigned its trade mark for heating equipment to a third party which in turn assigned it to the parent company of IHT. IHT sought to import heating equipment marked 'Ideal Standard' into Germany. The German company had, by this time, ceased to use the mark on heating equipment but continued to use it on sanitary fittings. It alleged trade mark infringement in Germany. The ECJ considered, inter alia, the question of whether prohibiting IHT from marketing the goods in Germany on the basis of trade mark infringement constituted an unlawful restriction on trade under Arts 30 and 36 (now Arts 28 and 30). A key difference from the *Hag* cases was that the initial division of the Ideal Standard mark and, indeed, its subsequent assignment were voluntary. The ECJ held that the *Hag II* principle nonetheless applied. Trade mark rights are both territorial in nature and independent of each other. Thus there is nothing to prevent a company voluntarily divesting itself of its trade mark in different territories to different third parties. The consent for such an assignment was not however the same consent as is required for the application of the doctrine of exhaustion of rights. For the latter, the owner of the right in the importing state (in this case

Germany) must directly or indirectly, be able to determine the products to which the trade mark may be affixed in the exporting state (in this case France) and to control their quality. That power is lost if, by assignment, control over the trade mark is surrendered to a third party having no economic link with the assignor. It was irrelevant whether that control was actually exercised. It was sufficient that there was the possibility of control, to disqualify a proprietor from opposing parallel imports. By separate routes the cases concerning exhaustion of rights and common origin have reached a similar destination. If the former have emphasised the narrow interpretation which must be accorded to the protection of trade marks if it interferes with the free circulation of goods, the latter have emphasised the important function of trade mark as a guarantee of origin which may limit the freedom to parallel import.

Trade mark protection and competition law in the EU

6.113   Articles 81 and 82 of the Treaty of Rome are designed to protect and promote fair competition . These principles may also conflict with registered trade mark protection, particularly in the context of licenses which may restrict the use of the mark between and within member states.

A market sharing agreement which prevents other traders from competing in a particular market may well fall foul of Art 81. Such a situation might arise if a proprietor who has a trade mark registered in different member states grants an exclusive licence in one country, on the grounds, for instance that the licensee does not attempt to market the product abroad. Similarly, in *Campari* (1978), the Commission held that an exclusive trade mark licence which restricted the right of the licensor to license other users within the same territory was, in principle, a restriction of competition likely to effect member states and therefore a breach of Art 85 (now Art 81). However, the Commission will also look at the effects of such a licence. If it decides the licence is actually beneficial to competition with other brands, as it did in the *Campari* case, it might grant it an individual exemption under Art 85 (now Art 81). Exclusive trade mark licences might also ride on the back of block exemptions granted to certain technology transfers and distribution and purchasing agreements, so long as the trade mark licence is ancillary to the technology transfer. In a recent interesting case, Laddie J in the HC held that it was arguably anti-competitive concerted practice for a group of trade mark proprietors to band together to sue a parallel importer

261

for trade mark infringement. The case, *Glaxo v Dowelhurst* (2000), preceded the action *Glaxo v Dowelhurst* (2000), which has been noted above (see **6.109**). In the earlier case, the defendants sought to amend their defences and counterclaims in order to challenge alleged anti-competitive practices by the claimants, a number of pharmaceutical companies. Laddie J noted that although trade mark rights did not offend against Art 81, if they were put to co-operative use they could do so. Thus even though Art 7(2) of the TM Directive (s 12(2) of the TMA 1994) allowed a trade mark proprietor to prevent the free market of goods in certain circumstances, this did not mean he was similarly entitled to do so in concert with others by mounting a 'collaborative attack' on parallel importers. *Glaxo v Dowelhurst (No 1)* raises interesting issues which again will need to be settled at the European level.

Parallel imports from outside the EEA

6.114   The terms of the TMA 1994 (following the TM Directive) ensure that, except in exceptional circumstances, a trade mark proprietor cannot prevent the parallel importation of goods bearing his mark into one state from another in the EEA where those goods have been put on the market in the EEA by him or with his consent (see **6.104** et seq). But are the trade mark proprietor's rights similarly exhausted if goods are first put on the market by him or with his consent outside the EEA and subsequently brought into the EEA by a parallel importer? This question has generated heated debate in the EU, which has been fuelled by the practice of retailers of selling branded goods acquired on what is known as the 'grey market'. Grey market goods are principally products made by a trade mark owner or a licensee and marketed in countries outside the EEA, which are then re-imported or imported for the first time into the EEA and sold at reduced prices. Price reductions are often possible because the goods are sold at different prices outside the EEA, perhaps because of currency fluctuations, to get rid of out of date stock or because they are of a different (perhaps inferior) quality. In the UK, large supermarket chains have been at the forefront of acquiring these grey market goods. In turn, brand holders, such as Calvin Klein and Levis, have objected to the sale of their goods at reduced prices in unauthorised outlets, claiming that as a consequence the image or reputation of their marks is impaired.

International exhaustion in the UK law before the TMA 1994

6.115 A number of cases decided under the TMA 1938 suggested that the UK did recognise international exhaustion within limits. In *Revlon v Cripps & Lee* (1980), the defendant imported shampoos from the US marked Flex. The UK registered proprietor of the same mark alleged infringement. It was held that there was no infringement as these proprietors formed part of the same group of companies and the manufacturer of Flex in the US had dealt with US wholesalers without any prohibition as to the export of the goods. The decision in *Revlon* was distinguished in *Colgate v Markwell Finance* (1990). In this case, the defendants were prohibited from importing Colgate toothpaste manufactured in Brazil. It was held that the 'Colgate' mark applied to the goods in Brazil, was a Brazilian mark and never intended to be used in the UK. Evidence used to support this conclusion was the fact the Brazilian product was inferior to that of the one sold in the UK. In essence, the CA said that although the 'Colgate' mark did show the source of the product, it undermined the other role of trade marks which was to allow the consumer to assume that goods would be of a uniform quality. Thus, at the time of the implementation of the TM Directive, the UK appeared to recognise international exhaustion so long as the public was not deceived as to the quality or source of the goods.

The decision in Silhouette

6.116 In *Silhouette v Hartlauer* (1998), the issue for the ECJ was whether the TM Directive intended to limit exhaustion to within the EEA or whether it intended to set a minimum standard which allowed separate countries to make their own rules relating to international exhaustion. Silhouette, an Austrian company manufactured high-priced fashion spectacles distributed under its Silhouette mark. In 1995, it sold outdated spectacle frames to a Bulgarian company, which, Silhouette claimed, was instructed to sell the frames only in eastern Europe. Hartlauer, also based in Austria, had a chain of outlets for cut-priced goods which were not supplied by Silhouette, which preferred more upmarket retailers. Hartlauer acquired the spectacles. The question for the ECJ was whether Art 7(1) should be interpreted to mean that the trade mark entitles a proprietor to prohibit a third party from using the mark for goods which have been put on the market under that mark outside the EEA. The ECJ concluded that the TM Directive neither introduced international exhaustion nor did it allow individual member states to adopt international exhaustion or not. In particular, the ECJ relied on the fact that the TM Directive was intended to approximate laws between member states in order to promote the free market of goods. Allowing individual states to decide on whether to adopt international exhaustion individually would have erected trade barriers between them.

6.117 The decision in *Silhouette* was confirmed in *Sebago v GB Unic* (1999) which involved the parallel importation of shoes into Benelux from El Salvador without Sebago's consent. It is possible to distinguish *Sebago* from *Silhouette* because in the latter the imported glasses were out of date, whereas in *Sebago* identical shoes to the parallel imports were still on sale in the Benelux countries. The ECJ was asked, in essence, whether there was consent within the meaning of Art 7(1) where the trade mark proprietor had consented to the marketing in the EEA of goods which were similar or identical to those in respect of which exhaustion was claimed or whether consent must relate to each individual item of product in respect of which exhaustion was claimed. The ECJ held the latter, explicitly reaffirming their decision in *Silhouette* that Art 7(1) covered exhaustion in the EEA only.

The debate

6.118 Reaction to the *Silhouette* decision was predictably mixed. It was welcomed by brand owners seeking to maintain control over the marketing of their goods and hence the value of their brands' reputations and by those EEA countries where manufacturers might lose out from the importation of cheaper goods from outside the EEA. Those in favour of international exhaustion however suggest that it favours the consumers with lower prices and, in an era of free trade, prevents the erection of tariff and trade barriers by indirect means. From a legal perspective, critics of *Silhouette* have argued that it is the trade mark's basic purpose which should determine whether there is international exhaustion. The essential function of the trade mark is as a badge of origin. However, *Silhouette* would allow a proprietor to object to any unauthorised dealings with his mark even though it continues to fulfil its essential function. Some have argued for the logic of the earlier UK position where international exhaustion was allowed unless the mark was deceptive (Cornish 'Trade Marks: Portcullis for the EEA' [1998] EIPR 172).

Not surprisingly the most forceful criticism of *Silhouette* has come from the UK, where the courts continue to privilege the trade mark's function as a badge of origin above its extrinsic features. In *Zino Davidoff* (see **6.110** above), the HC was concerned with the question of international exhaustion since the plaintiffs cosmetics had been imported from Singapore without its consent. Following *Silhouette*, the plaintiff sought to argue that their sale in the UK would be infringing. Laddie J held that it would not. He based his judgment on English contract law rather than the law relating to international exhaustion. In essence, he found that while *Silhouette* allowed the plaintiff expressly to restrict the sale of its goods in the EEA, English contract law as it has developed maintains a rebuttable presumption that, in the absence of a full and explicit restriction being imposed on all purchasers and all subsequent purchasers at the time of sale, the proprietor should be treated as having consented to his goods being imported into the EEA (for the rule applied in relation to patents, see *Betts v Willmott* (1871) (**2.103**)). In this case, Laddie J held that no such explicit restrictions had been laid down and the defendant's sale of the plaintiff's products in the UK was not infringing.

The future

6.119   It is submitted that the decision in *Zino Davidoff* obviously goes against the spirit of *Silhouette*. In the latter case, the ECJ had emphasised the importance of avoiding different rules concerning international exhaustion in member states, since this would inevitably impede the free movement of goods within the common market and hence undermine the intentions of the TM Directive. On the logic of *Zino Davidoff*, whether member states recognise international exhaustion would depend on how their laws relating to contract may be interpreted. The ECJ has now been asked to give a preliminary ruling as to whether consent of the brand owner to EEA marketing of his goods has to be express or direct or can it be given implicitly or indirectly. Secondly, it has been asked whether if, under the law of a non-EEA country in which the goods are distributed, the brand owner could have placed effective territorial restrictions on resale but did not do so, does this constitute consent to EEA marketing? While the ECJ will of course have its own opinion, it is most likely that the problems surrounding international exhaustion will need a political solution. This was the view expressed by the Advocate-General in *Silhouette*. The political outcome may be influenced by whether other states or trading blocks take a reciprocal approach (the US does not) and on the balance of economic interests within member states.

Interestingly, the questions raised by *Silhouette* are precisely those which, it is suggested, have plagued the interpretation of the TM Directive overall. In essence, the question for the future is to what extent trade mark protection will extend beyond the mark's role as an indicator of origin and recognise its value as the embodiment of an 'advertising function'.

Further reading

Kerly's Law of Trade Marks and Trade Names (13th edn, 2000)

Pickering *Trade Marks in Theory and Practice* (1998)

M Richardson 'Copyright in Trade Marks? On Understanding Trade Mark Dilution' [2000] IPQ 66

Self-test questions

1. David Simone, the world famous footballer who plays for Neasden Wanderers, learns that his cousin Frank Simone is planning to sell 'Simone' football shirts. Frank is also planning to publish a fan magazine called *Neasden Football* and an exposé of the club, a book entitled *The Wanderers: the Naked Truth*. David has applied to register 'Simone' as a trade mark for cosmetics and footwear including football boots. Neasden Wanderers have two registered marks, one consisting of the word 'Neasden' printed inside a football, which they use on their programmes. The second is the word 'Wanderers'. Both are registered inter alia for printed matter. Advise David and Neasden Wanderers on trade marks generally in relation to Frank's business plans.

2. Andrea has designed a hat, with a distinctive bell shape which is both decorative and an excellent design for protecting the head from high winds. She plans to make it out of cheap plastic and she has named it 'Bell Armour'. There is a French fashion house which produces a world-famous perfume, 'Belle Amour'. What trade mark protection can Andrea obtain for her hat?

3. To what extent are trade marks now protected from 'dilution' in the UK?

266

CHAPTER SEVEN

Confidential information

SUMMARY

The juridical justification for a law of confidence and its development

The three elements of the law of confidence

Element 1: confidential information
The form of confidential information; the springboard doctrine
Types of confidential information

Element 2: the confidential obligation
The limited purpose test; information given to third parties
Other relationships of confidence: employees and confidential information

Element 3: Unauthorised use or disclosure
The public interest defence and other defences

Remedies

The law of confidence: an introduction

7.1 The law of confidence has been seen as necessary to upholding certain standards both in public and private life (see for example *Coco v Clark (Engineering)* (1969)). According to Sir John Donaldson MR in *A-G v Guardian Newspapers* (1999), the 'Spycatcher' case,

> There is an inherent public interest in individual citizens and the state having an enforceable right to the maintenance of confidence. Life would be intolerable in personal and commercial terms, if information could

not be given or received in confidence and the right to have that information respected supported by the force of law.

In fact, the law of confidence has most often been used to protect commercial or trade secrets, such as customer lists or industrial know how, where economic interests will also be at stake. But the law of confidence may apply equally to any information provided it has the necessary quality of confidence (see **7.7** et seq). Prominent cases have concerned, for example, the private lives of the famous and the relatively obscure and, in the 'Spycatcher' case, the details of the UK's espionage operations. However, it is also important to remember that there may be occasions when the public interest would appear to demand the publication of secrets which otherwise would have the necessary quality of confidence. There has been considerable debate as to when public interest should override confidentiality, none more so than during the 'Spycatcher' case itself (see **7.47** et seq).

The nature of the law of confidence

7.2   The juridical justification for a law of confidence has been located in equity and in contract. More controversially, some have argued that it also has some basis in the law of property.

The equitable basis

7.3   It has been said that 'the equitable jurisdiction in cases of breach of confidence is ancient' (*Coco*). In two mid-nineteenth century cases, the courts clearly identified an equitable jurisdiction for breach of confidence actions, which would operate regardless of any contractual relationship between the parties. In both *Prince Albert v Strange* (1849) and the almost contemporaneous case of *Morison v Moat* (1851), a number of causes of action were advanced to justify the protection of confidential information, including breach of trust and contract, but in both cases the courts also identified breach of confidence as a separate cause of action. The ability of the court to act independently in equity in the absence of express or implied contractual obligations of confidentiality was confirmed in a number of key 20th century decisions, which again roughly coincided. According to Lord Greene MR in *Saltman v Campbell* (1948): 'If a defendant is proved to have used confidential information directly or indirectly obtained from a plaintiff without the consent, express or implied, of the plaintiff, he will be guilty of an infringement of the plaintiffs' rights.' He went on to say that the obligation to respect confidence is not limited to cases where the parties are in a contractual relationship. The CA judgment in *Seager v Copydex* (1967) confirmed that the court will act independently of the law of contract. The plaintiff, during preliminary negotiations with the defendants, revealed to them secret information about a carpet grip which he had invented. The negotiations broke down but the defendants produced a carpet grip of their own which apparently made use of the plaintiff's information. There was no contract between the parties. In his judgment, Lord Denning MR stated:

> The law on this subject does not depend on any implied contract. It depends upon the broad principle of equity that he who receives information in confidence shall not take unfair advantage of it. He must not make use of it to the prejudice of him who gave it without obtaining his consent.

In the third major case, *Coco*, Megarry J said: 'I think it quite plain from the *Saltman* case that the obligation of confidence may exist where, as in this case, there is no contractual relationship between the parties.' He described the applicable law as 'the pure equitable doctrine of confidence, unaffected by contract.'

Confidential information as property

7.4 Is confidential information also property? Certainly, it may have a considerable economic value. Generally, however, the view is that it is not. Confidential information is not recognised as property for the purpose of the Theft Act, although of course one can steal the physical medium upon which it is recorded (*Oxford v Moss* (1979)). What is at issue is the right to protect the confidentiality of the information, not its physical embodiment. A recent Law Commission Consultation paper, 'Legislating the Criminal Code: Misuse of Trade Secrets'(LCCP No 150 (HMSO) 1997), recommended that the unauthorised use or disclosure of a secret be a criminal offence. However, it is submitted that the basis for an action for breach of confidence remains in contract or equity.

Contractual obligations

7.5 Any competent lawyer will advise a client to seek a confidentiality agreement, before he discloses commercially valuable confidential information to another party. Limitations to express contractual terms might arise if publication of the information is held to be in the public interest (*Hubbard v Vosper* (1972)). Or an express contractual term might be held to be void or unenforceable if, for example, it is drawn too widely and therefore unreasonably restricts the actions of one party. A typical example might be a contractual term which applies to an employee once he leaves his employment (see below **7.30** et seq). Conversely, in certain circumstances, the courts will imply a contractual term in the absence of an express obligation to respect confidentiality (*Saltman; Wessex Dairies v Smith* (1935)). It is also possible for the court to identify both equitable and contractual obligations based on the same set of facts (*Robb v Green* (1895); *Saltman*). The relationship between the equitable and contractual bases giving rise to a breach of confidence are examined in greater detail in the discussion of employee confidentiality (see **7.30** below).

The elements of a breach of confidence action

7.6   There are three elements which will normally be required for a breach of confidence action to succeed. These were set out by Megarry J in *Coco*. They are:

- the information must have the 'necessary quality of confidence about it'

- the information must have been imparted in circumstances where the confidant ought reasonably to have known that the information had been imparted in confidence

- there must be unauthorised use or disclosure of that information to the detriment of the party communicating it.

Each of these elements will be looked at in turn.

Element 1: the confidential information

7.7   Confidential information must 'have the necessary quality of confidentiality about it' (*Saltman* per Lord Greene). But no single and clear definition of what constitutes 'confidential information' is to be found in the case law. Generally, the courts have offered a negative definition. In *Saltman*, Lord Greene stated that confidential information 'must not be something which is public property and public knowledge' (see also *Seager* per Lord Denning). According to Lord Denning in *Woodward v Hutchins* (1977), it should not be in the 'public domain'. In this case, the CA held that an incident on a 'jumbo jet' during which Tom Jones 'got high', which was known to all the passengers, was in the public domain. In *Coco*, Megarry J said, 'However confidential the circumstances of communication, there can be no breach of confidence in revealing to others something which is already common knowledge.' Furthermore, the law of confidence will not protect 'trivial tittle-tattle' (*Coco*). Nor will it protect 'useless' information, such as a betting system based on the age of the moon (*McNicol v Sportsman's Book Stores* (1930)). Generally, once any information is in the public domain it is no longer confidential (for exceptions, see **7.13** below). This statement, of course, begs the question of when does information enter the public domain. Or, put another way, when does it become sufficiently accessible to the public, that it is no longer confidential. According to Scott J in 'Spycatcher', the answer will depend upon the circumstances of the case. The court may, for instance, take a different view depending upon whether it is dealing with commercial information, government information or personal information. Each of these categories are considered separately below, although there are some broad principles which apply to them all.

Material in the public domain

7.8 A body of information which has been constructed by combining in a novel way information which is in the public domain may possess the necessary quality of confidence. As Megarry J observed: 'Novelty depends upon the thing itself, and not upon the quality of its constituent parts.' He went on, 'Indeed, often the more striking the novelty, the more commonplace its components' (*Coco*). To endow such information with the necessary quality of confidence, some product of the human brain, whether it be termed skill, ingenuity or originality, must have been applied to its creation. In *Coco*, the information related to the design of a moped engine, but the plaintiff failed to convince the court that his ideas were not 'common to the moped world'. More recently, it was suggested that confidentiality would not reside in a substantial collection of data all of which was in the public domain, in this case a list of features of contact lenses, because even though it had presumably required time and effort

271

to compile, it had required no particular skill (*Ocular Sciences*). Conversely, in *Exchange Telegraph v Central News* (1897), the plaintiffs transmitted horse racing information to subscribers by telegraph, one of whom gave the information to a rival wire service. It was held that although all the members of the public who attended the race meetings knew the results, even larger numbers of the public did not. It followed that publication by the plaintiffs to a limited number of subscribers did not place the information in the public domain. In *Schering Chemicals v Falkman* (1982), the information at issue was available to any member of the public who was prepared to undertake a lengthy and painstaking trawl through the scientific literature. The defendant, who had not made such a search, was held to have breached confidentiality.

Dissemination by the confider

7.9   Whether information has the necessary quality of confidence may depend upon not just how or how widely the confidential information is disseminated but also upon who publishes it. A number of cases have considered when action by the confider destroys the confidentiality of his own information. It has been held that publication of a patent specification including confidential information will destroy the latter's confidentiality. In *Mustad v Allcock* (1964), the plaintiff brought proceedings for breach of confidence after D, the ex-employee of a company it had purchased, disclosed confidential details of its fish-hook manufacturing machine to a competitor. Before the case came to court the plaintiff applied for and was granted a patent which covered the confidential information. The HL found that the patent disclosed the 'essential part' of the plaintiff's machine to the world, and so the plaintiff's action had destroyed the confidentiality of the information at issue. The 'secret, as a secret, had ceased to exist' (see also *Franchi v Franchi* (1967)). However, in *Cranleigh Precision Engineering v Bryant* (1966), the defendant, a director of the plaintiff, learned of a patent which affected the plaintiff's design, a fact he withheld from the plaintiff. He purchased the patent and then set up a rival company. He was found liable for breach of confidence despite his argument that the information contained in the patent specification was in the public domain. Here the information covered by the patent had not been published by the plaintiff, as was the case in *Mustad*. Rather, the defendant had used confidential information which had been available to him as a director of the company to take advantage of the patent himself. In *Dunford v Johnson* (1978), a company failed to impose an obligation of confidence on two shareholders over a confidential financial report because, inter alia, it had revealed the report to all its institutional shareholders.

Accessibility through analysis or reverse engineering

7.10   Placing a product on the market will not in itself destroy the confidentiality of information, which may be derived by reverse engineering of the product or by other analyses of it, provided it would require substantive work to acquire such information (*Ackroyds v Islington Plastics* (1962)). This was the view taken in *Terrapin v Builders Supply* (1967). The plaintiffs designed and marketed a novel type of portable building, which the defendants manufactured on their behalf. The defendants, making use of confidential information from the plaintiffs, manufactured and marketed similar buildings once its contract with the plaintiffs had expired. The defendants argued that by publishing detailed brochures and putting their buildings on the market so that a purchaser might analyse them, the plaintiffs had destroyed any confidentiality. This argument was rejected. The court found that a member of the public, without the benefit of the confidential information, would have had to employ considerable effort in order to analyse the buildings in this way. The information was not, therefore, accessible to the public. Conversely, it was recently held that encrypted information in a commercially available computer program did not have the necessary quality of confidence about it. Any purchaser with the skills to de-encrypt the program would have access to the information. The fact that the information was encrypted did not make it confidential (*Mars v Teknowledge* (1999)).

The form of confidential information

7.11   Unlike the situation in copyright, the law of confidence will protect information even if it has not been recorded in any material form. Confidential information may be communicated orally (*Seager*). It may also, unlike in copyright, consist of an idea rather than something written down. However, as a general rule, for an idea to be protected as confidential, it must be sufficiently developed to be commercially attractive and to be capable of being realised. With respect to an idea for a television programme, for example, this might require its extensive elaboration. Either way, the idea must have some originality or evidence of the application of ingenuity (*Fraser v Thames Television* (1983)). In *Fraser*, the plaintiffs' idea for a television series based on the experiences of a female rock band, 'Rock Bottom', was disclosed to the defendant over an extended lunch. The subsequent highly successful series, 'The Rock Follies', which was made without the plaintiffs' permission, not only had lead characters closely modelled on those in the real band, but also featured a number of their real-life experiences. It was held that the content of the idea was clearly identifiable, original, of potential commercial attractiveness and capable of reaching fruition. It was, therefore, protectable under the law of confidence. By contrast, in *De Maudsley v Palumbo* (1996), the plaintiffs had an idea for a night club which they communicated to the defendants at a supper party. Among its features were to be a 'high tech' industrial setting, a VIP lounge and all-night opening. The defendants subsequently opened the club as 'The Ministry of Sound'. The plaintiffs, who had no share in it, sued the defendants for breach of confidence. Knox J held that before the status of confidential information can be achieved by a concept or idea it is necessary to go beyond simply identifying a desirable goal. A considerable degree of particularity is required to show an idea capable of being realised as a finished product in the relevant medium. This did not exclude simplicity, but vagueness and simplicity were not the same. It was also necessary to show that the idea contained some significant element of originality.

The springboard doctrine 1: when does it arise

7.12   Suppose information is given by company A to company B in confidence which subsequently becomes public. B will be in a better starting position to compete with A than will other traders who must wait for the information to enter the public domain. Similarly, what if company A gives confidential information to company B which the latter realises can be gleaned from the publicly available information if sufficient effort is expended, as was the situation in *Terrapin*? Here again, by exploiting the confidential information, B can gain a competitive advantage both against A and also against other potential competitors, who will be put to the effort of collecting the information themselves. In other jurisdictions, such behaviour may fall foul of specific laws against unfair competition or misappropriation, or, as in the US, trade secrets laws. In the absence of such laws in the UK, the law of confidence offers the best protection against these practices. In *Terrapin*, it was held wrong that a person, who has obtained information in confidence, should, in either of the two situations outlined above, be allowed to use it as a springboard for activities detrimental to the confider. In *Seager*, where the defendants had copied the plaintiff's carpet grip, the details of which had been given in confidence, the CA considered the situation where the information was in part public and in part private. Lord Denning stated that the confidant should not get a start over others. He must either go to the public source to get the material in the public domain, 'or, at any rate, not be in a better position than if he had gone to the public source.'

The springboard doctrine 2: when does it expire

7.13   The springboard doctrine has now become an accepted part of the law of confidence, but it also gives rise to difficult questions. What if it places the original recipient of the confidential information under a continuing obligation of confidence even though the material involved has now entered the public domain and others are free to use it at will? If the information is published by the confider then the problem is solved, since no continuing obligation of confidence remains for any party including the original recipient. But where the information is published by a third party, the recipient may well remain under a continuing obligation of confidence, especially if he came across the information because of his special relationship to the plaintiff, as was the case in *Cranleigh* (see **7.9** above). A third situation arises where confidential information is released into the public domain by the recipient. Will the courts allow him to rely upon the fact that the information is public knowledge when it has become so by his own wrongful act? In 'Spycatcher', Lord Goff commented that once confidential information had entered the public domain there could not, under any circumstances, be a continuing obligation of confidence since the subject matter of the obligation had been destroyed, although the confider should be compensated for the damage caused (see also *Ocular Sciences*). However, prevailing judicial opinion is that, depending upon the particular facts of the case, the recipient may continue to be under an obligation of confidence, since it would be wrong for the recipient to be in a position to benefit from his own wrong doing. An example might be where the plaintiff and the defendant remain the only two companies competing in the market (*Speed Seal v Paddington* (1986) per Fox LJ).

7.14   The question then arises as to how long the obligation not to use the information should last. Given that the information is now free to be exploited by the public at large, should the recipient alone be indefinitely precluded from using it? In a commercial setting, courts have generally taken the view that the recipient's obligation should be finite. According to Lord Denning in *Potters-Ballotini v Weston-Baker* (1977):

> Although a man must not use such information as a springboard to get a start over others, nevertheless that springboard does not last for ever. If he does use it, a time may come when so much has happened that he can no longer be restrained.

It has been suggested that the restraint should remain only so long as the recipient would continue to have an 'unfair advantage'. In *Roger Bullivant v Ellis* (1987), the defendant was the managing director of the plaintiff's engineering firm. He left with confidential information and started a competing business. His contract of employment with the plaintiff had included a 12-month non-competition clause. The HC granted the plaintiff an interim injunction to prevent the defendant from contacting its customers. The defendant appealed. In the CA, it was held that in cases where the court was making an order restricting a defendant's freedom, in order to prevent him gaining an unfair advantage over the plaintiff, it was necessary to consider how long that advantage might reasonably be expected to last and to limit the order accordingly. In this case, since the contract of employment had specified a year, the order should last no longer. Typically, in such situations, the usual sanction against the confidant will be damages, as the court is likely to see an injunction as inappropriate once the information is in the public domain (*Seager, Coco*). Outside of commercial secrets there may be exceptions. In the 'Spycatcher' case, Lord Griffiths suggested that the agent who had disseminated government secrets continued to owe an obligation of confidence, and could be prevented through an injunction from publishing his book in the UK even though it had been widely distributed abroad, because financial compensation could never provide the government with an appropriate remedy.

Commercial secrets

7.15   These may include confidential information which is exchanged in the course of a business relationship, such as the situation in Seager

(**7.3**), or perhaps during an individual's employment. Unlike in the US, the UK courts have not given a general definition to trade secrets as such. A definition was offered by Megarry J in *Thomas Marshall v Guinle* (1979). The owner must believe that the release of the information injures him or helps his rivals. He must believe the information is not in the public domain. In both cases, his belief must be reasonable. Finally, the information must also be judged in light of the particular trade practices to which it pertains. However, the subjective elements of Megarry J's definition set it apart from the objective definitions of confidential information which have predominated in the case law, and hence it is by no means authoritative. The extent which the law of confidence protects trade secrets which arise in the course of employment and the particular obligations of confidentiality owed by an employee to an employer are looked at separately below (see **7.30** et seq).

Personal secrets

7.16   Personal information may be protected by an obligation of confidence (*Coco*). In the UK, the 'tabloid' newspapers have long competed by publishing personal information about the famous and not so famous. Increasingly, other sections of the media are seeking popularity by a similar route. Although there has been considerable discussion over a long period as to whether personal privacy laws should be introduced, which was particularly intense following the death of Princess Diana in 1997, arguments that they would be an unjustifiable incursion into press freedom have so far prevailed. For example, the Calcutt Committee which reported in 1990 suggested voluntary regulation of the press and no privacy laws (see the Report of the Committee on Privacy and Related Matters, Cm 1102). It remains to be seen whether the incorporation of the European Convention on Human Rights will establish a broader right to privacy in light of Art 8. In the meantime, the law of confidence has provided one line of defence for individuals against unwarranted press intrusion into their private lives. In *Argyll v Argyll* (1967), the leading modern case, the plaintiff sought to prevent her former husband, the Duke of Argyll and a national newspaper from publishing details of her private life which she had revealed to the Duke during their marriage. Ungoed-Thomas J held that marital secrets were protected by an obligation of confidence. Indeed, even subsequent adultery by one spouse, resulting in divorce, did not relieve the other spouse from the obligation to preserve earlier confidences. Extra-marital secrets received less protection in the later case of *Woodward*, which involved a number of pop stars. They sought to prevent the defendants, their former public relations officer and a national newspaper, from revealing personal details of their lives, such as, according to one headline, why Mrs Tom Jones threw her jewellery from a car window and Tom got high on a jumbo jet. In discharging an injunction, the CA held, inter alia, that because the defendants had sought publicity for certain favourable aspects of their lives, they were in no position to claim that other, less favourable aspects, were confidential. It was also true that much of the information was already in the public domain (see **7.7** above). The CA appeared to be influenced by the fame of the plaintiffs and the judgment has been criticised, not least because it would seem to allow a well-known individual no defence of confidentiality if he chooses to reveal only certain aspects of his private life (Gurry *Breach of Confidence* (1984) pp 99-101). Critics of the *Woodward* decision find the approach in *Stephens v Avery* (1988), which also concerned intimate personal confidences, preferable. The plaintiff had a lesbian affair with a Mrs Telling who was later murdered by her husband. She told Mrs Avery, a friend, details of the affair in confidence. Mrs Avery gave the information to a Sunday newspaper. The plaintiff sued Mrs Avery and the newspaper for breach of confidence and the defendants sought to have the action struck out. In rejecting the defendants' application, Sir Nicholas Browne-Wilkinson VC held that it was unconscionable for a person who had received information, including information regarding a sexual relationship, in confidence, to reveal that information, irrespective of the particular relationship between the parties. Nor did he believe that information relating to sexual conduct was 'mere tittle tattle'.

Immoral material

7.17 In *Stephens*, the court accepted that a duty of confidence would not be enforced if it related to matters which had a 'grossly immoral tendency'. It also accepted that there is no clear social consensus as to what constitutes immoral sexual conduct. Given that so few social values now rest on a clear consensus, it is submitted that this is an exception which will arise only rarely.

Government secrets

7.18 In the past half century, there have been a number of occasions when the state has sought to use the law of confidence to block publication of its secrets. The use of the law of confidence in this way has been criticised. It has been argued that 'state secrets' constitute a different category of information to confidential information. Indeed, since 1911, 'state secrets' have been granted particular protection by the Official Secrets Act (1911-1989). The fact that successive governments, over the past half century, have successfully employed the law of confidence to prevent publication of their secrets has, therefore, been seen by many as a worrying extension of its use. The judgment in *A-G v Jonathan Cape* (1976), which concerned the publication of the diaries of a former cabinet minister, Richard Crossman, was the first to hold that the law of confidence might be used to protect government secrets. However, the court tempered this extension of the law of confidence by introducing a public interest test, which is not applicable to commercial secrets. Not only must it be shown that the information at issue has the necessary quality of confidence, but also that it is in the public interest that the government should continue to keep the information secret. In the Crossman case, it was held that there was a public interest in the maintenance of the doctrine of joint responsibility in the cabinet, which might be prejudiced by the premature disclosure of views by individual members. However, there was no public interest in preventing publication of proceedings which, as in this case, were over 10 years old. The Australian case of *Commonwealth of Australia v John Fairfax* (1980), followed the Crossman decision. In this case, it was recognised that government secrets could be the basis of an obligation of confidence but also that, 'unless disclosure is likely to injure the public interest, it will not be protected.' The apparent tension between the state's interest in secrecy and the public interest in disclosure was considered at length in the 'Spycatcher' case, which concerned an attempt by the government to prevent a number of newspapers from publishing revelations by a former British spy, Peter Wright. The 'Spycatcher' case will be looked at in detail below when the public interest defence is fully considered (see **7.52**). In fact, the decision by the HL to allow publication by at least some of the defendants rested primarily on a recognition that the information at issue had already entered the public domain. In 1999, the government introduced a Freedom of Information Bill, which sets out to extend public access to information held by the government and other official bodies. There are, however, some notable restrictions to access, including information relating to the security services, and information which may be withheld by public authorities on the basis of risk or reasonable expectation of prejudice.

Professional confidences

7.19   There are a number of other relationships in which an obligation of confidence may be generated, including a number of professional relationships, for example, that between solicitors and their clients. In *Tournier v National Provincial and Union Bank* (1924), Bankes LJ stated that:

> The privilege of non-disclosure to which a client or a customer is entitled may vary according to the exact nature of the relationship between the client or the customer and the person on whom the duty rests. It need not be the same in the case of the counsel, the solicitor, the doctor and the banker although the underlying principle may be the same.

Element 2: the confidential obligation

7.20   The second element of a breach of confidence action is that the information must have been imparted in circumstances where the confidant ought reasonably to have known that the information had been imparted in confidence. In other words, a duty of confidence arises from the particular relationship between the parties.

The origins of the duty of confidence

7.21   Where the parties are in a contractual relationship, there may be an express contractual term which establishes a relationship of confidence. Or the court may imply such a term. But an obligation of confidence may also arise in equity. According to Megarry J in *Coco*, 'Where there is no contract, the information must have been imparted in circumstances importing an obligation of confidence' (see also *Marcel v Metropolitan Police Comr* (1991)). In *Lamb v Evans* (1893), no distinction was made by the CA between the duty of confidence placed on an agent by an implied contract and that imposed upon him by equity. Conversely, however secret and confidential the information, there can be no binding obligation of confidence if the information 'is blurted out in public' or is communicated in other circumstances which obviously undermine any duty to hold it confidential. The breadth and duration of the obligation of confidence depends on all the circumstances of the case ('Spycatcher' per Scott J).

Limited purpose test

7.22   The question arises of how to determine whether the information was communicated in circumstances which gave rise to an obligation of confidence. The most common test recognised by the courts is to ask whether the information was given for a limited purpose only. In *Saltman*, the plaintiffs were the owners of drawings of tools for leather punches, which they gave to the defendants, who manufactured the tools for them. The defendants used the drawings to manufacture tools on their own behalf. It was held, inter alia, that the defendants had an equitable obligation to keep the drawings confidential because they knew that they had been given to them for a limited purpose only, that is for the manufacture of tools for the plaintiffs' use. In *Ackroyds v Islington Plastics* (1962), the plaintiffs supplied the defendants with a special tool for the manufacture of 'swizzle sticks'. The defendants used it to make their own sticks, which they supplied to the plaintiffs' customers. The court found the defendants were under an obligation of confidence since the tool was entrusted to them solely for the manufacture of swizzle sticks for the plaintiffs 'and for no other purpose' and the defendants were obliged to use the equipment and the information solely for that purpose

7.23   The general view has been that the limited purpose test is an objective one. In other words, it is not necessary for the defendant actually to know that the confidential information was imparted for a limited purpose. It is sufficient if, given the circumstances in which the information was imparted, he *ought* to have known. The circumstances might include the confider's own attitude or behaviour in confiding the information, ie did the confider act in a way commensurate with the information being confidential. For instance, if the confider was an employer, did he ensure that his employee was aware that he was being given confidential information. The objective nature of the test was considered in an interesting Australian case, *Smith Kline & French Laboratories (Australia) (SKF) v Secretary to the Department of Community Services and Health* (1990). The applicant, SKF, imported a controlled drug, Cimetidine, into Australia. To obtain approval to import the drug, it sent information relating to it to the relevant government department. Some years later, Alphapharm, which manufactured and imported generic drugs, also sought to import Cimetidine into Australia. The department, in order to evaluate the generic product, intended to make use of the information supplied by SKF. SKF claimed that the information had been made available to the department for the sole purpose of assessing its own application. It sought an injunction to prevent the department from using it for any other purpose. It was held by the court that the information was confidential, thus satisfying the first part of Megarry J's trilogy. But was the department bound by the obligation of confidence? SKF alleged that the department knew or ought to have known of the limited purpose for which it was supplied. It was found, on the facts, that the department did not *actually* know that the data was supplied on the understanding that it would not be used to evaluate generic data, but *ought* it to have known? The court assumed that the test was objective. The obligation of confidence arose not only where the defendant knew, but where he ought to have known in the circumstances. In this case, the court found that although there was an 'implicit' understanding on the part of both SKF and the relevant departmental secretary that the information would not be revealed to third parties, there was no similar understanding on the part of SKF as to what else the department might do with the information. The court would not impute to the department the placing or the acceptance of an obligation which restricted the manner in which it might discharge its functions, as would be the case if SKF had succeeded. In other words, in the circumstances, it could not be held that the department 'ought to have known' that it should not use the information for the further purpose of evaluating the generic drug.

7.24 It was also suggested in *Coco* that a general test of whether information is given in confidence should be objective. Megarry J said:

> It may be that hard-worked creature, the reasonable man, may be pressed into service once more; for I do not see why he should not labour in equity as well as law. It seems to me that if the circumstances are such that any reasonable man standing in the shoes of the recipient of the information would have realised that upon reasonable grounds the information was being given to him in confidence, then this should suffice to impose upon him the equitable duty of confidence.

However, in the recent case of *Carflow v Linwood* (1996), Jacob J held that although an objective test may be appropriate for finding a contractual obligation of confidence or if the information was given for a limited purpose, with respect to the equitable obligation of confidence, a subjective test is more appropriate. This was because 'equity looks at the conscience of the individual'. In other words, in situations where the obligation is equitable, the question should be 'what did the parties themselves think they were doing by way of imposing or accepting obligations?' and not 'what would a reasonable man think they were doing?' In *Carflow*, the plaintiffs produced a steering wheel lock for which they had a registered design. The defendants showed a similarly designed prototype of the lock to a buyer for Argos some time before the plaintiffs' lock went on sale. One question for the court was whether the buyer had been placed under an obligation of confidence when he had been shown the prototype. Jacob J said that he had not. Applying a subjective test, Jacob J did not believe that either the buyer or the defendants thought that the information was being given in confidence. Although he thought the subjective test most appropriate to the circumstances, he also found that an objective test would have a similar result. The reasonable man would not assume an obligation of confidence was being imposed merely because a prototype was shown. On the contrary, the reasonable man would assume that there were other independent intellectual property rights, such as copyright or design right, which would protect the prototype. As a consequence, he would not assume that he would be placing himself under an obligation of confidence in respect of matter which could be protected by other means. It remains to be seen whether the approach in *Carflow* will be followed in future cases. It goes against the run of previously decided cases, where the test has generally been held to be an objective one. Indeed, Jacob J himself returned to the objective test of the 'reasonable man' in *Mars v Teknowledge*, in assessing whether the de-encryption of the plaintiff's commercially available software could be said to be a breach of confidence. He held that it could not.

Confidential information given to third parties

7.25 According to Lord Keith in 'Spycatcher', 'It is a general rule of law that a third party who comes into possession of confidential information which he knows to be such, may come under a duty not to pass it on to anyone else.' If this were not the case, the confidant might remove the obligation of confidence by wrongly disclosing the information to a third party. In *Schering*, the plaintiffs marketed a drug, Primodos. The second defendant was given confidential information about the drug by the plaintiff, so that he might do public relations work. In fact, he planned to use the information in a television documentary made by Thames Television, the third defendant. Thames were aware of the

283

circumstances in which the second defendant had acquired the information. The CA upheld an interlocutory injunction against both the second and third defendants. According to Lord Denning, if the second defendant was in breach of duty, then Thames could not take advantage of his breach. In *Fraser v Thames* (**7.11**), Hirst J held that to fix a duty of confidence, the third party must know the information was confidential. He said: 'Knowledge of a mere assertion that breach of confidence has been committed is not sufficient.' There are a wide range of cases where a third party has been held liable, encompassing situations where the confider and confidant are linked by contract or where the obligation of confidence lies in equity. In the early case of *Prince Albert v Strange*, the defendant, Judge, was restrained from exhibiting copies of etchings, which Strange, who had obtained them 'surreptitiously', had given to him. Typically, a third-party case might involve the communication of personal information to the press, such as in *Argyll v Argyll*, where the newspaper was restrained from publishing the marital secrets. Another common situation arises when an employee confides confidential information relating to his former employment to his new employer. In 'Spycatcher', the government sought to prevent newspapers printing confidential information passed on to them by an ex-secret agent. In this case, Scott J posed the question as to whether there can be circumstances where a duty of confidence is owed by the original confidant, but will not necessarily lie on every third party who comes into possession of the confidential information because it may be that a public interest in publishing the information will apply to the latter and not to the former. Sir John Donaldson agreed that the newspapers' duty to the Government was not necessarily the same as that of the ex-spy. However, if the confidant's breach causes the information to enter the public domain, then the third party will have no obligation to keep it confidential.

7.26   There are two situations where a third party who receives information may be in breach. First, he may know the information is confidential at the time it is given to him or, second, he may find out only later. In the first case, the third party may be fixed with three different kinds of knowledge. The first is actual knowledge (for example, Judge, in *Prince Albert v Strange* (**7.25** above)). The second is imputed knowledge. This has often been imputed to companies which have been formed by confidants to exploit the confidential information that they have obtained (for example, in *Cranleigh* (**7.9**)). The third is constructive notice, where the third party is affixed with notice if he wilfully fails to make proper inquiries. Here the third party will be held to be in a similar position to the confidant, who knew or *ought to have known* that information given to him was for a limited purpose. It is submitted that third party constructive notice is established by an objective test: are the circumstances such that a reasonable person in his position would have made inquiries at the time he acquired the information? For instance, in *London & Provincial Sporting News Agency v Levy* (1928), the plaintiffs were turf commission agents who informed subscribers of the betting prices offered at race meetings. The subscribers were under contract not to pass the information on. A subscriber (a bookmaker) passed the information to a second turf commission agent who, in turn, passed it to a news agency. It was held that the latter two defendants knew or ought to have known that the information came from the plaintiffs, 'or at any rate that they had a very certain suspicion that it was the plaintiffs' news and had deliberately refrained from asking a direct question.' In the second situation where the third party acquires the information but is unaware that it is confidential or that it has been given in breach of confidentiality, his liability arises only from date at which he is informed or given notice of the fact that the information was confidential.

Confidential information disclosed involuntarily

7.27   As a general rule a duty of confidence arises from the particular relationship between the parties involved. However there are situations in which confidential information is disclosed where no such relationship exists. For instance, what happens if the information is obtained accidentally or else surreptitiously? Under these circumstances, the courts have been willing to accept that the recipient of such information may well be bound by a duty of confidence. As early as 1913, Swinfen Eady J stated that 'the principle upon which the Court of Chancery has acted for many years has been to restrain the publication of confidential information improperly or surreptitiously obtained...' (*Ashburton v Pape* (1913)). It has been widely recognised that it would be inequitable if a confidant is to be held accountable under the law of confidence for disclosing information which was willingly communicated to him by the confider, while an individual who engages in dishonesty or subterfuge to obtain what he knows to be confidential information is not. This is especially so when, in the case of industrial espionage or media 'snooping', for example, the acquisition of confidential information can prove immensely profitable. The Australian case of *Franklin v Giddins* (1978) set out the judicial basis for potentially broad protection. Here the defendant had stolen a cutting from the plaintiff's uniquely high-yielding nectarine tree. The court found that the defendant had behaved 'unconscionably and in contravention of the plaintiff's rights' and that the latter was entitled to equitable relief. Likewise, in the US, the decision in *duPont v Christopher* (1970) recognised a cause of action for the discovery of a trade secrets by any 'improper' means, in this case by taking aerial photographs of the plaintiff's factory. However, the extent to which the law of confidence in the UK will protect secrets gained outside a confidential relationship remains uncertain. *Malone v Metropolitan Police Comr* (1979) took a narrow approach. The plaintiff's telephone had been tapped by the police who used the information gained to prosecute him unsuccessfully for handling stolen goods. Malone sought a declaration that the tapping of his telephone by the police had been unlawful and an injunction to restrain future tapping. Sir Robert Megarry VC, in rejecting the application, took the view, inter alia, that the plaintiff had no right of privacy in his conversation. Nor did he believe that there was a general right to confidentiality in telephone conversations. Even if there were, he considered that the interception by the police had been justified since it was of material assistance in an attempt to uncover a criminal act. He reasoned that to use the telephone involved an inherent risk that the user will be overheard by an 'unknown', in the same way as if confidential information is imparted on a bus or train. In such circumstances, he did not see why someone who overheard the secret should be under any legal obligation to keep it confidential. Indeed, he went further and perhaps surprisingly concluded that no realistic person would rely on the telephone to protect his confidentiality against those who might overhear the conversation 'by tapping or otherwise'. (See now the Interception of Communications Act 1985.)

7.28   There was some criticism of the *Malone* decision for circumscribing the remit of the law of confidence in this way. Later cases, have suggested the courts' willingness to take a more expansive view. In *Francome v Mirror Group Newspapers* (1984), the defendant newspaper had acquired tapes of telephone conversations of the plaintiff, a leading jockey, from an undisclosed source. The tapes were alleged to show breaches of Jockey Club rules and of the criminal law by the plaintiff. The defendant successfully obtained an interlocutory injunction against the *Mirror* newspaper to prevent publication of the tapes. In the CA, Fox LJ distinguished *Malone*, which was concerned with authorised tapping by the police, against the present situation, where the phone had been tapped illegally. In this case, it could not be said that the plaintiff had accepted the risk that his conversations would be overheard in the same way he might have accepted the risk that he would be overheard because of accidents or imperfections in the telephone system itself. Following this reasoning, Fox LJ considered that there was a serious issue to be tried and granted the injunction.

7.29 The *Francome* decision suggests that where there is no relationship between the parties, the court's view as to whether or not there is an obligation of confidence might be based upon how the information was acquired. However, in the 'Spycatcher' case, Lord Goff suggested that a duty of confidence might exist even where an individual comes across confidential information 'innocently', such as 'when an obviously confidential document is wafted by an electric fan out of a window into a crowded street', or 'a private diary, is dropped in a public place, and is picked up by a passer by', although it is an open question as to whether he would apply the same rule to personal and commercial information (see Hull 'Analysis: Stealing Secrets: A Review of the Law Commission's Consultation Paper on the Misuse of Trade Secrets' [1998] IPQ 422). It has been suggested that one approach to achieving greater consistency in the law would be for the court simply to consider whether the person who acquires the information ought reasonably to have known it was secret, rather than to concern itself with how the information was acquired (Thompson 'Breach of Confidence and Privacy' in Clarke *Confidentiality and the Law* (1990) p 74). It will be interesting to see whether the introduction of the Human Rights Act which includes a right to privacy will affect the use of the law of confidence in this area. Certainly, the introduction of new technologies, such as the internet, will provide further opportunities for surreptitious access to confidential information by the government and by private individuals.

Other relationships of confidence: employees and confidential information

7.30 The law has long recognised that an obligation of confidence may arise out of particular relationships. Examples are the relationships between a doctor and patient, a priest and penitent, a solicitor and client, a banker and customer. The relationship which has generated the most amount of case law, reflecting its central importance both economically and socially, is the relationship between employer and employee. It is this relationship which is examined below.

7.31 The general rules of the law of confidence will apply to the employee/employer relationship. However, the relationship between employee and employer also gives rise to a number of particular problems concerning the use of information. Typically, an employer will wish to limit as far as possible the ability of an employee to compete using information acquired during the course of his employment. On the other hand, an employee, particularly a former employee, may well seek to use this same information in pursuit of his own interests even if these conflict with those of his (ex) employer. The conflict engendered by the competing claims of employer and employee frequently focuses on the boundary between what the employer will claim is his confidential information and what the employee will claim is, in reality, the general knowledge or 'know-how' of his trade or business, which he should be allowed to take elsewhere. In balancing these competing claims, the courts have drawn a distinction between the duty owed by employees and former employees. In the first situation, the courts have emphasised the duty which is owed to an employer by an employee. In the second, the court has, by contrast, sought to protect the ex-employee's freedom to earn a livelihood without unreasonable constraint.

Duties during employment

7.32 The duty of confidence may be based in equity as well as in contract. In the context of employment, where the parties are linked by a contract of employment, the duty of confidence is founded on that contractual relationship (*Vokes Ltd v Heather* (1945)). In the absence of any express term, an undertaking by the employee to serve his employer with 'good faith and fidelity' will be implied into the contract of employment (*Robb v Green* (1895) per Smith LJ). Since the last century, the courts have viewed the duty of confidence, during the course of employment, as a central aspect of the general duty of good faith or fidelity (*Faccenda Chicken v Fowler* (1986)). Fundamental to the general duty of good faith and fidelity is the duty of an employee not to compete during the duration of the employment contract, including, as a general rule, the duty not to compete in his spare time. In the latter circumstance, the courts are likely to identify a conflict if the employee knows of trade secrets which may be useful to a competitor and if he occupies a position with the employer where the expectation would be that he owes an exclusive duty to him. So a 'manual worker', working by the hour, may be under less constraint as to how he uses his spare time than a more senior employee (*Thomas Marshall*). In certain limited circumstances, an employee may make preparations while he is employed in order to compete with his employer after he has left. But these will not include taking away a card index file of customers (*Roger Bullivant* (see above **7.14**)) or, as in *Wessex Dairies v Smith* (1935), soliciting customers on the final day of employment in order to set up a rival milk round. It has also been held that it is wrong to memorise lists of names of customers for later use (*Printers & Finishers v Holloway* (1965)). However, merely recalling rather than memorising information will not be restrained (*Coral Index v Regent Index* (1970)). An employee may even have a positive duty to disclose information, which may be of benefit to his employer, which he encounters during his term of employment. This was the conclusion reached in *Cranleigh* (**7.9**). The extent of this positive duty will again depend upon the position of the employee. For instance, in *Cranleigh*, the defendant was managing director of the company, and therefore owed a fiduciary duty to his employer which went beyond the general duty of good faith and fidelity. A similar duty may not extend to an employee in a less responsible position.

The Faccenda Chicken case

7.33   In 1986, in *Faccenda*, the CA reviewed the general principles behind breach of confidence cases involving employees. In his judgment, Neill LJ considered both the extent of the employees' duties and the nature of the information which was owed protection. Although, the case was concerned with a post-termination breach, the judgment has a wider relevance. The facts are relatively straightforward. The defendant, Fowler, was employed as a sales manager by the plaintiff company, which marketed fresh chickens. Fowler had the novel and profitable idea of using a fleet of travelling salesmen to sell fresh chickens direct to retailers from refrigerated vans. Subsequently, Fowler resigned from the plaintiff and set up a competing business covering the same geographical area. He also employed a number of the plaintiff's former salesmen. During their employment, Fowler and the other salesmen had acquired information concerning customers' names and addresses, routes, the quality and quantity of the goods and the prices charged. The plaintiff contended, inter alia, that the defendants had abused the confidential information they had acquired during their employment. At first instance, Goulding J had divided workplace information into three general categories:

- easily accessible information which was not confidential

- confidential information which an employee could not use or disclose during his employment, but which, in the absence of an express covenant, he was at liberty to use subsequently

- 'trade secrets' which he was not at liberty to disclose or use either during his employment or after.

Goulding J placed the information carried away by Fowler in the second category. But since there was no express covenant, Fowler was held not to be liable. The plaintiff appealed. The CA reached the same conclusion as the trial judge, but disagreed on one vital point. Neil LJ held that there was no second category of information which could be protected by an express restrictive covenant. Instead, there were two categories of information: trade secrets which would be protected post-employment either by an express or implied contractual term and the rest, including information which may have had the necessary quality of confidence while the employee was employed, but ceased to do so once he had left. In this case, the information at issue did not amount to a trade secret, and so did not remain confidential post-employment.

The Faccenda definition of 'trade secrets'

7.34   It has been suggested that the subjective approach of Megarry J's definition of trade secrets in *Thomas Marshall* does not fit with the general run of case law (see **7.15**; also the comments of Carnwath J in *Lancashire Fires v Lyons* (1996)). In *Faccenda*, Neill LJ did not attempt to define trade secrets per se. He cited examples of trade secrets or their 'equivalent', including 'secret processes of manufacture such as chemical formulae' or 'designs and special methods of construction'. He also left the category open by adding, 'other information which is of a sufficiently high degree of confidentiality to amount to a trade secret' including, albeit in circumstances different to those obtaining in this case, information about

290

prices. Neil LJ then went on to identify four factors which are relevant to differentiating between trade secrets and other information, including 'merely confidential information' which would not be protected post-employment. The first is the nature of the employment. An employee who is accustomed to handling confidential information as part of his job may be expected to protect trade secrets better than one who is not. The second is the nature of the information. Is it the sort of information which meets the standard of a trade secret? In *Faccenda*, the example was offered of information which was given only to a limited number of employees. Thirdly, did the employer impress upon the employee the confidentiality of the information? Merely saying that information is confidential does not make it so, but a warning that the information is confidential will assist the court in finding that it is. Thus, in *Worsley v Cooper* (1939), the defendant C was an employee of a the plaintiff paper merchants, who set up on his own. He told his customers that he could obtain paper from the same sources as his former employers. The latter claimed that this information was confidential. The court found that no warning had been given to C that the information as to the papers' sources was to be treated as confidential either during or after his employment and C was not found to have breached confidence by using this information to compete. Finally, Neil LJ in *Faccenda* identified the fourth question to be whether the confidential information could be easily isolated from other information which the employee acquires during his employment. In *Faccenda*, the CA found that the information about prices could not be isolated from the other information which was not protectable post-employment. Below (**7.40**) the controversy surrounding the *Faccenda* view that, post-termination, only 'trade secrets' can be protected is examined. But first it is necessary to look at how the courts have sought to draw a distinction between confidential information, however defined, and the know-how and general knowledge which the employee is able to take away from his employment.

Confidential information versus 'know how'

7.35 In a recent CA decision on employee secrets, *FSS Travel v Johnson* (1998), Mummery LJ cited with approval (as had Neill LJ in *Faccenda*) the distinction drawn by Cross J in *Printers & Finishers* between trade secrets which are 'owned' by the employer and the general skill and knowledge which an employee is entitled to take with him. In *Printers & Finishers*, the defendant was a manager of the plaintiffs' flock printing factory. While still in their employment, he contacted another company V about setting up a competing flock printing plant. In addition, he showed employees of V around the plaintiff's 'secret factory', showed them samples of the plaintiff's products and ordered a 'cyclone' machine of the plaintiff's design for the use of V. The plaintiff sought to restrain the defendant from misusing its confidential information. According to Cross J, if the contested information could 'fairly be regarded as a separate part of the employee's stock of knowledge which a man of ordinary honesty and intelligence would recognise to be the property of his old employer and not his own to do as he likes with' then that information would be protected as confidential. By contrast, general knowledge of the plaintiff's plant and process, of the difficulties encountered in production and ways around them which the employee has discovered 'for himself by trial and error during the employment' were not trade secrets. In this case, according to Cross J, the defendant's 'skill in manipulating a flock printing plant' which he had acquired during his employment could not be separated from 'his general knowledge of the flock printing process' and Cross J doubted whether 'any man of average intelligence and honesty would think that there was anything improper in his putting his memory of particular features of his late employers' plant at the disposal of his new employer.'

7.36 Clearly, the distinction between confidential information and know how is not always an easy one to make. It was examined once more by the CA in *FSS Travel*. The plaintiff specialised in producing computer programs for the travel industry. The defendant J was employed as a computer programmer. There was a term in J's contract that for a period of one year after leaving the plaintiff's employment, he would not engage in any competing business. J left and took up employment with a competitor. The plaintiff sought to enforce the post-termination covenants. At first instance, it was held inter alia that the plaintiff had trade secrets to protect but that the scope of the restrictive covenant was unreasonable. The plaintiff appealed. The CA dismissed the appeal but on the grounds that there was no confidential information capable of being protected. According to Mummery LJ, the determination of whether the employee's knowledge constitutes confidential information or know how is a question of fact, to be decided by examining all the evidence, considering not only the four factors which had been identified in *Faccenda* (see above **7.34**) but also the extent to which the information is in the public domain and the likely damage to the employer if the information is disclosed. During his employment, J had acquired skill, experience, know-how and general knowledge relating to the computer systems rather than a separate identifiable body of objective trade secrets to which the plaintiff was entitled. The express covenant was therefore invalid as the latter had no trade secrets legitimately protectable by the imposition of a covenant. The CA emphasised that the plaintiff's lack of precision in its pleadings, and the absence of solid evidence of trade secrets was fatal to its case.

Post-employment obligations

7.37   The duty of good faith and fidelity owed by a former employee is not as great as the duty owed by an employee during his employment. During employment, there is an implied term in the contract of employment that the use or disclosure of confidential information, even though it may not amount to a trade secret, will be a breach of the duty of good faith. By contrast, post-employment, the implied term will cover the obligation not to use or disclose trade secrets, but it will not cover all the information acquired by an employee during the course of his employment. It will not cover Goulding J's second category in *Faccenda*, that is information which is 'confidential' in the sense that it would be a breach of an employee's duty of good faith to disclose it while he is employed. In *Printers & Finishers*, Cross J gave as an example of this sort of information the printing instructions which were given to the defendant by the plaintiff. During his employment, it would have been a breach of confidence for the defendant to disclose these instructions to 'a stranger'. But, according to Cross J, many of these instructions were not really 'trade secrets'. While the defendant was clearly not entitled to take a copy of the instructions away with him, 'in so far as he carried them in his head', he was entitled to use them for his own benefit or for the benefit of a future employer. In effect, upon leaving his employment, they had become part of his general knowledge or know-how.

Post-employment restrictive covenants

7.38   Since the *Faccenda* judgment, there has been much debate as to whether Goulding J's second category of information, while not protected by an implied term, can be or should be protectable post-employment by an express term in a restrictive covenant. In *Faccenda*, Neill LJ disagreed with Goulding J, and clearly expressed the opinion that a restrictive covenant would only restrain an ex-employee if it could be shown he was divulging a trade secret or the equivalent of a trade secret. Before examining the dissent from this finding, it is useful to look at the nature of restrictive covenants, themselves.

7.39   In dealing with restrictive covenants, the courts have always been concerned to ensure that they will not be used unreasonably to prevent competition, as this is assumed to be broadly against the public interest (*Herbert Morris v Saxelby* (1916); *Faccenda*). The public interest at stake is 'that a man should be free to exercise his skill and experience to the best advantage for the benefit of himself and of all those who desire to employ him' (*Herbert Morris* per Lord Atkinson). Accordingly, the courts will not uphold a restrictive covenant whose sole aim is to protect an employer generally from competition, rather than to protect some specific subject matter for which the employer can legitimately claim protection, such as trade secrets (*Stenhouse Ltd v Phillips* (1974) per Lord Wilberforce; *FSS Travel*). As it was put by Lord Atkinson in *Herbert Morris*:

> He [an employer] is entitled to have his interest in his trade secrets protected, such as secret processes of manufacture which may be of vast value. And that protection may be secured by restraining the employee from divulging these secrets or putting them to his own use. He is also entitled not to have his old customers by solicitation or such other means enticed away from him. But freedom from all competition per se apart from both these things, however, lucrative it might be to him, he is not entitled to be protected against. He must be prepared to encounter that even at the hands of a former employee.

It follows, according to Neil LJ in *Faccenda*, that a trade secret can be protected post-employment by an express term in a restrictive covenant. However, the second category of information identified by Goulding J, which is less than a trade secret, cannot. To allow such protection would unreasonably expand the scope of the subject matter of restrictive covenants and inhibit competition. In effect, according to the CA in *Faccenda*, Goulding J's second category of information becomes, post-employment, an aspect of the know how and general knowledge which is acquired by the employee as part of his job and which cannot be subject to restraint.

Faccenda criticised

7.40   Neil LJ's austere view, arguably obiter, that only trade secrets may be protected by express or implied contract terms post-employment was challenged both by legal commentators and in later cases. Following *Faccenda*, there was widespread surprise that a suitably worded restrictive covenant, which was reasonable in its scope, could not prevent a former employer from deploying his know-how to compete with his employer at least for a limited period or within a limited geographical area. (Critics of the CA cited *Printers & Finishers* in support of the idea that it could, whereas in *Faccenda*, Neill LJ cited the same case as authority that it could not!) In *Balston v Headline Filters* (1987), Scott J questioned whether the CA was right to disagree with Goulding. He observed that he did not believe that the CA in *Faccenda* could have 'intended to hold that confidential information that could not be protected by an implied term of a contract of employment ipso facto could not be protected by a suitably limited express covenant.' The same point was taken up by the CA in *Lancashire Fires v Lyons* (1996), where Bingham LJ suggested, again obiter, that a covenant to prevent a former employee working for a competitor was a reasonable way of protecting Goulding J's second category of information. However, in this case the information at issue was held to fall into Goulding's third category of employee know-how and hence the point was not pursued.

Faccenda approved

7.41 A different approach, which it is submitted better overcomes any problem which may be posed by the *Faccenda* decision, was taken by the CA in *Lansing Linde v Kerr* (1991). Here the approach was to enlarge the category of information which might be protected post-termination by allowing for a flexible view of what might constitute a 'trade secret' (although, to be fair, Neill LJ had, himself, left the category open). In *Lansing Linde*, the plaintiff company, which manufactured, distributed and sold forklift trucks, employed the defendant as a divisional director. The defendant signed a contract which restrained him from working for any competitor, worldwide, for 12 months following termination. After he left the company, he became managing director of a competitor. The plaintiff sued for breach of contract and to enforce the restrictive covenant. The CA considered the question of whether the defendant was in possession of confidential information which could be protected post-termination. According to Staughton LJ a trade secret will generally be information used in a trade or business, its owner must limit the dissemination of it or at least not encourage or permit its widespread publication and its publication must cause real harm to its owner. As such, it can include not only secret formulae for the manufacture of products, as mentioned in *Faccenda*, but also a much wider variety of information, including, as in this case, the names of customers and the goods which they buy. These may not be trade secrets in 'ordinary parlance', but they still justified post-termination restrictions. Here, it was held that the defendant did have 'trade secrets' (or 'confidential information') which could be protected, but the protection claimed was too wide. According to Butler Schloss LJ also in *Lansing Linde*,

> we have moved into the age of multi-national businesses and world wide business interests. Information may be held by very senior executives, which, in the hands of competitors, might cause significant harm to the companies employing them. 'Trade secrets' has, in my view, to be interpreted in the wider context of highly confidential information of a non-technical or non-scientific nature, which may come within the ambit of information the employer is entitled to have protected, albeit for a limited period.

The CA in *FSS Travel* (**7.36**) appears to have followed *Faccenda* and *Lansing Linde* by giving protection only to trade secrets following termination, but maintaining a highly flexible approach to what these might be. It should be remembered that in this case, as in *Lansing Linde*, the CA was considering an express term in a restrictive covenant and came to the conclusion that it was unenforceable because the information it sought to protect did not constitute a 'trade secret'. As a result of this most recent decision, it is submitted that the criticisms of *Faccenda* aired in *Balston* and *Lancashire Fires* are unlikely to be repeated.

Element 3: Unauthorised use or disclosure

7.42   The third element required for a breach of confidence action is that there must be unauthorised use of the confidential information, and that use must be to the detriment of the party communicating it (*Coco*). Breach can be either by use or disclosure. Whether or not a breach has occurred is a matter of fact and evidence. Three elements need to be shown:

- that the confidant has used or disclosed the confidential information

- that the information was obtained from the confider directly or indirectly

296

- that the use or disclosure went beyond the purpose for which the information was confided.

There has been some controversy, however, as to whether it is also necessary to show detriment and this is considered separately below (see **7.46**).

Misuse and unauthorised disclosure compared

7.43 In *Saltman*, Greene MR stated:

> If a defendant is proved to have used confidential information, directly or indirectly, obtained from the plaintiff without the consent, express or implied, of the plaintiff he will be guilty of infringement of the plaintiff's rights.

In *Saltman*, the confidential information consisted of a set of drawings given by the plaintiffs to the defendants, in order for the latter to manufacture tools for leather punches on the plaintiffs' behalf. The defendants were found to have breached the relationship of confidence because they used the drawings to make tools and punches on their own behalf. Their use went beyond that authorised by the plaintiffs. The line between breach by disclosure and breach by use may be a thin one. The former might arise when an ex-employee sells his employer's trade secrets to a third party and the latter when he makes use of these same trade secrets to compete on his own account. In *Thomas Marshall*, Sir Robert Megarry VC examined the relationship between use and disclosure. The plaintiff, which brought and sold textile products, employed the defendant as a managing director. There was an express clause in the defendant's contract not to 'disclose' during or after employment any confidential information relating, inter alia, to the trade secrets of the plaintiff. Sir Robert Megarry VC found that the defendant had breached his implied duty of fidelity and his fiduciary duty as director. The defence argued that the express clause only prevented 'disclosure' of business secrets and not the defendant's own use and was able to point to another clause which explicitly prevented both 'use' and 'disclosure'. On this argument, the defendant succeeded. But Sir Robert Megarry VC, stated:

> I can conceive of methods of use which would amount to making a disclosure. If an employee were to use his secret knowledge in such a

297

way as to make it plain to others what the secret process or information was, that might well amount to a disclosure. The mode and circumstances of use may be so ostentatious that they plainly constitute a disclosure. But apart from such cases, I do not think a prohibition on disclosure prevents use.

The defendant's state of mind

7.44 To be fixed with a duty of confidence, it must be shown that the defendant knew or ought to have known the information was given to him in confidence. The question of whether or not this is an objective test has been looked at above (see **7.23**). Once it has been established that the defendant had the requisite knowledge, his state of mind at the time of the breach is irrelevant. A defendant may be found liable even if he was unaware that his act amounted to a breach. In *Seager*, the plaintiff had disclosed his 'Invisgrip' carpet grip to the defendants during prolonged negotiations over his earlier 'Klent' grip. After the negotiations broke down, the defendants sought to patent an 'Invisigrip' which, like that of the plaintiff, had a special 'V-tang' shape. It was the defendants' belief that so long as they did not infringe the plaintiff's patent they had done nothing wrong. In the CA, Lord Denning acknowledged that the defendants 'were quite innocent of any intention to take advantage' of the plaintiff but nonetheless he found them in breach for using the information 'unconsciously'. Other defendants have been held liable even though the breach of confidence had simply been 'by error or oversight' (*Interfirm Comparisons v Law Society of NSW* (1977)). Occasionally, the willingness of the courts to find for a plaintiff has been increased by particularly reprehensible behaviour on the part of a defendant (an example is *Argyll v Argyll* (**7.16** above)).

The extent of misuse

7.45 In the case of both patents and copyright, infringement will follow only if a certain level of copying is identified. In the case of copyright, the copying must be of a substantial part of the copyright material (judged qualitatively). For patent infringement, there must be copying of the essential elements of the patent. There are however no fixed rules as to how much confidential information must be misused or disclosed to found an action for breach of confidence. This may mean that an action for breach of confidence has certain advantages, as is illustrated by the recent case of *Cantor Fitzgerald v Tradition* (2000). The plaintiff company was an inter-dealer broker in bonds. Its former managing director joined with a number of other former employees who had been responsible for developing the plaintiff's bond-trading computer systems to work for a rival company, Tradition. The system used by Tradition had similarities to the plaintiff's and the plaintiff alleged breach of confidence and copyright. Although the plaintiff succeeded in showing breach of copyright of two of its program modules, it failed to do so in respect of its source code, which the court found had actually been reproduced in the defendant's system. Nonetheless, the defendants had disclosed the plaintiff's source code to Tradition while its system was being set up and this was found to be a breach of confidence (for the copyright aspects of the case see **3.88**). Furthermore, it is also true that while a breach of confidence action will not protect trivial tittle tattle it will protect ideas, which may not be protected by copyright (*Fraser* at (**7.11**)).

Must there be detriment?

7.46 It is unlikely that a claimant will bring an action for breach of confidence unless it expected to or had already suffered by the defendant's actions. However, despite the fact that Megarry J's third element specifies that for a breach to occur the unauthorised use must be of 'detriment' to the confider, there is by no means agreement on this point. Even *Coco* is unclear. Megarry J himself says he can 'conceive of cases' where a plaintiff might bring an action without suffering detriment. He gives as an example a case where the information might show the plaintiff in a favourable light but injure a relation or friend whom the plaintiff wishes to protect. In *Seager*, Lord Denning suggested that breach of confidence involves 'prejudice' to the confider. During the 'Spycatcher' case, Lord Keith raised the question once more. He made the obvious point that detriment is usually present in commercial cases. But his comments suggest that the necessary detriment in the case of personal secrets can be so minimal as to be practically meaningless. It was sufficient that the confider did not want the information to be given to people whom he would prefer not to know, even though the disclosure would not be positively harmful to himself. Indeed, Lord Keith went further and suggested that since 'as a general rule' it is in the public interest that confidences should be respected, then the general detriment which a breach causes to this broad public interest may be sufficient, even if there is no specific detriment to the confider. In the same case, Lord Goff suggested it was still an open question, since although detriment would 'nearly always form part of the case', it 'may not always be necessary'. Meanwhile, Lord Griffiths required detriment or potential detriment in both personal and commercial cases. In fact, the question of detriment is unlikely to be an issue in commercial cases, while in cases of personal secrets, the courts are often willing to assume detriment if the other elements of breach of confidence are present. The exception arises in cases where public information is at issue, and where the state must positively show why the information should remain confidential. This issue is looked at below.

Defence 1: The public interest defence

7.47 It has been suggested that behind the law of confidentiality lies the belief that there is a public interest in ensuring that 'confidences should be preserved and protected by the law' ('Spycatcher' per Lord Goff). It has also been long maintained by the courts that in certain circumstances, for example if the confidence concerns an 'iniquity', the obligation of confidence should not be recognised. More recently, the courts have taken the view that on occasion the public interest in knowing certain information may out-balance the public interest in information remaining confidential. The so-called 'public interest' defence has been recognised in relation to information which emanates from government and the public sector, as well as information arising from commercial and personal relationships.

The origins of the defence

7.48 The origins of a defence of iniquity are usually traced to the judgment of Sir William Page-Wood VC in *Gartside v Outram* (1856), who held that an employee had a duty to the public to disclose information regarding fraudulent practices by his employer, there being 'no confidence as to the disclosure of an iniquity'. Later in *Weld-Blundell v Stephens* (1920), the CA affirmed that in certain circumstances, such as when confidential information relates to a proposed or contemplated crime or a civil wrong, the duty of confidence may be overridden by a duty to the public to disclose.

The defence in contract and equity

7.49 Initially the defence of iniquity or public interest derived from a

300

contractual analysis of the duty of confidence. The courts would not imply a term of confidentiality into a contract whose enforcement would be contrary to public policy. In *Initial Services v Putterill* (1968), the plaintiffs ran a laundry. The defendant, who was their sales manager, left and took with him documents which he handed to the *Daily Mail*. These documents and information supplied by the defendant suggested, inter alia, a price fixing agreement between the plaintiff and other laundries, which should have been registered under the Restrictive Trade Practices Act 1956 but was not. The allegations were published by the *Daily Mail*. The plaintiffs claimed that by disclosing the information to a third party, the defendant was in breach of an implied term of his contract of employment. Lord Denning accepted that while there was an implied duty of confidence in the contract, it was subject to exceptions, including 'any misconduct of such a nature that it ought in the public interest to be disclosed to others.' Such was the case here, and the defendant was held to have a reasonable defence to the action. However, it is now well established that the defence will also apply where the obligation of confidence is an equitable one (*Fraser v Evans*). The present balancing exercise, in which the court will weigh up on a case-by-case basis whether or not public interest lies in disclosure of information or in maintaining its confidentiality, has arguably moved the defence away from any narrow dependence upon either contractual or equitable principles (see for example the criticisms offered by Gummow J in the Australian case of *Corrs v Collector of Customs* (1987)).

The scope of the defence

7.50   In *Garside v Outram*, Sir William Page-Wood VC appeared to limit the defence to the situation in which the confidence concerned an 'iniquity', hence its original sobriquet of the 'iniquity defence'. In *Initial Services*, Lord Denning said that the defence had a far broader scope, covering 'any misconduct of such a nature that it ought in the public interest to be disclosed to others, including crimes, frauds, misdeeds, both those actually committed and those in contemplation.' Two years later in *Fraser v Evans*, Lord Denning said that, '[iniquity] is merely an instance of a just cause and excuse for breaking confidence.' In *Beloff v Pressdram* (1973), Ungoed Thomas J said that the defence covered:

> matters carried out or contemplated, in breach of the country's security, or in breach of law, including statutory duty, fraud, or otherwise destructive of the country or its people, including matters medically dangerous to the public; and doubtless other misdeeds of similar gravity.

7.51 By the time that *Lion Laboratories v Evans* (1984) was decided, the defence was already being referred to as 'the public interest defence' rather than the iniquity defence. In *Lion Laboratories*, the question arose as to whether 'a just cause or excuse' had to rest on actual misconduct on the part of the confider. The plaintiff manufactured the Lion Intoximeter, which the UK police used exclusively when 'breathalysing' motorists. Two ex-employees had contacted a national newspaper with evidence including internal correspondence which raised doubts as to its reliability. The plaintiffs obtained an *ex parte* injunction against the ex-employees and the newspaper restraining them from disclosing the information. The defendants appealed, contending that the judge had not given sufficient weight to the public interest in allowing publication of the material when granting the injunction. In response, the plaintiff argued that since the confidential information did not show any misconduct on its part, the defendants could not rely on the public interest defence . It was held by the CA, in discharging the injunction, that there need be no evidence of wrongdoing to raise the public interest defence. The defence rested upon showing that 'there was a legitimate ground for supposing it is in the public interest for [the information] to be disclosed.' Stephenson LJ then went on to perform a balancing exercise, weighing up the public interest in disclosure against non-disclosure. In this case, the CA, unlike the HC, found that the balance came down squarely in favour of disclosure. By contrast, courts have not generally considered that sexual misconduct (or, more properly, 'alternative sexual conduct') negates the obligation of confidence (see *Stephens v Avery* at **7.16**; and more recently *Michael Barrymore v News Group Newspapers* (1997)). The exceptional earlier case is, of course, *Woodward v Hutchins*, where Lord Denning expressed the view that as the plaintiffs had actively sought to present themselves in favourable light, it was in the public interest that the true picture should emerge (see **7.16** above).

The Spycatcher case

7.52 The decision in *Lion Laboratories* suggested that the public interest defence no longer rested upon the unconsionableness of maintaining the confidentiality of details relating to particular behaviour (or, more properly, misbehaviour) on the part of the confider. Instead, it is submitted it is now possible to see the defence as having evolved into a pure balancing exercise between competing public interests. The approach taken by the courts in the 'Spycatcher' case suggests this to be the case. The AG sought to prevent a number of English newspapers publishing details of the UK's espionage operations as revealed in 'Spycatcher', a book written by a disenchanted agent, Peter Wright, and, in the case of the 'Sunday Times', from serialising the book. In denying an injunction, the HL based their decision on the fact that the material, which had been widely disseminated abroad, no longer had the necessary quality of confidence. However, along the way, the courts at every level considered the public interest defence in some detail.

7.53   Although various conclusions were reached as to whether the public interest demanded the publication of some or all of this material, there was a broad consensus that it was necessary to proceed through a balancing exercise. According to Lord Goff, the most important limiting principle to the scope of an obligation of confidence is that,

> the public interest in preserving confidentiality, may be outweighed by some other countervailing public interest which favours disclosure. This limitation may apply...to all types of confidential information. It is this limiting principle which may require a court to carry out a balancing operation, weighing the public interest in maintaining disclosure against a countervailing public interest favouring disclosure.

Lord Goff went on to state that although this limiting principle was once 'narrowly stated' as applying to 'crime or fraud', 'it is now clear that the principle extends to matters of which disclosure is required in the public interest'. Accordingly, the balancing exercise did not merely involve weighing up whether it is better for the public if the information is disclosed, but whether the danger to the public is of such gravity as to make disclosure vital. There was also a general view expressed that to justify an iniquity defence it was insufficient to argue that publication of the allegations of iniquity, if true, would justify an iniquity defence or that allegations of iniquity had been made. It must be shown that they are likely to be true or, alternatively, that there is a prima facie case that the allegations have substance or a reasonable attempt has been made to verify their truth.

The balancing exercise in Spycatcher

7.54   By applying the balancing principle to the facts in 'Spycatcher', it was held by Scott J in the HC and Bingham LJ in the CA that while in relation to Peter Wright's breach of confidence, the most 'pressing social need' would be to maintain the principle that spies do not publish their memoirs, in relation to the newspapers, public interest in freedom of the press might be said to favour publication.

To whom should disclosure be made

7.55   In 'Spycatcher', the disclosure of the confidential information by the newspapers was made to the general public. Behind the public interest defence lies the principle that limited disclosure may be sufficient to satisfy the public interest. Only if proper channels of complaint are lacking or fail to take action may wider dissemination be justified. In *Initial Services*, Lord Denning said that disclosure should be '...to one who has a proper interest to receive the information.' In this case, he held that the defendant was arguably justified in making his disclosure to the public at large through the press. Conversely, in *Francome*, the CA took the view that, pending trial, disclosure to the police and the Jockey Club about the plaintiff's alleged misconduct would be sufficient to satisfy the public interest. In reaching this conclusion, Lord Donaldson MR made the still apposite observation that newspapers are all to apt to confuse their own interest in publishing a story with that of the public interest. According to Lord Goff in 'Spycatcher', alleged iniquity in the Secret Service was a 'classic example' where limited disclosure was sufficient, as there are 'a number of avenues for proper complaint.' These had been enumerated in the judgment of Lord Donaldson and included the Prime Minister and the Leader of the Opposition. Lord Donaldson doubted that these controls would, in themselves, be insufficient to support the public interest, but conceded that, at bottom, 'if the newspapers seriously concluded that parliamentary control had broken down and that the allegation of significant wrongdoing was supported by compelling evidence, I would accept their right and duty to make the allegation public.' A more recent example is *Robert Bunn v BBC* (1998). The plaintiff was a former employee of the Robert Maxwell Group. He admitted to the police that he had conspired to defraud. The BBC was making programmes about the Serious Fraud Office (SFO) and wanted to refer to statement. It was held that the public interest in the BBC revealing the workings of the SFO was not sufficient to outweigh the public interest in an accused person being able to make a full disclosure to the police without fear it will be used for other purposes. It was not as though Mr Bunn had failed to reveal the 'iniquitous' behaviour to the police. He had already done so.

Defence 2: the confidential information is insufficiently identified

7.56 An action for breach of confidence will fail if the plaintiff does not identify the information at issue sufficiently clearly (*John Zink v Wilkinson* (1973)). In *Ocular Sciences,* Laddie J gave two reasons for this rule. First, when a plaintiff seeks an injunction, the injunction would be of uncertain scope and so difficult to enforce. Second, the defendant must know what case he has to meet in order to mount a defence. For instance, he may wish to argue that certain items were in the public domain (see also *CMI-Centers v Phytopharm* (1999)). Similarly, it may be an abuse of process to cite information in the action which is not, in fact, confidential (*Searle v Celltech* (1982)). In *Ocular Sciences,* the plaintiffs had previously used the defendant company and its directors to manufacture contact lenses. In their statement of claim, the plaintiffs listed as confidential information 'more or less everything' to do with manufacturing contact lenses. During the trial, they dropped their claims to the confidentiality of many of these items. Laddie J held that the plaintiffs had made 'reckless claims' to confidentiality, although he granted an injunction to prevent disclosure of a far more limited category of information which he accepted was in fact confidential.

Remedies

7.57 Given the 'private' nature of the information which by definition forms the subject of a breach of confidence action, it is not surprising that search orders are particularly suited for uncovering evidence of a breach. Indeed, the *Anton Piller* case was itself an action for breach of confidence. As with other breaches of intellectual property rights, the primary concern of the claimant, in a breach of confidence action, is to bring the breach to an end as quickly as possible with damages typically only a secondary consideration. Again, like other breaches of intellectual property rights, if the claimant obtains an interim injunction, the defendant is likely to abandon its use of the confidential information. As a result, an interim injunction usually brings a breach of confidence action to an end, without the need for a trial and consequent remedies. Generally, the principles enunciated in *American Cyanamid v Ethicon* (1975) apply to an action for breach of confidence (*Francome*). The balance of convenience is usually in favour of granting relief ('Spycatcher').

Injunctions

7.58 It is possible to identify two common situations where the question of an injunction might arise. Where the breach of confidence is continuing the court will normally order injunctive relief. In the second situation, the breach has already occurred, and as a result of the defendant's actions the information has now become public. Is it appropriate for the defendant to be restrained, by use of an injunction, from making further disclosure or use of the information? The authorities are by no means decisive on this issue. In *Terrapin*, it was suggested that there could be a continuing obligation not to use the information as a springboard despite the fact it was now public knowledge. In *Coca*, the question was raised but not answered. In 'Spycatcher', Lord Goff took the view, obiter, that once the subject matter of the breach of confidence action had been 'destroyed' (ie had been made public) an injunction to prevent further disclosure of the information was generally inappropriate. The proper remedy for the plaintiff was in damages or an account of profits. He took the same view towards the defendant who is continuing to benefit from the use of the information, having previously employed his unique access to it as a springboard, he doubted that an injunction would be appropriate, suggesting instead that a remedy might lie in a constructive trust or restitution. In *Roger Bullivant*, (see **7.14** above) the court dealt with the latter situation by granting a time-limited injunction. More recently, in *Ocular Sciences*, Laddie J preferred Lord Goff's approach. Even if the continued use of the confidential information, in this case concerning the production of contact lenses, produced an 'unfair advantage for the defendant', where the information was no longer confidential the proper remedy was not an injunction but the imposition of a financial penalty.

Damages

7.59 In cases where breach of confidence is based on contract term, either express or implied, the courts may award compensatory damages (*Nichrotherm Limited v Percy* (1957)). However, where the breach is an equitable one, the situation is less clear. Courts have traditionally had discretion to award an account of profits, typically an equitable remedy, which is generally designed to satisfy the principle that no one should be permitted to profit from his own wrongdoing ('Spycatcher' per Lord Goff). It follows that for an account to be ordered there will be knowledge on the part of the defendant. An account of profits has been ordered in commercial cases (*Satnam Investments v Dunlop* (1999)). In 'Spycatcher',

Lord Keith thought it appropriate that the *Sunday Times* should be ordered to account to the Crown for the profits accruing from its publication of Peter Wright's memoirs. Most recently, in *AG v Blake* (2000), the HL, Lord Hobhouse dissenting, held that in exceptional circumstances an account of profits might be ordered for breach of contract. The defendant, Blake, was a former member of the security services who had been convicted of spying and sentenced to 42 years' imprisonment, from which he had escaped in 1966. He lives in Moscow and in 1990 wrote his memoirs, for which he was to receive substantial payment from the publisher. He had signed an undertaking not to disclose any official information gained during the course of his employment, whether or not it was confidential. The lower courts found that the information disclosed in his memoirs was no longer confidential and there was no public interest in preventing its publication. Should Blake, however, be allowed to benefit from the breach of his undertaking? The HL thought not. In his leading judgment, Lord Nicholls identified the exceptional circumstances which justified an account of profits in this case. They included the fact that no member of the security services should have a financial incentive to break an undertaking and the fact that much of the appeal of Blake's book resulted from its account of previous breaches of his undertaking.

7.60 Since the nineteenth century, courts have also had discretion to award damages for future loss instead of or together with an injunction. In fact, the courts have also ordered damages for past infringement, that is where an injunction may be inappropriate. The legal basis for such an award has remained a point of contention. In *Seager,* it was that held that the remedy of an account of profits was inappropriate and an enquiry as to damages was ordered. The court may have been influenced by the fact that it did not believe the defendants had acted deliberately. In *Seager v Copydex (No 2)* (1969), the court held that the basis for assessing the amount of damages should be by analogy with tort of conversion on the basis of what a willing purchaser would have paid a willing vendor for the information. In cases where personal, rather than commercial, information has been disclosed the amount of damages is obviously hard to determine and seldom compensates the plaintiff for his or her distress. Courts have also ordered the delivery up or destruction of infringing material in breach of confidence actions or its destruction. In *Franklin v Giddens*, where the defendant has taken cuttings from the plaintiff, the court ordered the delivery up of the resulting nectarine trees.

Further reading

F Gurry *Breach of Confidence* (1984)

J Hull *Commercial Secrecy: Law and Practice* (1998)

E France 'Privacy and Openness: Data Protection, Privacy and Confidentiality' in A McDonald and G Terrill (eds) Open Government (1998) p 45

Self-test questions

1. Barbara is a factory foreman at Bedlow Ltd which manufactures mattresses. Over the years, she has come to understand the production process well and has adjusted the machinery to produce more hard wearing mattresses. Her husband, Alan, is sales manager. He has had an excellent and long-term relationship with Bedlow's customers. By accident, Alan has received a letter meant only for Bedlow's directors outlining a plan to introduce a revolutionary new mattress, while Barbara has overheard one director on the telephone, making plans to join an Italian rival. Meanwhile, Barbara and Alan have been offered better paying jobs by Sleepy Ltd, Bedlow's main British rival. Naturally, Sleepy would be interested in all the relevant information which Barbara and Alan have about the mattress business and Bedlow. How much can they safely reveal without a breach of confidence?

2. In your opinion does the public interest defence provide an acceptable balance between the need for confidentiality and the need for certain information to be published for the public good?

3. What particular difficulties are presented by the relationship between employer and employee in relation to confidentiality? How have the courts dealt with these difficulties?

Index

Index